The Next
Canadian
Century

By the same author

A Dictionary of Canadian Economics

Controlling Interest

The Next Canadian Century

BUILDING A COMPETITIVE ECONOMY

David Crane

Published in 1992 by
Stoddart Publishing Co. Limited
34 Lesmill Road
Toronto, Canada
M3B 2T6

TYPESETTING: Dale Bateman/ArtPlus Limited

Printed and bound in Canada

Stoddart Publishing gratefully acknowledges the support of the Canada Council, Ontario Arts Council and Ontario Publishing Centre in the development of writing and publishing in Canada.

For Françoise Hébert, my wonderful wife

Contents

Tables

Acknowledgements

THIS BOOK COULD NOT HAVE BEEN WRITTEN without the help of many others. The *Toronto Star*, through the encouragement and support of Beland Honderich and the late Martin Goodman and, more recently, John Honderich and Ian Urquhart, has enabled me to gain rich experience in trying to understand the changes taking place in the world, whether from the vantage point of the World Economic Forum in Davos, Switzerland, or in the details of the City of Mississauga's economic plan. The work of the Canadian Institute for Advanced Research, led by one of our most remarkable Canadians, Fraser Mustard, has been invaluable. So has the work of Peter Nicholson, of the Bank of Nova Scotia, and others on the National Advisory Board on Science and Technology, and that of David Pecault of Canada Consulting in his research and insights for Ontario's Premier's Council and for NABST.

The work of the Science Council of Canada and the Economic Council of Canada also has been extremely helpful. For more than 20 years, the Science Council has laboured, when few wanted to listen, to alert Canadians to the imperatives of a new science-based economy, and the Economic Council has worked equally hard to help Canadians understand the importance of education and training and the critical role played by productivity performance in raising our standard of living. The decision of Finance Minister Donald Mazankowski to terminate these two invaluable centres of research is a travesty and a great loss to Canada. The output of Statistics Canada, which the *Economist* has justifiably called one of the best statistical agencies in the world, also was of great help. At the international level, the research and statistics of the Organisation for Economic Co-operation and Development (OECD) in Paris has been of great value, and the same must be said of the International Monetary Fund and the World Bank in Washington.

Last, but certainly not least, this book would not have been written without the support of Jack Stoddart, the patient but firm direction of Donald G. Bastian, and the skilful editing of Carlotta Lemieux.

Introduction

THIS BOOK WAS WRITTEN while Canada was in the midst of an intense debate over whether it would still be in existence a year from now, let alone at the start of the next century. Writing it was my personal leap of faith that Canadians would in the end decide that the country they had created together over the past 125 years was worth preserving and, equally important, that together they could look forward to even greater accomplishments in the future. Resolving the constitutional issue should allow Canada to get on with the enormous task of nation building that lies ahead. What is needed now is nothing less than a transformation of Canada from the old economy of resource extraction and big chimney industries to a new economy based on knowledge and ideas, which, through science, technology, and innovation, will produce the high-value goods and services that can support high-skill and high-pay jobs.

Unless it has the capacity to create new wealth based on ideas and knowledge, Canada will face a long period of economic decline and a growing inability to support the very things we value as a society: our commitment to sharing, as reflected in our health-care system, social programs, child care, regional development, and equalization payments; our respect for education, as shown in the large amount of our income that we annually devote to learning; our desire for our own cultural expression on the North American continent, as reflected in our support for Canadian films, books, magazines, and television programming as well as museums, theatres, and festivals; our concern for the environment, as illustrated by our great national and provincial parks and our crusade against acid rain; and our optimistic confidence in the potential of all races and creeds, as shown in our commitment to multiculturalism.

The challenge is enormous, because change will touch almost every aspect of Canadian life. New technologies will transform both the things we make and the way we make them. The information revolution has already radically changed the nature of banking and created global financial markets. Computerized reservation systems have become the key assets of airlines. Semiconductors, digitalization, and software will truly shape Marshall McLuhan's "global village." The computer and communications will alter almost everything we do and the way we live and work, which is why Canada must be a leader in the new information age. Other technologies, from biotechnology to advanced materials, will transform medicine, agriculture, food, and chemicals, as well as changing the role of Canada's resource industries. The recognition that the health of the environment is now fundamental to our future will also mean making important changes in our way of life.

If Canada is enterprising, it will create new opportunities to develop the new goods and services of the sustainable economy. Intense competition from the three economic superpowers, the United States, Japan, and Germany, as well as from the fast-changing developing world — ranging from South Korea, Hong Kong, and Taiwan to Mexico, Brazil, and Russia — will pose difficult challenges for many Canadian industries and jobs. So will the dash to turn the coast of China into a giant Hong Kong, and India's plan to use its large number of engineers and software specialists to join the high-tech world. But all these societies also represent great opportunities for us if we can develop a "Canadian catalogue" of goods and services that we can sell to them.

If Canada is to build this new wealth-creating economy, sweeping changes will be essential. There will have to be new institutions of partnership, like those emerging, for example, between industry associations and unions for skills development. There will have to be institutions to develop new knowledge and to bring Canadian business into the age of science and technology. Again, there are some hopeful signs; for instance, the Ontario and federal Centres of Excellence, which bring universities and industry together in precompetitive research and development; and the Canadian Institute for Advanced Research, which has brought some of Canada's brightest scholars and researchers home to develop their new ideas here and to inspire a new generation of bright young Canadians.

Experimentation will be essential. The University of Waterloo's bold approach to co-op education is one example; the university's engineering students can go to Japan and work with Japanese companies as part of their co-op program. The establishment in Quebec of the union-run Fond de solidarité du Québec, which directs Quebec savings into new business ventures, is another example. But the new economy will mean many other changes, including ways of organizing the workplace that give employees power; and a recognition by unions of the importance of costs, profits, and efficient work organizations — as well as the recognition by business that employees can cooperate more easily if they have a collective voice through a union.

Much of the initiative to create a new knowledge-based economy that can raise our productivity and our standard of living will depend on the millions of individual efforts by teachers, researchers, entrepreneurs, and workers, but government, too, must play a major role. This has already been recognized at the provincial level. Alberta is pursuing its vision for the year 2000, British Columbia has its Science Council, Ontario has its Premier's Council, and Quebec has its strategy for 13 key industry clusters. Even cities are searching for new ways to bootstrap themselves into the knowledge economy — Calgary, Montreal, and Mississauga, for example, are developing their own economic strategies. Government is important because it sets the vision for the country, and this in turn provides the frame of reference for countless decisions from coast to coast. Government provides the means of consensus on the Canadian agenda and the policies that facilitate and support the urgent changes we must make.

There is a second leap of faith in this book on how we prepare for the twenty-first century — namely, an optimistic confidence in the capabilities of Canadians. These capabilities can be seen in the hundreds of high-tech entrepreneurs who struggle against great odds yet produce sophisticated products they can sell all over the world. Similar capabilities can be seen in the innovative activities of our teachers and some of our schools, in some of our social agencies that try despite great difficulties to bring alienated high school dropouts back into the mainstream of society, and in the street workers who spend their time teaching illiterate adults how to read and write.

Sir Wilfrid Laurier's famous statement that the twentieth century belongs to Canada was not, apparently, first said by him. According to John Robert Colombo, it was Nova Scotia Attorney-General James W. Longley who in 1902 declared: "The beginning of this century marks an epoch of phenomenal progress in British North America. The nineteenth century was the century of the United States. The twentieth century is Canada's century."[1] Longley may have been off by a century; but if there is a lesson to be learned from the twentieth century it is that if Canada is to realize its potential, it will have to earn it through creativity and innovation, and by having and international outlook. This is a footloose world, and opportunities are everywhere. While this book sets out the many problems Canada faces as we head towards the twenty-first century, its underlying message is that we do have the people to build a productive new economy and to be active participants in the challenging new world that is emerging. But it is up to us — by being open to entirely new ways of doing things — to realize this potential. The rest of the world won't do it for us.

The Next Canadian Century

1

The Canadian Challenge

A S CANADIANS ENTERED THE 1990s, the last decade of the twentieth century and the forerunner to the twenty-first, every-thing seemed to be going wrong. Permanent plant shutdowns and rising unemployment spread through the country's industrial heartland. While some companies relocated in the United States or Mexico, once-proud industrial superstars, such as Canada's steel giants, floundered in red ink and a downsizing unrivalled since the devastating days of the 1930s Great Depression. Canada's farmers and fishermen fared no better. Canadian grain farmers on the prairies had to cope with falling prices and shrinking markets, and Saskatchewan appeared headed for long-term decline. Atlantic fish-ermen and fishworkers lost jobs as the fisheries catch was reduced and fish plants closed. Big Oil, once thought to be relatively immune to recession, flowed red ink as prices fell. Layoffs permeated the Oil Patch, not only in oil companies but in all the related drilling and other service industries. Canada's forest and mining companies also were confronted by big losses, mill shutdowns, layoffs, and down-graded credit ratings.

Unlike previous recessions, this one hit the service sector hard, and total services employment actually declined. Trust companies went broke and developers put downtown projects on hold. Even the big accounting and legal firms reduced their staff, and a succession of well-known retail names closed their doors. Television stations were no longer licences to print money. And advertising agencies had to cope with flat billings and layoffs. Not even that once mighty trio of billionaires, the Reichmann brothers, escaped unscathed with their huge Olympia & York real estate empire; falling rents and disappearing tenants meant that they could not keep up their payments to their creditors. In the public sector, schools, hospitals, and government departments also were exposed to the cost-cutting knife as jobs disappeared, services were reduced, and new projects were put on hold.

At the same time a massive public debt— $328.4 billion, or 48.3 per cent of gross domestic product (GDP) in 1991 — hobbled the ability of governments to kick-start the economy; meanwhile, the Bank of Canada's obsessive anti-inflation policy compounded the difficulties of the business sector by forcing up real interest rates and the exchange rate of the Canadian dollar. Canadians found themselves forced to divert a growing share of annual wealth production to foreign creditors as a rising net foreign debt (about $280 billion at the end of 1991 and growing by about $20 billion a year) made Canada one of the world's most heavily indebted countries and therefore increasingly vulnerable to the demands of Japanese, German, and U.S. life insurance companies, pension funds, and other purchasers of Canadian bonds. The Canadian way of life was being financed by increasing indebtedness to the rest of the world — a situation that could not continue indefinitely. To top it all off, Canadians were confronted with the question of whether the country would even survive into the mid-1990s. It is little wonder that Canadians were in a testy, frustrated, and angry mood, as well as being frightened about their own future.

Despite the knowledge that recessions always end, many Canadians felt that the decade ahead would be one of diminished expectations, with less economic security and few hopes for an improvement in their standard of living. Brian Neysmith, president of the Canadian Bond Rating Service, predicted that the 1990s would probably be a decade of declining living standards and limited growth. "You have to plan for a very, very slow-growth Canadian domestic society," he said, adding, "There's going to be material declines in the standard of living."[1] With 1.5 million Canadians unemployed by March 1992, with a growing number of older unemployed workers lacking the skills for new jobs, and with an increasing number of workers in their early twenties already experiencing successive periods on unemployment insurance or welfare, Canadians were entitled to ask what had gone wrong in a country that had so much promise and was said to be the envy of the world.

The issue was not what had been accomplished in the past. Canadians have built a civilized, decent society that has one of the

TABLE 1

Average Annual Wages and Salaries, 1967–90

(per hour in constant 1989 dollars)

Year	$ Per Hour	% Change
1967	9.50	
1968	10.29	+8.3
1969	10.81	+5.1
1970	11.27	+4.3
1971	11.84	+5.1
1972	12.27	+3.6
1973	12.81	+4.4
1974	13.21	+3.1
1975	13.78	+4.3
1976	14.60	+6.0
1977	14.50	−0.7
1978	13.89	−4.2
1979	13.75	−1.1
1980	13.94	+1.4
1981	14.03	+0.6
1982	14.00	−0.2
1983	13.65	−2.5
1984	13.70	+0.4
1985	13.77	+0.5
1986	13.80	+0.2
1987	14.00	+1.4
1988	14.13	+0.9
1989	14.05	−0.6
1990	14.29	+1.7

SOURCE: *OECD Economic Outlook, no. 50* (Paris: OECD, 1991).

world's highest standards of living. And Canadian wealth has been used in worthy pursuits — a society with a deep commitment to social justice, as exemplified in the health-care system and social safety net; in equalization payments to the poorer provinces and a constitutional commitment to regional development; and in legal aid, pay equity, accessible higher education, and support for cultural expression. What was at stake was whether Canada would have the kind of competitive economy that could sustain and build on the distinct Canadian society in the future, maintaining the quality of public goods and services. Could Canada build a new economy, based on knowledge, ideas, and innovation, to replace an economy that was based on the extraction of natural resources and old-style mass-production industries? In other words, could Canadians find new ways of creating wealth in an increasingly open and competitive global economy, one in which even small companies in small towns had to worry about what a competitor might be doing far away in South Korea or Mexico? For this new economy to emerge, far-reaching changes in Canadian attitudes, priorities, and institutions would be needed; the 1990s could not be a time for half-measures or tinkering. While the 1991 recession would eventually end, a massive restructuring of the Canadian economy was needed as well.

It was not hard for Canadians, facing the daily challenge of supporting their families, to know that something was wrong. Many people felt poorer, and with good reason. According to the Economic Council of Canada, average hourly real wages, which rose 4.9 per cent a year from 1968 to 1976, declined 0.2 per cent a year, after inflation, from 1977 to 1990. In 1990, the average hourly real wage was 2.1 per cent lower than it had been in 1976. Other surveys from Statistics Canada revealed a similar picture. In 1988 the average Canadian worker earned $29,969, which, after inflation, was 1.6 per cent lower than the average pay cheque in 1977. In other words, Canadians had experienced more than a decade of no growth in income — the first time this had happened since the Great Depression of the 1930s.[2]

Family incomes also stagnated through the 1980s, even though a growing number of families had two income earners and a growing number of teenagers were working long hours in fast-food chains and other low-wage activities. Between 1980 and 1989 there was virtually no increase, after inflation, in average family income. According to Roger Love and Susan Poulin of Statistics Canada, this experience "contrasted sharply with earlier decades where family income at the end of the decade was substantially higher than at the beginning."[3] Average after-tax family income in 1989 was only 0.5 per cent higher than in 1980, compared with a 22 per cent real (after-inflation) increase between 1971 and 1979. The identical statistics are not available for the 1950s and 1960s, but pre-tax average family income rose 27 per cent after inflation in the 1950s and 34 per cent in the 1960s. "The 1960s was clearly the period of greatest growth followed by the 1950s," another Statistics Canada report on income distribution said. "During the 1970s, the real increase was still significant, though down sharply from the growth of the previous decade. The 1980s has seen much less growth compared to the three previous decades."[4] Moreover, if many married women had not entered the workforce, family incomes would in fact have fallen — a matter of concern for the increasing number of single-parent families.

There are several explanations for the stagnation in living standards in the 1980s. One is the changing mix of jobs. High-paying manufacturing positions disappeared, and there was an increase in the number of lower-paying service positions (as well as high-paying service ones). As companies strove to reduce costs, they eliminated manufacturing jobs and middle layers of management, and closed plants: between 1980 and 1991, 246,000 jobs disappeared in manufacturing, while the number in service industries rose by 1.8 million. With a growing percentage of workers employed in services (66 per cent in 1980 and 72 percent in 1991), where average weekly incomes (not including overtime) are only 81 per cent of those in manufacturing and resources, it is not surprising that average incomes declined. Although the services sector provides many of Canada's best-paying positions in finance, real estate, law, accounting, advertising, and medicine, a large proportion in this sector are still "McJobs" in fast-food restaurants and shopping mall stores. Steel giant Stelco cut its workforce more than half to 12,890 and Northern Telecom added 900 new jobs in Canada between 1981 and 1991, bringing its total to 21,700, but McDonald's added 29,000 full- and part-time jobs, bringing its total to 60,000. Likewise, the growing share of new jobs in small business meant lower incomes, since small businesses pay less, provide fewer benefits, and offer less job security than large businesses.

But the underlying explanation for Canada's stagnating standard of living through the 1980s has been its poor performance in productivity, the weakest performance among the major industrial countries. Between 1979 and 1990, productivity rose at an annual average rate of 0.2 per cent in Canada, compared with 0.3 per cent in the United States, 2.0 per cent in Japan, and relatively high rates elsewhere. Similarly, manufacturing output per hour rose an average of only 1.8 per cent in Canada between 1979 and 1989, compared with 3.2 per cent in the United States and 5.5 per cent in Japan. If our productivity performance is persistently weaker than that of other major countries, we shall inevitably fall behind those other countries in living standards. U.S. economist Paul Krugman

TABLE 2

Canada's Productivity Performance in the Business Sector

Percentage Changes at Annual Rates

Country	Total Factor Productivity			Labour Productivity		
	1960–73	*1973–79*	*1979–90*	*1960–73*	*1973–79*	*1979–90*
CANADA	2.0	0.8	0.2	2.8	1.5	1.2
United States	1.6	-0.4	0.3	2.2	0	0.7
Japan	5.9	1.4	2.0	8.6	2.9	3.0
Germany	2.7	1.8	0.8	4.6	3.1	1.6
France	4.0	1.7	1.7	5.4	3.0	2.6
Italy	4.6	2.2	1.3	6.3	2.9	1.9
Britain	2.3	0.6	1.6	3.6	1.6	2.1
Belgium	3.9	1.5	1.4	5.2	2.8	2.4
Denmark	2.8	1.2	1.3	4.3	2.6	2.1
Finland	3.2	1.5	2.5	4.9	3.2	3.6
Holland	3.1	1.5	0.9	4.8	2.8	1.5
Sweden	2.7	0.3	0.9	4.1	1.5	1.7
Switzerland	2.0	-0.4	0.4	3.2	0.8	0.9

SOURCE: *OECD Economic Outlook, no. 50* (Paris: OECD, 1991).

explains that "productivity isn't everything, but in the long run it is almost everything. A country's ability to raise its standard of living over time depends almost entirely on its output per worker."[5]

To some extent, Canada's poor productivity performance had been concealed because GDP per capita has been rising. But this has been because of the growing proportion of Canadians in the workforce, not because of productivity gains; so, as we saw above, the income of individual workers has not been growing. As Michael Porter's report on Canada's economy explained, "in the long run, productivity determines the standard of living by setting wages, profits, and ultimately the resources available to meet social needs." A country with rising productivity constantly upgrades the products it makes, develops more efficient ways of making products, and moves into higher-value exports, the Porter report said. "It is also an economy that has the capability to compete in entirely new industries, absorbing the resources made available from improved productivity in existing industries."[6]

Productivity depends on much more than the efforts and attitudes of workers, though these are of course important. Productivity in the economy and in individual businesses, government agencies, schools, and hospitals is affected by red tape, bureaucratic and inefficient organizational structures, out-dated job classifications, and other sources of high costs. At the same time, it is highly dependent on the education, skills, and training of workers — and on their ability to use new technology — as well as on investment in the latest state-of-the art technology. To be highly productive, employees need the best available technologies, but the potential of these technologies can only be captured if the people using them are well educated and if the structure of the workplace gives them the opportunity to employ their skills.

Productivity also depends on good management, and this could be a major cause of Canada's poor performance. It is the job of management to make sure that capital and technology, employees, and raw materials and components are used effectively; so management decisions on workplace organization, relations with employees, investment in training, investment in new technologies and in research and development, quality systems, and long-term corporate vision all influence productivity. Likewise, unions can influence productivity by deciding whether they will pursue issues such as worker training and cooperate in workplace restructuring in collective bargaining, or whether they will resist change. Governments, too, shape productivity, not just in the economic climate they create through policies that determine inflation, interest rates, and economic growth, but also through the type of rules and regulations they set for the economy, the tax system, competition policy, infrastructure spending, education and training policies, science and technology policy, health policy, and the design and incentives of social policy.

Canada's "most serious weakness," the Porter study said, is that "since the early 1970s, Canada has ranked near the bottom of all major countries in productivity growth." In manufacturing, Canada had the worst productivity growth of all the G-7 countries (the United States, Japan, Germany, France, Italy, Britain, and Canada). Between 1979 and 1989, our unit labour costs rose faster than those of most industrial countries and more than twice as fast as those in the United States, "which is the most important competitive benchmark for Canadian industry."

TABLE 3

Average Annual Rates of Change in Manufacturing Output Per Hour

Country	1960–73 (%)	1973–79 (%)	1979–89 (%)
CANADA	4.5	2.1	1.8
United States	3.3	1.6	3.2
Japan	10.3	5.5	5.5
France	6.4	4.6	3.4
Germany	5.7	4.2	2.0
Italy	6.4	5.7	4.0
Britain	4.2	1.2	4.8
Denmark	6.4	4.2	1.4
Netherlands	7.3	5.4	3.7
Sweden	6.4	2.6	2.2

SOURCE: U.S. Bureau of Labor Statistics, as cited in National Academy of Sciences, *The Government Role in Civilian Technology* (Washington: National Academy Press, 1992).

Judith Maxwell, chairperson of the Economic Council of Canada, contends that "the deterioration in productivity growth in the past two decades explains a lot of the political and social tensions in Canada."[7] In prolonged periods of stagnation in living standards, social consensus can break down and strains can emerge in public support for social and other programs. Much of Canada's modern social system, including health care, social assistance, and regional development, was set up in the 1960s when high productivity growth could still be taken for granted. But when that growth slows or halts, these programs become a growing burden, and pressures mount for their dilution or dismantling as government revenues fall off and debt burdens mount.

As much as anything, Canada's deficit and debt problems are a consequence of its failure to restore stronger productivity growth after the oil shocks of the 1970s, as other industrial countries did. If Canada had maintained higher productivity growth, it would not have the debt and deficit problems that now hold the economy in a straitjacket. A high-productivity economy is a high-wage economy; but as Maxwell points out, to compete as a low-wage economy by paying low wages and accepting low productivity growth means conceding that Canada's standard of living is too high. As a result of poor productivity, Canadians have not been able to maintain the

TABLE 4
Production Per Employee, 1980–88

	(1980 = 100)	
Country	Total Manufacturing	Metalworking/Machinery
CANADA	115	123
United States	142	149
Japan	129	155
France	126	126
Germany	126	113
Britain	154	n.a.
Netherlands	135	130
Sweden	128	134

SOURCE: OECD, *Indicators of Industrial Activity* (Paris: OECD, 1989).

good life. "In essence, many Canadians — mainly those under 40 — have not been able to achieve their expectations for higher incomes and a better quality of life. This is a painful shock for a frontier country built on the implicit promise that each generation would do better than the last."[8] Considering Canada's mediocre record in investing in innovation through research and development, as well as the fact that its investment in new machinery and equipment (the way new technology is introduced into the economy) has been the lowest of any G-7 country as a share of GDP for the past 30 years, it is not surprising that Canada's performance has been so dismal when measured against its potential.

Even in the best circumstances, Canada faces what British economist Vivien Walsh calls "the small country squeeze."[9] It is in the development and use of new technologies that countries have the greatest scope for new economic growth; and the big economic powers, such as the United States, Japan, and Germany, have the greatest financial and scale capacities to develop the industries of the future, putting inevitable pressure on Canadian companies that are trying to move into these same areas. At the same time, dynamic newly industrializing countries, such as South Korea, Taiwan, Thailand, Mexico, and Brazil, are increasing pressure from below by moving competitively into more mature industries.

Small size does not rule out success in technology, though, as the experience of Sweden and Switzerland shows — not to mention examples such as Northern Telecom, Spar Aerospace, and CAE Industries in Canada. But it does mean that small countries have an even more urgent need than large ones to have clear economic strategies and the businesses that can make these strategies work. Moreover, as Walsh points out, there are many factors that will determine whether an economically smaller country, such as Canada, will be successful. "These will include past investment, determining current levels of industrialization; natural resources; geographical location and a variety of historical factors; the innovativeness and strategic orientation of firms and scientific and technical skills, experience and knowledge of the population as well, of course, as the policy instruments adopted by governments."[10] The competitiveness of the economy is not just the sum of the competitiveness of all its businesses, says Walsh. It depends on other factors as well, including some intangible ones, "which amount to the ethos and culture of a nation as well as its industrial and institutional infrastructure and which provides a more or a less-stimulating environment for innovation, entrepreneurship, marketing and export."

At the same time, says Walsh, small countries may find that much of their production consists of semi-processed raw materials or parts and components for other countries (in Canada's case, for the United States). If suppliers and customers are in another country, "the small country becomes characterized by units that are isolated from each other, as well as dependent on the rest of the world. The 'normal' inputs and outputs that one would expect in a national economy with horizontal and vertical relationships between firms are eroded." In other words, the clusters of activity in which suppliers, customers, producers, research institutes, and educational institutions all interact with one another to create a dynamic potential for innovation and growth are much harder to establish.

Canada is handicapped in the new economy, because much of its past investment and hence its industrial base has been tied to the production of semi-processed resources at low cost, rather than being directed to science, technology, and innovation in order to develop advanced, high-value products. In the past, science, technology, and innovation have not ranked high in the country's agenda, notwithstanding the remarkable success of individual Canadians and some businesses. As a result, many talented Canadians have been forced to move to the United States and, more recently, also to Japan in order to make use of their research and other abilities. Moreover, Canada lacks a growth agenda for the future to facilitate and accelerate a shift to a high-value economy based on ideas and knowledge, an economy that can provide high-skill jobs with high pay — which means that talented Canadians will continue to leave.

Canadians have been inundated with warnings about the future, but with little result. Senator Maurice Lamontagne, in a series of farsighted reports in the early 1970s, warned of the urgent need to change course; and the Science Council of Canada, in a succession of reports, sounded the same urgent message through the 1970s and into the 1980s. But high resource prices through much of the 1970s made business and government complacent about the need to build a new economy, and there was complacency again as a result of the speculative environment and easy growth of the mid-1980s (which was attributable to a low Canadian dollar and to soaring demand in the United States because of the Reagan administration's high-deficit fiscal policy). A 1989 C.D. Howe Institute report on Canada's future priorities never once mentioned the need for a new economy based on science, technology, and innovation.[11] But by the late 1980s, the message began to sink in among some Canadians, and it became more pronounced in the early 1990s — though Canada still lacks a strategy for the twenty-first century.

In a 1988 speech, Larkin Kerwin, then president of the National Research Council, stressed that "Canadians must face some very unpleasant facts: Among the industrialized nations of the world, we rank as technological illiterates; we have become incompetent in the unfolding scientific civilization." As Kerwin said, "we cut down more trees than any other country, yet we import chain saws. We have an elaborate healthcare system, yet we import stretchers. We import 76 per cent of our machinery, 40 per cent of our electrical products, 80 per cent of our healthcare equipment." And in an attempt to pay for what we buy from the rest of the world, "we continue to export relatively raw natural resources at a time when there is a surplus of virtually every commodity in the world, including food. Simply put, we are not able to compete because we lack the knowledge to do so effectively."[12]

In the same year a Science Council of Canada statement, *Gearing up for Global Markets*, warned that "although the Canadian economy is flying high, this country's industry faces testing times. Ahead is a new era of intense international competition that will be technology-driven."[13] Canada was going into the Canada–U.S. free trade agreement without any kind of economic strategy to restructure its industry or upgrade its workforce so that it would be able to compete in the new environment; and at the same time, the country faced growing competitive pressure from the technological progress emerging in Asia and other parts of the world. "To prepare for the world of the 1990s, it is necessary to act quickly and aggressively, while corporate Canada prospers," the Science Council said. But this warning was ignored, and a year later Canada began its slide to the recession of the early 1990s.

The Canadian Institute for Advanced Research, a remarkable body set up in the early 1980s to help create a new economy with new institutions, warned in another 1988 report, *Innovation and Canada's Prosperity*, that "Canada, as an economically small country, faces critical problems of adapting its institutions, policies, and practices to a radically new environment." In the new global economy, science, engineering, and technology have acquired the power "to transform the comparative advantage and prosperity of nations," the report said, so that "science-based innovation has become the driving force for the technological and corporate change that creates new tradeable goods and services." Moreover, the report emphasized, innovation applies as much to institutions and their management as it does to new processes for production or the development of new products and services.[14]

The report stressed that the ability of a country and its industries, universities, and workers to transform technological advances into competitive processes and new products and services will determine the country's ability to participate in the new economy; and it noted that "Canada has an appallingly weak capacity to perform in industry, long-term, applied research that either may establish the basis for significant new products or services or may not, at the time of execution, prove relevant to the targeted area." Canada, it said, urgently needs new institutions to reach a consensus on a national agenda for innovation and a national policy to enhance the country's science, technology, and innovation capacity.

In a powerful expression of business concern, David Vice, then president of Northern Telecom and chairman of the Canadian Manufacturers' Association, warned in a 1989 report on Canada's future: "Our history has largely been one of passively accepting the economic direction determined first by Britain, and then by the United States. We have been dominated by, and accepted as given, world market prices for our natural resources without articulating clearly for ourselves our economic future and how to get there. In the global economy that will make the leap forward into the 21st century, this is a recipe for disaster."[15] Canada is becoming poorer relative to other countries, is losing ground to its competitors, and is failing to build its capacity to generate wealth in the future, the report argued, and it said that although Canadians might find this hard to believe (it was written before the 1990–91 recession), "today's prosperity is masking the erosion of the nation's underlying capacity to create wealth. Prosperity had blinded us to the need to keep pace with economic change, to adjust our economy to new conditions of international competition."

A 1991 confidential paper from the Department of Industry, Science and Technology in Ottawa told the federal cabinet that high economic growth was unattainable in the 1990s without significant advances in competitiveness through improved productivity growth: "The private sector on its own cannot fully realize the potential of the Canadian economy. A comprehensive national strategy to improve competitiveness is needed to improve Canada's international trade performance, reduce pressure on the budget deficit and avoid an erosion in Canadians' standard of living relative to other major industrialized economies."[16] The paper said that only about 3 per cent of companies in Canada have any research capability and "most have no technical staff capable of identifying or acquiring best practice technology." In fact, 70 per cent of manufacturing companies, it claimed, had no engineer on staff, and Canadian industry spending on science, technology, and innovation was "weak" by the standards of leading industrial countries.

TABLE 5
Investment in Machinery and Equipment

	Annual Average as % of GDP	
Country	*1960–89*	*1980–89*
CANADA	7.4	7.4
United States	7.5	7.9
Japan	12.3	10.4
Germany	8.6	8.4
France	8.8	8.6
Italy	9.9	10.1
Britain	8.5	8.2
Sweden	7.7	8.2

SOURCE: OECD, as quoted in Michael E. Porter and The Monitor Co., *Canada at the Crossroads* (Ottawa: Business Council on National Issues and Ministry of Supply and Services, 1991).

In a 1991 presentation to Prime Minister Brian Mulroney, Peter Nicholson, a senior vice-president of the Bank of Nova Scotia and chairman of the National Advisory Board on Science and Technology's committee on national science and technology priorities, warned that we "face a declining relative standard of living, unless we become much more adept in applying science-based technology to create a continuous flow of innovation and productivity growth. There is no more serious challenge facing Canada today." Nicholson added, "If our economy continues to lose its vitality, all the fiscal, social and political strains in the federation will become unmanageable."[17]

Much the same warning was contained in the powerful 1991 report by Michael Porter and the Monitor Co.[18] "Canada today is at an economic crossroads" and "the core of its economic prosperity is at risk," stated this report. Although the country's heritage of resources, its proximity to the huge U.S. market, and the relatively high tariffs that once protected Canadian industry have allowed Canada to achieve one of the world's highest standards of living, these same advantages "have led to an array of policies, strategies and attitudes on the part of governments, business, labour and individual Canadians that leave the economy in many respects ill-equipped to respond to a rapidly changing competitive environment." Noting that the restructuring of the Canadian economy was underway, the report stressed that "signs are already accumulating that Canadian industry is encountering difficulties as it confronts this changed and more competitive environment. If the current trajectory continues, the standard of living of Canadians seems destined to fall behind." Reinforcing the risk of this, the Porter study said, was the long-term trend of rising unemployment in Canada. As the *Economist* asked, "What's a nice country like Canada doing in a mess like this?"[19]

At the time of writing, the federal government is in the midst of its own Prosperity Initiative, with a vast advertising and public relations budget — just when the government has said that it can no longer afford to maintain crucially important national institutions such as the Science Council of Canada and the Economic Council of Canada, with their capacity for ongoing research into the country's future. It remains to be seen whether the Prosperity Initiative will amount to anything more than a public relations exercise.

One of the major forces shaping Canada's future is the Canada–U.S. free trade agreement, which is to be extended to include Mexico. This trade pact reinforces the trend to a world divided into three economic competing and potentially hostile blocs: a triad of North America, dominated by the United States; Europe, dominated by Germany; and Asia, dominated by Japan. The next 10 years could also see growing conflict between different economic systems which, while they are all based on market systems, represent different flavours of capitalism with differing roles for government and different business and other institutions.

For Canadians, the key issue is whether the free trade agreement will integrate Canada into the U.S. economy and make it so dependent on the U.S. market that it loses its capacity to sustain a society that has different policies and institutions from the United States. For example, the former chairman of the U.S. Federal Reserve, Paul Volcker, told a 1991 monetary conference organized by the Kansas City Federal Reserve Bank that a currency union or arrangement in North America is almost inevitable. "If we came back here five years from now," he said, "I would not be at all surprised to find a fixed exchange rate between the peso, the U.S. dollar and the Canadian dollar."[20] If this happens and the Canadian dollar is formally tied to the U.S. dollar, Canada will lose all control over its monetary policy and its role in fighting inflation or unemployment. Yet businesses that are worried about competing in the continental market may become strong proponents of a fixed exchange rate to bring greater certainty to trade and investment decisions. One prominent Canadian economist, Tom Courchene, has already argued that the exchange rate should be pegged.

"The trend towards regionalization counterposed against the authority of individual countries to set economic policy could lead to a new set of challenges for national governments," the United Nations Centre for Transnational Corporations warns. "Regional integration implies increased competition among firms in the region, which often respond by shifting their activities according to where they make the most economic sense, irrespective of national borders."[21] This raises a special threat for Canada, as was pointed out in a 1991 survey of Japanese business executives conducted by the Japanese consulate in Toronto. Many of the Japanese executives questioned whether Canada would benefit from a North American free trade agreement expanded to include Mexico. Canada was disadvantaged, the report said, "because the United States maintains a large market advantage and Mexico has an inexpensive labor advantage, whereas Canada is weak in both areas." This, it said, was the reason why Canada immediately had to "restructure its industries to become more competitive" if it was to "survive" in a unified North American market. Otherwise, Canada could become the attic of North America.[22]

In turn, the United Nations has warned, in a report with special significance for Canada, that corporations in regional blocs may "put competitive pressures on the national policy systems that regulate economic activity in individual countries. . . . For example, a country with policies of high taxation and extensive social benefits may find its fiscal base eroded, if business shifts to neighboring countries with lower taxes following regional integration." Indeed, said the U.N. study, "a whole range of policies, including industrial, environmental and social policies, may face increasing pressures to change as a result of integration with countries with different policy frameworks. Integration may thus lead not only to competition among firms but competition among policy systems, and national governments are likely to find it necessary to adapt their policies to reflect the new environment."[23]

As part of this process, transnational corporations are now looking at regions rather than at individual countries as their relevant market and production spaces. This explains why, since the free trade agreement, there has been so little Japanese investment in Canada apart from natural resources and real estate. Japan is putting its investment in Mexico, where labour costs are low, and in the United States, where it is closer to major customers and is better protected against the vagaries of U.S. trade laws and "buy American" policies than it would be in Canada. Nor does the free trade agreement give corporations investing in Canada assured duty-free access to the U.S. market. Even if Canada succeeds in rolling back the tariff imposed by the United States on Canadian-produced Honda automobiles, the damage has already been done: Japanese (and other) foreign investors will be more cautious about investing in Canada to serve the U.S. market.

Since the free trade agreement came into effect, many of our federal and provincial policies have been subjected to intense comparison with those of the United States (including taxation, labour standards, regional development, unemployment insurance, and social assistance), and the argument is increasingly being made by business groups that we cannot afford to be different from the United States. This should be no surprise, since one of the principal motives behind business support for the Canada–U.S. free trade deal was to bring Canadian policies into closer harmonization with those of the U.S. This was put most bluntly by Gordon Bell, then president of the Bank of Nova Scotia, who told a 1987 business audience in Toronto, "By and large, the opponents to freer trade hold an interventionist view." If they block the trade deal, Bell said, "they will seek much more vigorous use of subsidies, quotas, regulations and governmental decisions as to winners and losers — all those government instruments that the free trade agreement would proscribe."[24]

Since these harmonization pressures will be felt in almost every area of national and local life, it is crucial to identify the areas that are most important to Canadians — for example, health care, culture, public infrastructure, the planning process of our cities, social policy, the fostering of Canadian companies, the environment, and the workplace. If Canada is to be more than the attic of North America and more than one big U.S. branch plant, it must work hard and creatively to be different — perhaps as the Scandinavia of North America.

This effort to resist U.S. pressure for harmonization will be even more difficult because the free trade agreement will mean an increased assertion of north-south forces between the United States and Canada and a decline of east-west commercial links within the country. National symbols will face new threats, as is already evident in the airline industry and the continuing cultural inroads of U.S. media, such as satellite broadcasting. More of Canada's distribution by rail and truck will take place through the United States, with less traffic on the Trans-Canada Highway and Canadian rail systems. Canada's electronic highway — the national telecommunications system — could be threatened by new network links through the United States unless ways are found of sustaining and enhancing the nation's electronic spine.

Canada itself was established in defiance of the strong southward pull of the United States. Transcontinental railways, prairie immigration, the national broadcasting and telephone systems, the first national airline, national systems of fiscal equalization, national standards in health care, the use of crown corporations as vehicles for national objectives and regional development — all were designed to offset the pull of the United States and to build a nation in which the various regions were linked to one another. The free trade agreement will profoundly weaken these east-west ties. We can see signs of this already.

For British Columbia, the free trade agreement means close links with Washington and Oregon in the Pacific Northwest. For Alberta, it means closer links with Denver, Colorado, and, through energy trade, with California. Winnipeg is looking to new ties with Minneapolis through the Red River corridor. Ontario is increasingly a part of the Great Lakes economy, which encompasses six Great Lakes states, along with upstate New York. And both Quebec and the Atlantic provinces are looking to New York and New England. As these north-south ties intensify, how much will Canadians still have in common? If the economic ties are north-south, who cares about the Trans-Canada Highway? And why should rich provinces spend money on equalization payments to poorer provinces if those provinces use the money to pay for U.S. imports? A Canada in which the major cities — Vancouver, Calgary, Edmonton, Winnipeg, Toronto, Montreal, and Halifax — are all looking south could easily become one in which Canadians have little or nothing to say to one another.

In 1981, U.S. journalist Joel Garreau wrote a provocative book, *The Nine Nations of North America*, in which he predicted that Canada and the United States would break apart into nine different regions. While Quebec would stay on its own, Atlantic Canada would become part of New England; Ontario would be part of what Garreau called the foundry, which would include Great Lakes industrial states such as Michigan, Illinois, and Ohio; the prairies would be part of the breadbasket, along with the main U.S. Midwest agricultural states; most of Alberta and British Columbia, the Far North, and northern Ontario would be part of the empty quarter, which would include U.S. states such as Montana, Colorado, Arizona, and

Utah; and the coastline of British Columbia, together with the coastlines of Washington, Oregon, and California, would become Ecotopia.[25] All this may have seemed far-fetched at the time. But today it is clear that a restructuring of trade and other links on the continent will put strong pressures on the ties between the different parts of Canada, making it imperative that we have policies to ensure that a sense of Canadian identity and purpose is sustained.

Now that the free trade area is to be expanded to include Mexico — and, perhaps later, other countries in Latin America — further changes are likely in the dynamics of the North American continent. As Mexico's population approaches 140 million by 2025, and as Mexico's wealth and industrial capacity increases, Canadians could find that the once special Canada–U.S. relationship is overshadowed by a more important U.S.–Mexico relationship. Moreover, Canada will be pressed to participate in new continental institutional arrangements covering labour mobility, the environment, energy, monetary and fiscal policy, and trade and other relations with the rest of the world.

M. Delal Baer, director of the Mexico Project at the Center for Strategic and International Studies in Washington, has even suggested that the three countries revisit the spirit of Jean Monnet's Commission, which set out the strategy and rationale for the European Community. "The three nations of North America, in more modest fashion, have also arrived at a defining moment," he says, calling for the appointment of a wiseman's North American commission to operate when the three-way trade deal is in place. Among other things, the commission could "adopt a forward-looking agenda on themes such as North American competitiveness, links between scientific institutions, borderland integration, the continental ecological system and educational and cultural exchanges. The historic import of NAFTA calls for marshalling creative resources as never before to consider the future of North America."[26] The problem is that in this type of arrangement, the United States would always have the majority vote.

Building a new Canadian economy with greater ties to the global rather than solely North American economy could be one way of protecting Canada's interests and preventing them from being subsumed in a new North American relationship. This could also be a unifying theme within Canada. But it can only happen if Canadian business has the initiative to look beyond the U.S. market and to accept the implications of a global market in deeds as well as words.

For a start, this means paying much greater attention to the future of the resource industries, which still generate most of Canada's trade surplus (along with the auto industry). All of the sectors — from grains and fish to oil, natural gas, forest products, and mineral products — have been hard hit during the 1991 recession. According to the World Bank, non-fuel commodity prices in real or after-inflation dollars were at a postwar low in 1991. Based on 1979–81 prices = 100, non-fuel commodity prices fell to 71.1 in 1988 and to 58.2 in 1991. Commodity prices were expected to remain low until the middle 1990s before increasing again; but by the year 2000, they were still expected to be well below the real levels of 1979–81.[27]

One new factor, as the World Bank explained, is the entry of the former Soviet Union republics into the world commodity market. Indeed, once Russia and the other republics achieve economic reforms and begin to make or attract the necessary investments, they could become formidable exporters. Russia could become the new Canada, exploiting its vast forests for paper and lumber pro-

---

TABLE 6
Real Commodity Price Changes

Commodity	Average Annual Rate of Change		
	1980–90 (%)	1991 (%)	1990–2000 (%)
Petroleum	-6.6	-20.3	0.2
Non-petroleum commodities	-5.1	-6.7	0.5
Agriculture	-6.4	-5.2	1.1
Food, including cereals	-6.6	-4.9	1.3
Raw materials	-5.6	-6.4	0.6
Timber	-2.5	3.3	1.7
Metals and minerals	-2.8	-11.3	-0.9

SOURCE: World Bank, *Global Economic Prospects and the Developing Countries* (Washington: World Bank, 1992).

duction in both the European and the Asian markets, competing against Canadian producers, and competing against Canada for investment dollars. Japanese and South Korean companies are already moving into Siberian forests. Russian aluminum production has forced layoffs at Alcan. Other minerals, such as copper, nickel, lead, zinc, uranium, and gold, also could become major Russian exports by the end of the decade. Likewise, Russia and the Ukraine could again become major agricultural producers and net exporters, eliminating Canada's single largest export market for wheat.

There will be other forces, too, that will limit the scope for Canada's traditional raw material exports. One is the emergence of lower-cost producers in the developing world and the attraction these reserves now have for mining companies (for example, copper in Chile and various metals in Mexico), though these reserves will present investment opportunities for Canadian mining companies. Similarly, new and faster-growing sources of pulp and paper are emerging in Latin America and elsewhere. Meanwhile, the growing move to paper recycling means that more production will shift closer to major U.S. cities, where used papers for recycling can more easily be obtained. Ontario and Quebec forest communities can be expected to face more shutdowns, because although many of the paper machines have been upgraded, they date back to the 1920s and cannot compete with new technologies from Scandinavia. The high cost of western Canada's coal production and its need for huge government subsidies can be seen in the disastrous experience of coal projects in northeastern British Columbia. In addition, relatively weak oil prices mean that new megaprojects, such as Hibernia or Alberta tar sands plants, make little economic sense on their own and represent a misallocation of governments' scarce dollars to support new industrial development. At the same time, Canada's oil production from conventional sources in Alberta will decline over the next decade, and this will mean less work for drilling and other service companies within Canada. Canadian oil companies, like Canadian mining and forest companies, will have to diversify abroad and develop high-value products in Canada if they are to prosper.

Savings in materials and the substitution of materials are other factors affecting the growth of Canada's resource industries.

According to a World Bank study, the growth of consumption in most minerals has slowed markedly over the past decade. While future growth, especially in the developing countries, will increase demand, other developments will constrain the rate of increase. One of these is the pressure to save materials, both for environmental reasons and because of costs. "Thinner coatings of tin, nickel and zinc as well as the use of thinner- and smaller-gauge aluminum and copper lead to savings of these metals," the World Bank study found. "The oil price shock of 1973 stimulated the automobile industry to downsize and substitute for better fuel efficiency, by means such as smaller batteries (which use lead)," while "fibre optics technology almost totally eliminated copper use in telecommunications."[28] Similarly, plastics and aluminum have displaced steel in automobiles.

But an even bigger challenge will come as advances are made in the exciting new world of advanced or new materials: composites, new alloys, ceramics, fibre optics, polymers, and new superconductive materials. Plastics that are stronger than steel, new materials constructed atom by atom, "intelligent materials" that are sensitive to changes in their environment, and ceramics that can be made flexible will transform many of the ways we make things, from buildings and bridges to computer chips and automobiles. Because

---

TABLE 7
Growth in World Consumption of Metals

	Average Annual Rate of Increase	
Metal	1961–73 (%)	1973–88 (%)
Steel	5.7	0.7
Aluminum	9.9	1.7
Copper	4.6	1.3
Lead	4.2	0.9
Zinc	5.9	0.6
Nickel	6.2	1.9

SOURCE: Buom-Jong Choe, "Global Trends in Raw Materials Consumption," Working Paper 804, International Economics Department (Washington: World Bank, 1991).

of the revolutionary potential of these materials, countries such as the United States and Japan are investing billions of dollars in research and development.

Canadian resource companies do not have a strong presence in the development of new materials. Instead, as Science Council of Canada chairperson Janet Halliwell has pointed out, Canadian resource companies emphasize "low costs of production above all else," with low investment in high-value products from the resources. This low investment, Halliwell argues, "is part and parcel of what might be called Canada's 'implicit' or 'unconscious' industrial strategy. Too often Canadian resource-based companies, by and large, have chosen to compete primarily on the basis of price rather than on the basis of product and service innovation (or quality or timeliness to market)."[29]

Yet despite Canada's emphasis on process, it has little to offer the rest of the world in technologies for the mining, oil and gas, or forest industries — or, for that matter, in agricultural and fisheries technologies. Canada's only strength is in the engineering of resource projects. Instead of developing their own technologies, Canadian resource companies use those imported from Scandinavia, Germany, Japan, and the United States. Magnus Ericsson of the Stockholm-based Raw Materials Group believes that there will be a huge market for mining technology and related environmental technology in Russia and the other former Soviet republics, as well as opportunities for Western mining companies to buy a stake in the mining industry of the former Soviet states. The Soviet Union was the world's leading producer of iron ore, nickel, lead, manganese, and potash, and was strong in copper, gold, diamonds, platinum, chromite, and zinc. But the main mining companies moving into these states are Finnish, German, and French.[30]

The resource issue is crucial because resources are the source of so much of the foreign exchange that is needed to help pay Canada's way in the world and because these industries are so important to so many different communities and regions in Canada. As the Porter report observed, "Canada has the largest world export share in the crude materials sector, a rather unusual pattern for a wealthy, industrialized nation." Resource-based exports account for nearly half Canada's total exports. "Canada's tendency to export unprocessed or semi-processed natural resources has persisted, in contrast with other advanced nations," Porter pointed out, adding, "Sweden has capitalized on competitive advantages in process technology and sustained its competitiveness in resource-based industries, even though its natural resource positions themselves no longer represent an advantage."[31] Canada has not followed suit, though industrial countries are moving to materials-saving systems and new materials, and developing countries are opening up their own resource supplies.

The weakness of a resource-based economy was spelled out in Porter's monumental book, *The Competitive Advantage of Nations.* "While the possession of abundant natural resources may support a high per capita income for a sustained period of time," he said, a resource-dependent economy "is one with a poor foundation for sustained productivity growth." In the case of Canada, he said, few industries outside the resources sector "possess international competitive advantage."

Porter argues that, eventually, "dependence on natural resources will leave a nation vulnerable to depletion, new foreign sources or technological changes that reduce or eliminate resource needs." But resources present another kind of challenge: they can provide a high standard of living for a time without forcing a country to upgrade its other capacities, and this makes it hard to move beyond a natural resource economy and develop other industries. Countries with high levels of resource wealth may bypass the evolution of an innovation-based economy and move from a resource economy to a wealth-driven economy that spends its time in mergers and acquisitions, and investments in financial assets, activities that eventually lead to economic decline because "an economy driven by past wealth is not able to maintain its wealth." As a result, "diminishing competition, adversarial labor-management relations, and protection may arise as attention in the economy shifts towards preservation of the status quo. Nations such as Canada and Norway face this risk," says Porter.[32]

Economists used to call this the Dutch disease. A country that has large resources usually has a lower level of industrial technology, according to Hiroshi Kakaza of the International University of Japan. He describes how overconcentration on resource production, investment, and exports, particularly by foreign investors, creates "an adverse environment for the introduction and diffusion of industrial technology. In a resource-based economy, the technology adopted tends to be highly capital-intensive," and resource exports "push up the real exchange rate which discourages the introduction of appropriate technology for manufactured exports."[33] While it would make no economic sense for Canada to turn its back on its resource industries, the clear lesson is that Canadian resource industries rapidly have to improve their commitment to research and development, advancing their capabilities in new materials while also working much harder to strengthen Canadian capabilities in production technologies and engineering that can be sold around the world, as Inco had been trying to do.

Similarly, Canada has to find ways of looking beyond its dependence on the U.S. market. Although the United States will continue to offer great opportunities for Canadian exporters, it will have only modest economic growth through the 1990s, an OECD analysis says.[34] While North America will grow about 2.5 per cent a year through the 1990s, with an acceleration of "rust belt" companies and blue-collar jobs to Mexico, the European Community could grow 3–4 per cent a year, and the Asia-Pacific region is likely to grow 5–6 per cent a year, with Japan itself growing 3–4 percent a year. Asia's share of world income could rise from 24 per cent in 1989 to 35 per cent by 2010, and to over 50 per cent by 2040.

Prospects for Latin America and southern Asia, notably India, also are promising as economic reforms proceed. Whether or not U.S. President George Bush's proposal for hemispheric free trade, his Enterprise for the Americas, will proceed remains to be seen. But other regional trade groupings in Latin America are proceeding, and the market of 350 million people could double to more than 700 million by 2025; yet little Canadian trade is conducted in this direction. India, with a population that will exceed 1 billion people, has great potential as a major economy if it can continue with economic reforms and if it can resolve religious and ethnic conflicts. Rapid development of the coastal provinces of China could make the region of the South China Sea one giant and dynamic Hong Kong. Similarly, the former Soviet states, particularly Russia and the Ukraine, could become major destinations for both trade and investment.

Despite all these opportunities, Canada, with close to 75 per cent of its exports destined for the United States and most of its foreign direct investment in the United States, is not effectively participating in the rapidly evolving global economy. "It is ironic that Canada — probably the world's most multicultural nation — is in fact one of the least international in economic terms," says Bank of Nova Scotia chairman Cedric Ritchie. "Never mind that 25 per cent of our national output is exported, ranking us among the leading trading nations, at least statistically. The truth is that more than 75 per cent of those exports are to the United States. Many of them are shipments between parents and subsidiaries on opposite sides of a commercially integrated border. In fact, Canada has by far the *least* diversified trade among the world's major countries. And surveys regularly confirm that Canadian business, as a whole, is among the least outward-looking in the industrialized world."[35]

Even where Canada sells to other parts of the world, the bulk of its exports consists of raw materials; for instance, Canada sells coal and other resources to South Korea — and imports cars, television sets, and semiconductors. Canadians, says Ritchie, must become sophisticated world traders like the Dutch, Swedes, and Swiss. This means, though, that Canadians must have businesses that are run by executives who can look beyond North America and be able to produce the sophisticated goods and services that other countries want to buy. Since 1987, U.S. exports to Mexico have more than doubled. In this same period, Canadian exports there have actually declined, which suggests that Canada lacks the mix of high-value goods and services that Mexicans want to buy.

So Canada has to make a renewed effort to develop its manufacturing and tradable service industries. Yet there is a tendency to disregard the decline of manufacturing, despite the warning of top executives such as Sony's Akio Morita, who told an Ottawa conference that "such a trend is destructive. for in the long run, an economy that has lost its manufacturing base has lost its vital centre."[36] A prosperous economy needs a healthy manufacturing base, he stressed, adding that if this was not understood, Canada would "find itself on the sidelines of the great game called international business." Moreover, warns Charles McMillan, former policy adviser to Prime Minister Brian Mulroney and a professor of international business at York University, Canada's service industries also lack the strategy and resources to join in the new global competition. "In many respects, business as well as governments at all levels have frittered away a decade of enormous growth, he says, by failing "to establish the underlying infrastructure in manpower and technology necessary to compete globally in the next decade." While some Canadian service companies are successful — for example, in banking, insurance, and engineering — "few Canadian companies have either the managerial outlook or the necessary cash flow to enter the European, U.S. and Japanese markets on any sustained basis." McMillan predicts a growing trade deficit in services, which amounted to $7.2 billion in 1989. This will be made worse by the trend of foreign-owned subsidiaries to buy a growing share of services from their foreign parents.[37]

First of all, though, Canadians have to understand the new economy and how it works. Fraser Mustard of the Canadian Institute for Advanced Research puts it this way: the standard of living of a country depends on its capacity to produce. "When productive capacity increases, the citizens of a nation can choose to have more consumer goods, more health care, better education, a cleaner environment, or more of any number of other valuable goods and services. If total capacity does not grow, any increase in the production of one good or service must be accompanied by a reduction in some other good or service." This means that society must pay close attention to the productive or wealth-creating part of the economy.[38]

Mustard breaks the economy into the wealth-creating sector (which consists of the manufacturing and resource industries, plus tradable services such as transportation, communications, finance, engineering, design, and other business services) and the consumption sector (which consists of non-market areas such as health, education, social services, and public administration; and market areas such as retailing and other personal services). While the majority of Canadians work in the consumption sector, the health of this sector depends on the health of the wealth-creating sector. Without a strong wealth-creating sector, Canadians cannot afford the quality of health, education, and other services that they want, and they cannot enjoy rising disposable income for personal consumption. Canada has tried to have rising consumption while neglecting wealth creation, by going deeper into debt to the rest of the world. In 1990, Canadians had to make net payments of $24 billion to service their foreign debt; and because the surplus on trade in goods and services was only $2 billion, Canada went into debt another $22 billion to the rest of the world. This pattern is not sustainable, and it can effectively be reversed only by improving our ability to develop new goods and services to sell to the rest of the world.

To accomplish this, Mustard argues, Canada must become an innovative economy, an economy that is driven by new ideas and knowledge and by the potential of science and technology — a high-skills, high-pay society producing high-value goods and services. The alternative is to become a lean and mean economy attempting to compete in the world through declining real wages and a stagnating standard of living, a society increasingly unable to afford the health care, social systems, cultural activities, and other basic features of the Canadian way of life.

As we look around the world, it is clear that the societies that are investing the most in innovation are the most dynamic. One yardstick is the amount of spending on research and development. Only 1.4 per cent of GDP is being spent on research and development in Canada, compared with double that rate in big countries such as the United States, Japan, and Germany, as well as in smaller countries such as Sweden and Switzerland.

In other countries, the role of new knowledge is well understood by the political and business leadership. Japan is seeking leadership in technology, marketing, and management, or "brain capital," says U.S. management expert Peter Drucker. "Every major Japanese industrial group now has its own research institute, whose main function is to bring to the group awareness of any important new knowledge — in management and organization, in marketing, in finance, in training — developed world-wide."[39] The same attention is paid to new science and technology. Newly industrializing nations also are moving ahead on R & D and management systems. According to a report on science and technology in the Pacific Region, South Korea wants to raise R & D spending from its current rate of 2 per cent of GDP to more than 3 per cent by 1996; Taiwan wants to grow from its current 1.2 per cent to 2.5 per cent by 2000; and Singapore wants to grow from its current 0.9 per cent to 2 per cent by 2000.[40] Canada, however, has no target and no plan for an innovative economy that will provide a high quality of life for its people. There is no strategy for Canada's future.

Part of the problem, says economist Richard Lipsey, is that Canadians have been made prisoners of outdated economic thinking — neoclassical economics — and this is still the economics being taught each year to thousands of university students. In a major report for the Canadian Institute for Advanced Research, Lipsey argues that while the neoclassical approach has made an important contribution through its emphasis on the role of competition and markets, it is inadequate to deal with the new economy that is based on ideas and innovation. Neoclassical economics gives government a role to deal with market failures, such as policies to protect the environment, but it gives little role for government to encourage innovation through intervention, despite the central role that ideas and innovation play in dynamic economies. Lipsey holds that a new theory of economic growth is needed.[41]

There is no disputing the fact that technological change is "the major engine for economic improvement," as Lipsey argues. "The most important thing we've learned is that ideas matter [and] technological change is to be understood as the history of ideas — new ways of doing things, new ideas for making new products or new ways of making existing products." Paul Romer, a brilliant young American economist who is one of the leaders in developing a new theory of economic growth (and is a fellow of the Canadian Institute for Advanced Research), argues that a simple way to understand the role of ideas in the economy is to think of them as recipes, or new ways of rearranging raw materials.

The sand we find on a beach has no real value; but silicon inside a computer, he says, has high value: "Think about all the possible combinations you could form that amounted to about 30 pounds of copper, iron, carbon, aluminum, silicon, plastics and a few other things thrown in together. Almost all those combinations would be worthless rubbish that you would pay someone to take away. But a very small fraction of them would turn out to be incredibly valuable objects, like a VCR or a personal computer." Economic growth, then, "is growth in value that comes from putting what would otherwise be worthless objects into manufactured, valuable combinations."[42] To get this kind of economic growth, someone first has to come up with the idea, the instructions, or design, what Romer calls the recipe. Increasingly, these people are scientists and engineers who are working with advances in fundamental knowledge. Then someone has to organize what Romer calls the "cooking," which takes place through the mines, paper mills, chemical refineries, factories, transportation and communications systems, and management skills. "But without a constant flow of new ideas, economic growth would come to a halt. We would just run out of ways to create new values for new wealth." The trouble is that countries often end up spending much of their time trying to prop up activities that have exhausted the current set of ideas, such as bailing out a steel mill or subsidizing an uneconomic oil project, instead of investing in new ideas to create new growth. This is mainly because established industries, backed by unions and banks, have a much more organized voice in the economy than new ideas and industries, which are scattered and lack the power of large organizations or the ear of government.

Romer is very much an optimist about the future, arguing that humankind had barely scratched the surface in developing new recipes for economic growth — recipes that are compatible with the compelling case for sustainable development to protect the planet and our environment. The cow, which is a living petrochemical refinery, shows how much progress can lie ahead, Romer says. "As far as humans are concerned, the cow converts grass, water and a few other nutrients into milk. With no human intervention, the cow searches out inputs, maintains the temperature and other conditions needed for its reactions within a very narrow band, protects against invasion by pathogens, automatically repairs most malfunctions, and most astonishingly, physically replicates itself." If nature can put together such a factory by trial and error, says Romer, "there have to be unimaginably wonderful things yet to be found just by combining hydrogen, oxygen and carbon."

But the issue is how to create the kind of society that can generate ideas for the future and convert them into economic growth. This is a bigger challenge than finding ways for individual companies to come up with a new product. It implies sweeping changes in institutions, since societies that learn how to develop and innovate acquire the capacity to become even better innovators. As Romer argues, the twenty-first century will belong to the nation that invents institutions that can support high levels of applied and commercially relevant research and development in industry.

This has major implications for Canada's future. As Fraser Mustard argues, "in a society such as Canada, in which wealth has primarily come from natural endowment, the socioeconomic culture of the society, its institutions and its policies are largely geared to extracting that wealth and distributing the benefits." But when a society becomes an ideas-driven or innovation society, its culture changes as well. The dependence on ideas and knowledge, along with the skills and initiative of workers, requires a degree of partnership and cooperation that does not exist in a resource-based economy. Economic success depends on all groups in society, since everyone has a stake in the success of the wealth-creating component of the economy. This does not mean that Canadians stop developing their resources and just make computers and other high-tech products. It means that all economic activities must be based on innovation and ideas, which means that resources will continue to be important, but in a very different way.

Canadians everywhere are concerned about their economic future, not only because they want better lives but because a failure to solve the economic problems will mean the unravelling of Canada's social system — from health care and social welfare to accessible education, clean and livable cities, culture and recreation — and will threaten Canada's unity as a nation. In a world of enormous challenge and opportunity, there is no reason why Canada cannot be a more active participant. But if it is to do so, it must overcome its problems of high debts and low productivity. As individuals, Canadians are up to the challenge. But without new institutions, approaches, and policies, the talents of the Canadian people cannot be used and opportunities will be lost, as they have been through the 1980s. Only by moving to create a new economy, based on ideas and innovation, can Canada successfully move into the twenty-first century.

2

Aging Canadians and Young Mexicans

THERE IS NO BETTER PICTURE of what the world will look like as it enters the next century than that of Canada and Mexico. Canada, like the other nations of the rich industrial world, will be an aging society with slowing population growth. It will be increasingly worried about paying for an elderly population and about how to cope with labour shortages. As Canada grows older, it could become less entrepreneurial in business and more conservative in politics; and it will face relentless competition from Mexico — although, if Canada is smart, it will move to capitalize on opportunities in the much faster-growing Mexican economy. Without aggressive policies to create an Information Age economy using ideas and innovation to create wealth and high incomes, Canada could stagnate; but if it upgrades the skills of its people and uses new technology, it could become more productive and better off even while its population ages.

Meanwhile, in Mexico, where there is a young and fast-growing population that is typical of much of the developing world, the emphasis will be on education, investment, jobs, and exports. As a youthful country, Mexico will be highly entrepreneurial, luring young Canadians as well as Mexicans. And as Mexicans gain experience and education, they will move into many of the industrial sectors that once belonged to countries such as Canada. Mexicans will not be content to be a low-cost labour pool for rich countries; they will pursue new technologies and high-value activities. Because of the rising productivity and rapid rates of family formation, Mexico's economy will show strong growth and its people will enjoy a fast-rising standard of living. Within 20 years, Mexico could have an economy about the same size as Canada had in 1990. (Today, Mexico's economy is barely 40 per cent that of Canada's.) Forty years from now, Mexico will almost certainly have a bigger economy than that of Canada. But Mexico's rapid growth will cause it to pay more attention to the environment.

Twenty years from now, perhaps less than 30 per cent of Canada's population will be under the age of 20 while roughly half of Mexico's population will be that young. According to United Nations forecasts, Canada's population will grow from 26.5 million in 1990 to 31.9 million in 2025, an increase of just 5.4 million people. Over the same 35 years, Mexico's population could soar by nearly 62 million, from 88.6 million in 1990 to 150.1 million in 2025 (although the World Bank's estimate is 142 million Mexicans in 2025). In other words Mexico could add the equivalent of two Canadas to its population over the next 35 years.

In many ways, Canada and Mexico are proxies for the world at large. During the next several decades, a major reshaping of the world will take place as developing countries with young populations expand and as their economies accelerate, while the rich industrial nations experience slow population growth or even declining populations and face sweeping changes in the world's economic, technological, and military balance of power. Yet if the situation is properly handled, the industrial countries of the North and the developing countries of the South could both enjoy a new era of sustainable growth and shared prosperity. Mishandled, the world could face turbulence, environmental chaos, uncontrollable migrations, religious and nationalistic fanaticism, and economic protectionism and decline.

Between now and the year 2000, the world population will increase by nearly a billion people. That is more than 10 new Mexicos. There will be a similar increase in the first decade of the next century. Almost all of these new inhabitants of our planet will live in what we call the Third World, the developing world or, more simply, the South. This demographic reality will shift industries and jobs to countries that are home to hundreds of millions of restless

TABLE 8
World Population

	1990	2025
	millions	
World total	5,292.2	8,504.2
Industrial world	1,206.6	1,353.9
Developing countries	4,085.6	7,150.3
Africa	642.1	1,596.9
North America	275.9	332.0
United States	249.2	299.9
Canada	26.5	31.9
Latin America	448.1	757.4
Mexico	88.6	150.1
Brazil	150.4	245.8
Colombia	33.0	54.2
Argentina	32.3	45.5
Asia	3,112.7	4,912.5
China	1,139.1	1,512.6
Japan	123.5	127.5
South Korea	42.8	51.6
North Korea	21.8	33.1
Indonesia	184.3	285.9
Philippines	62.4	111.5
Thailand	55.7	80.9
Vietnam	66.7	117.5
Bangladesh	115.6	235.0
India	853.1	1,442.4
Iran	54.6	113.8
Pakistan	122.6	267.1
Turkey	55.9	87.7
Europe	498.4	515.2
Britain	57.2	59.7
France	56.1	60.4
Germany	77.5	70.9
Soviet Union	288.6	352.1
Oceania	26.5	38.2

SOURCE: U.N. Population Fund, *The State of the World Population 1991* (New York: United Nations, 1991).

young Third World workers who, with their Sony Walkmans, know that a better life is possible. If they do not get those jobs, they will migrate to where that better life exists, to countries such as Canada that are part of what we know of as the industrial world, the First World or, more simply, the North.

The second reality is that Canada, like the other rich countries of the North, will be an aging society with such a low birth rate that it will soon be unable to sustain its population without sustained immigration. The low birth rate could lead to a shortage of versatile new workers and a consequent loss of that vitality that comes from a steady influx of young workers who want to do things differently. On the other hand, this will accelerate automation and encourage the faster adoption of new technologies, which could make us more productive and better off. With an aging society, we will have to do more about high school dropouts and the retraining of older workers; we will not be able to be as casual about people who fall by the wayside as we were when the baby boomers were entering the job market. In the future, we won't be able to waste anyone.

The slowdown in our population growth should also lead to better child care and to flexible working hours, not just because we want more women to work but also because, as can be seen in Sweden, good child care and maternity leave actually raise the birth rate. Pensions and changes in the retirement age will become bigger workplace issues, and the requirements of an aging society will focus more attention on the design and costs of health-care programs and social policy. Another result will be a continuing change in the multicultural composition of Canada and continuing debate over the goals of immigration policy. Yet no matter what we do, we cannot escape the forces of demographic change.

In 1950 there were about 2.6 billion people in the world, of whom 32 per cent, or 832 million, lived in the industrialized countries and 68 per cent, or nearly 1.8 billion, lived in the developing countries. Today, according to estimates of the United Nations Population Fund,[1] the world's population has reached 5.4 billion, and just 23 per cent, or 1.2 billion people, live in the industrial countries; the developing countries are home to the other 77 per cent, or 4.2 billion. By 2025, when today's high school students will have reached middle age, the world will have a population of 8.5 billion, with only

16 per cent, or 1.4 billion people, living in the industrial world; the other 84 per cent, or 7.1 billion, will live in the developing world. Between now and 2025, the world population will increase by 3.1 billion people, and 94 per cent of that increase will occur in the developing world. And by the year 2150, Europeans and North Americans will account for less than 7 per cent of the world's population.

The current decade, the 1990s, will see a larger increase in human numbers than any decade in history. The world's population "is increasing by three people every second — about a quarter of a million every day. Close to 95 million people — roughly equivalent to the population of Eastern Europe or Central America — will be added every year during the 1990s; a billion people — a whole extra China over the decade," warned the United Nations[2] in 1990.

So the world of the future will have to recognize a far greater economic and political role for the countries of the South. This large and diverse group of nations, ranging from India, China, Iran, Turkey, and Nigeria to Korea, Mexico, Brazil, and Indonesia, along with the newly liberated economies of Eastern Europe and the Commonwealth of Independent States, will drive much of the economic growth during the next 25 to 30 years; and because of their great potential for growth, these nations will attract large flows of investment and production.

One leading U.S. expert, David Hale of Kemper Securities, argues in fact that "growth prospects for the world economy during the next 10 years are potentially the most exciting since the early years of the 20th century."[3] "As a result of the fall of communism and the spread of liberal economic ideas to the Third World, over 3 billion people are now poised to re-enter the global marketplace for goods and capital after periods of absence ranging from 40 to 80 years." The World Bank, in a forecast of prospects for the developing world, including Eastern Europe and the states of the former Soviet Union, predicts economic growth of 4.9 per cent a year through the 1990s, well above the 3.2 per cent growth rate of the 1980s. With economic growth outpacing population growth, per capita incomes are expected to grow 2.9 per cent a year through the 1990s or more than double the 1.2 per cent a year experienced through the 1980s.[4] With the world economy growing an average of 2.8 per cent a year through the 1990s, the world's output in the year 2000 will reach

US$29.4 trillion in 1990 dollars, or some 32 per cent higher than the 1990 level of US$22.3 trillion. By 2030, the world economy could reach US$69 trillion, in 1990 dollars, the World Bank says, with real per capita incomes in developing countries tripling.

Other countries that lack a significant trade and investment presence in these potentially fast-growing nations will lose out on many of the opportunities for future world growth. That is why it is vital that Canadian companies look beyond the easy market of the United States to the much bigger future market in the rest of the world. Despite our multicultural population, we have few trade links with the developing world.

On the basis of current fertility and mortality rates and assumptions of improved family planning, it is predicted that China's population of 1.1 billion could reach 1.5 billion — more than that of the entire industrial world — by the year 2025. India could see its population climb from 853 million today to 1.4 billion in 2025. But U.N. projections show other big countries as well in 2025; they include Nigeria (281 million people), Indonesia (286 million), Pakistan (267 million), Brazil (246 million), Bangladesh (235 million), Mexico (150 million), Vietnam (118 million), and Iran (114 million). A growing number will become more competitive and more important players in the global economy. Korea, Taiwan, Thailand, Malaysia, Singapore, Indonesia, and perhaps the Philippines, as well as India and China, in Asia and Mexico, Brazil, Venezuela, Chile, Colombia, and Argentina in Latin America all have the potential to prosper.

The Western world, in contrast, will show little population growth. The United States is expected to add 50 million people between now and 2025 to reach a population of 300 million (compared to an increase in Canada of 5.4 million, to reach not quite 32 million people in 2025), according to the same U.N. estimates. With Mexico's projected growth, a trilateral free trade area in North America would expand to a market of 482 million people in 2025, compared to 364 million people today; 52 per cent of the population growth would take place in Mexico, which would add more people than the United States and Canada combined.

The 12 members of the European Economic Community (including East Germany), which now have a combined population of 325 million people, are projected to have almost zero population growth to 2025, reaching only 328 million people by then. Similarly, Japan's population is expected to remain almost flat, rising from 124 million people now to 128 million people in 2025. The former states of the Soviet Union will add 64 million people, reaching 352 million by 2025; but this growth will occur in the Asian republics, which have more in common with the developing world than with the industrial world.

Massive population growth is also expected to take place in Third World megacities. In 1965, 11 of the world's 20 largest urban centres were in the industrial world, led by New York, Tokyo, London, Osaka, and Moscow. By the year 2000, according to the United Nations,[5] only three of the 20 largest urban centres will be in the industrial world. The top five cities will be Mexico City, São Paulo, Tokyo, Calcutta, and Bombay. Other leading cities will be Shanghai, Seoul, Teheran, Rio de Janiero, Jakarta, Delhi, Buenos Aires, Karachi, Beijing, Dhaka, Cairo, Manila, and Bangkok — as well as New York, Tokyo, and Los Angeles. The projected growth of megacities in the developing world poses huge environmental, social, and economic challenges — ranging from health and sanitation to infrastructure, poverty, and jobs.

The huge growth in world population has alarmed many experts, and it certainly poses great risks to the environment, to world stability, and to international migration. "We are not on a course towards a sustainable civilization," John Wheeler, former chairman of the OECD's Development Assistance Committee, has warned.[6] As the world population increases, so does the potential for damage to the environment. A large and growing number of poor and hungry people are causing soil erosion and destruction of the rain forests as a result of their daily quest for survival. Meanwhile, increased industrial production and consumption by the developing world, as several billion people strive to improve their standard of living, also pose a major threat because of the use of today's technologies. That is why perhaps the greatest challenge that will face Canada and other industrial countries in the twenty-first century will be to provide significant technological and financial resources so that developing countries can raise their standard of living in a way that is compatible with sustainable development.

The United Nations' forecast that the world population will stabilize at about 10.2 billion late in the twenty-first century depends on the world's reaching a fertility rate of 2.1 children per woman (the rate at which a population replaces itself but stops contributing to a continued increase) by the year 2035. In its 1991 report, the U.N. Population Fund pointed out that this hinges on a doubling of funding for population programs by the year 2000 so that its projection of a 3.3 fertility rate per woman (the number of children an average woman would have in her lifetime) can be reached by the end of the century.[7] A 20-year delay in reaching the 2035 target would add nearly 3 billion more people to the world's population.

Indeed, according to the executive director of the U.N. Population Fund, Nafis Sadik, its long-term projections are now under review: "It seems that the projections of a 'stable' total of 10.2 billion — or only about twice today's population — by 2085 may have been too optimistic. Some analysts now believe that 10 billion will be reached by 2050, and growth will probably go on for another century after that, unless some substantial further progress can be made in reducing fertility."[8] One reason for slow progress is that rich countries, including Canada, are not providing the support that is needed for family planning programs. As the Development Assistance Committee of the OECD warns, "Action — or the lack of it — in population policy during the 1990s will decide whether the world population will eventually double or triple." The difference between 10 billion and 15 billion people will have enormous environmental, economic, and geopolitical consequences for all of us.

Canada and other industrial countries have promised to do more to help the developing world adjust. But there is reluctance to reduce trade barriers to products of the developing world, and promises of financial help have not been met. Foreign aid from the industrial world, as a share of gross national product (GNP) has remained flat at 0.36 per cent in both 1980 and 1990, well short of the promised target of 0.75 per cent. The most generous aid providers are Norway (1.17 per cent of GNP), the Netherlands (0.94 per cent), Denmark (0.93 per cent), and Sweden (0.90 per cent). Canada's foreign aid peaked at 0.54 per cent of GNP in 1975 and was down to 0.44 per cent in 1990. Budget cuts have promised further constraints in Canadian foreign assistance, leading to a rebuke from the OECD, which "noted with regret" Canada's cutbacks. It charged that "the aid budget had borne a disproportionate share of the over-all expenditure restraints, given Canada's proud record in drawing attention to the global importance of development issues and its concern for alleviating poverty."[9]

With its young population, the developing world will be under enormous pressure to create jobs — about 40 million jobs a year. From 1990 to 2000 the world labour force is expected to grow by close to 400 million people, according to a major study by the International Labor Organization (ILO).[10] Of the roughly 360 million new jobs that will be needed around the world, more than 90 per cent will have to be created in developing countries; if these jobs are not created, there will be huge migration flows from the poor coun-tries to the rich. The ILO study makes clear that this pressure will continue through the first 25 years of the next century. Nearly 900 million new jobs will have to be created in that period; of these, 875 million, or almost 98 per cent, will have to be in developing coun-tries. While Canada and the United States will have to create 11 mil-lion new jobs between 1990 and 2000, for example, Latin America (including Mexico) will have to create 42 million; similarly, Canada and the United States will have to create another 12 million jobs between 2000 and 2025, but Latin America will have to create 107 million. India alone will need 10 million new jobs a year for the next 10 years, according to its planning commission.

To create many of these jobs, developing countries will move aggressively to develop industries that can use lower-cost labour to compete in world markets, as some, such as Asia's Four Tigers, have already done. This will inevitably displace existing industries and jobs in Canada and other industrial nations. Mexico is targeting the auto industry as one that will be developed. Some Canadian auto parts producers have already located operations in Mexico, and the major U.S., Japanese, and European auto companies are developing a new production base in Mexico to serve global markets. South Korea, likewise, is building a diversified industrial base, investing heavily in modern steel production, chemicals, consumer electron-ics, semiconductors, industrial machinery, shipbuilding, and autos and auto parts. Other countries that are aggressively developing their industrial capacity include Turkey, Malaysia, Thailand,

Indonesia, Taiwan, and Brazil. Many of these countries have no intention of remaining sources of low-cost labour for the rich countries, so they are investing in higher education and are building up their own science and technology capacities to absorb, modify, and build on the technologies they import from the industrial nations.

Despite the debt constraints of the 1980s, many developing countries enjoyed dynamic growth in the diversity of their manufactured exports. While textiles, clothing, and footwear were the most important manufactured exports, there was "spectacular growth" in exports of office equipment, motor vehicles, chemicals, and building materials, according to the International Finance Corporation (IFC), a division of the World Bank that helps finance the growth of businesses in developing countries. "In total, developing countries now export nearly US$250 billion worth of manufactures to the United States, Japan, and the EC," the agency says, adding that "the dominant role that textiles, clothing, and footwear have played in (less developed country) exports is eroding as new export industries grow up. Developing countries now export large volumes of automobiles and components and a formidable range of electric and electronic products. Many of these products were virtually unknown as developing country exports at the start of the 1980s."[11]

Korea and Taiwan are now both competitive manufacturers of their own personal computers, which they sell under their own brand names in Canada and the United States. Although East Asian countries such as Korea, Taiwan, and Hong Kong did the best in expanding and diversifying their exports in the 1980s, Turkey, Pakistan, Malaysia, Mexico, and the Dominican Republic also did well, the IFC said.

These countries are bound to become much more important industrially over the next 10 to 15 years, capitalizing on both a steady supply of lower-cost labour and an increasingly better-educated workforce. "In the long run," says Richard Freeman, a Harvard University economist, "the low wages and available labor in the less developed countries will transform the historic division of labor between the developed and less developed countries from one in which the former manufactured goods from raw materials and inputs imported from the latter to one in which the advanced countries provide services and knowledge while the less developed countries produce mass-production manufactured goods."[12] A wide range of industries, such as clothing, textiles, shoes, toys, metal stampings, steel, consumer electronics, autos, and auto parts, will shift activities to the developing world to serve growing local markets as well as markets in Canada and other industrial countries. Next to trade protectionism, the biggest risk these countries face is that the industrial world will withhold its new technologies, creating a wider science and technology gap between the rich and poor countries.

The irreversible trend, says James Austin, a business professor at Harvard University and an expert on developing countries, is that "the economic importance of the Third World is great and becoming even greater." The developing countries produced about 20 per cent of the output of the world's market economies in 1987 and accounted for 25 per cent of the world's imports. They import machinery, manufactured goods, fuels, foods, chemicals, and raw materials, and 60 per cent of what they buy comes from the industrial countries — including more than 90 per cent of their machinery imports, 88 per cent of chemicals, and 77 per cent of manufactured goods. They also supplied 28 per cent of the world's exports, with 70 per cent of their sales going to industrial countries.[13]

Developing countries, with lower labour costs and increasing accessibility to the technologies of mature industries, are gaining competitive advantage over the industrial countries in many areas. "By the 1980s, for example, Brazil's manufacturing output exceeded Britain's. In 1986 Taiwan exported US$36 billion of manufactures and generated a trade surplus exceeded only by Japan and West Germany," says Austin.[14] In other words, the developing countries have become "fierce competitors" in a variety of manufactured products, increasing their share of manufactured imports by industrial countries from 11 per cent in 1960 to 25 per cent by the mid-1980s. Third World companies are starting to show up in lists of the world's multinationals, such as the world's largest bicycle manufacturer, the Munjal Co. in India, along with Hyundai, Daewoo, Samsung, and Lucky-Goldstar in South Korea, Sampo and Tatung in Taiwan, Embraer in Brazil, and Pemex in Mexico. And as Austin points out, "as we move toward and into the twenty-first century, developing countries will become even more important in the global economy."

The world trading organization, the General Agreement on Tariffs and Trade (GATT), argues that these changes should be encouraged. Canada and other industrial countries, it says, "are entering an era in which they can less and less afford the lower economic growth that accompanies blocked or delayed structural adjustment."[15] With a future of close to zero population growth and an aging workforce, Canada cannot afford protectionist policies for clothing, for example, by supporting an industry in which we are not really competitive. This forces Canadians to pay too much for clothing. Instead, we should be diverting our efforts to develop industries in which we can be more productive and can benefit from better jobs. Canada needs that productivity to pay for an aging society. "In the absence of a much faster rate of productivity gain in the industrial countries than that recorded in the past decade, the ageing of the population will imply a choice among lower levels of pensions and health care for retirees than are currently anticipated, sizeable cutbacks in other areas of government expenditure and increased taxes on active workers," GATT warns.

Some experts believe that we are quickly moving towards a world market for labour. One of those who holds this view is William Johnston, a senior research fellow at the Hudson Institute in the United States, who in 1990 completed a study of world workforce trends for the U.S. Department of Labor. "Human capital, once considered to be the most stationary factor in production, increasingly flows across national borders as easily as cars, computer chips, and corporate bonds," Johnston contends. "Just as managers speak of world markets for products, technology, and capital, they must now think in terms of a world market for labour."[16] Johnston sees a great "mismatch" in the world labour market: a large portion of the world's skilled and unskilled workers live in the developing countries while most of the best or well-paid jobs are being generated in the cities of the rich industrial world. This, he contends, will have a number of significant impacts in the 1990s and beyond:

- There will be large-scale movements of people around the world, including immigrants and temporary workers, with the greatest movement coming from young and highly educated workers moving from developing countries to the major cities of the Western world.

- Some industrial countries will open their borders to increased immigration by foreign workers, especially workers with education and skills. In fact, industrial countries could find themselves competing for certain types of foreign workers.
- The industrial countries will move to common labour standards, and world standards might even evolve in areas such as workplace safety and employee rights. The European Economic Community's plans for a single internal market, to be in effect by January 1, 1993, include a social charter that attempts to harmonize workplace rules and standards, along with mutual recognition among the 12 member states of skills levels and accreditation. The Canada–U.S.–Mexico free trade negotiations provided an opportunity for a North American social charter, but it was not taken up.

While the workforce in industrial countries ages, the developing countries will have the advantages of youth. "By 2000, workers in most developing nations will be young, relatively recently educated, and arguably more adaptable compared with those in the industrial world," says Johnston. "Very young nations that are rapidly industrializing, like Mexico and China, may find that the youth and flexibility of their workforces give them an advantage relative to their indus-

TABLE 9
Enrolment in Engineering Schools

Country	1980	1988
CANADA	76,020	78,487
Mexico	160,522	287,359
Brazil	156,726	141,702
China	363,146	732,941
India	—	494,711 (1987)
South Korea	209,636	224,983
Philippines	225,254	257,452
Japan	396,856	444,675

SOURCE: *UNESCO Statistical Yearbook 1990* (Paris: UNESCO, 1990).

trialized competitors with older workforces, particularly over those in heavy manufacturing industries, where shrinkage has left factories staffed mostly with workers in their forties and fifties."

Moreover, the young workers of the developing countries will increasingly be better educated; and as education improves, their workforces will be able to handle the most modern manufacturing and construction technologies. But developing countries are not stopping there. Increasingly, they are pushing university education as well, because they want to join the ranks of modern nations rather than remaining low-cost labour pools for the rich Western world. Some countries, such as South Korea, have made higher education, especially in science and engineering, a key element in their strategy to become modern nations with a high standard of living. The newly industrializing countries realize also that economic development will cause wages to rise, so they cannot count on low labour costs for an ongoing competitive advantage. This explains the growing number of students from developing countries who are taking graduate courses in Western universities; they are part of the developing world's thrust to build highly competitive and productive societies. In 1990–91, more than half the doctoral students enrolled in engineering in Canadian universities came from other countries, the largest number being from Asia; likewise, nearly 40 per cent of the doctoral students in mathematics, computer science, and physical sciences came from abroad. UNESCO statistics show that Brazil and China are now graduating more scientists than Canada, while Brazil, China, the Philippines, South Korea, and Mexico are all graduating more engineers than Canada.[17]

This means that developing countries will find it easier to adopt the latest technologies and will become more competitive in areas of high technology as well as in the services related to new technologies, notably offshore computer services. Jamaica, Barbados, the Philippines, Malaysia, China, and other countries are already taking advantage of the telecommunications revolution and are providing basic data-entry workers for the computer systems of big companies in Toronto, New York, and Tokyo. India's skills in computer software and engineering are being used by Western software and engineering companies, employing the latest telecommunications systems. And most major Japanese software houses now have software pro-

TABLE 10
Enrolment of Postgraduate Students in Engineering, 1988

CANADA	8349
Mexico	3532
China	36,408 (1986)
India	15,112 (1985)
South Korea	9973
Philippines	609
Turkey	5012
Japan	29,454

SOURCE: *UNESCO Statistical Yearbook 1990* (Paris: UNESCO, 1990).

TABLE 11
Scientists and Engineers Employed in R & D per Million People

CANADA	2243 (1987)
Mexico	215 (1984)
South Korea	1325 (1988)
Singapore	1287 (1987)
Japan	5029 (1988)
Switzerland	2299 (1986)
Sweden	2724 (1987)
Netherlands	2518 (1987)
Norway	2882 (1989)
United States	3317 (1987)

SOURCE: *UNESCO Statistical Yearbook 1990* (Paris: UNESCO, 1990).

duction facilities in China. In the future, we will increasingly look to the developing countries to help fill our skilled and professional manpower needs in what will fast become a global labour market.

Although the rapid population growth of the developing world poses environmental, political, migration, and economic challenges to Canadians, it also presents great opportunities. The next generation of nations will have vast development needs: power plants, highways, urban transit, housing, and airports, as well as environmental technologies and services, financial systems, hospitals, training institutes, telephone systems, for example. As these countries progress, they will develop large middle-class communities that will become markets for Western products. According to the World Bank, South Korea's economy has grown from US$3 billion in 1967 to US$236 billion in 1990; Mexico's has grown from US$22 billion to US$238 billion, Hong Kong's from US$2 billion to US$60 billion, Thailand's from US$4 billion to US$80 billion, and Brazil's from US$19 billion to US$414 billion. And these countries still have a great deal of growth ahead of them.

Some Canadians are already active in the developing world. Bell Canada is supplying cellular phones in Mexico, and Northern Telecom has seen its exports to Mexico grow from just $4 million in 1987 to an expected $100 million in 1991. Spar Aerospace has built satellite receiving stations for China. Atomic Energy of Canada Ltd. is building nuclear power plants in South Korea. SNC Engineering is managing a huge transit project in Thailand. But Canada can do much more. World Bank statistics and those of other development banks that Canadians help finance, such as the Asian Development Bank and the Inter-American Development Bank, show that Canadian companies have failed to capitalize on the business that is available from bank-financed projects. Similar opportunities will arise through the recently created European Bank for Reconstruction and Development, which Canada has helped finance.

The result is that, so far, Canada has a significant trade deficit with the developing countries: more than $4 billion in 1991. Instead of exporting computers, machinery, and fine chemicals to developing countries, we are exporting mainly commodities, such as coal, wheat, and wood pulp; and because of the small number of Canadian-based international corporations, only a few Canadian companies are investing in developing countries.

It is clear, then, that population pressures in the rest of the world will have major significance for Canada's future. But demographic changes at home will have a similarly profound impact. As already noted, Canada is an aging society. As we move into the twenty-first century, there will be more older people dependent on pensions and in need of greater health care, and fewer young people coming into

TABLE 12

Canada's Changing Population Profile

	1961	1971	1981	1990	2001	2011
0-4	2,256.4	1,816.2	1,783.4	1,860.4	1,735.6	1,708.6
5-9	2,079.5	2,254.0	1,776.8	1,842.2	1,845.3	1,763.6
10-14	1,856.0	2,310.7	1,920.9	1,820.4	1,927.4	1,875.8
15-19	1,432.6	2,114.3	2,314.9	1,856.0	1,922.6	1,972.5
20-24	1,183.6	1,889.4	2,343.8	1,998.1	1,970.7	2,013.6
25-29	1,209.3	1,584.1	2,177.6	2,373.3	2,022.3	2,071.0
30-34	1,271.8	1,305.4	2,038.6	2,366.6	2,158.2	2,087.1
35-39	1,270.9	1,263.9	1,630.3	2,171.3	2,416.1	2,185.1
40-44	1,119.0	1,262.5	1,337.9	1,973.3	2,429.0	2,418.0
45-49	1,015.3	1,239.0	1,255.4	1,545.7	2,215.5	2,424.6
50-54	863.2	1,052.5	1,243.5	1,274.5	2,020.0	2,205.6
55-59	705.8	954.7	1,179.9	1,210.1	1,593.8	2,003.0
60-64	583.6	777.0	979.3	1,154.8	1,282.6	1,568.0
65-69	487.1	620.0	844.3	1,042.8	1,139.1	1,229.8
70-74	402.2	457.4	633.4	782.3	1,010.9	1,043.5
75-79	274.2	325.5	432.7	600.0	818.0	870.3
80+	227.6	341.6	450.6	639.3	1,019.8	1,224.1
Total	18,238.2	21,568.3	24,343.2	26,511.2	29,527.5	30,664.0

SOURCE: Statistics Canada Census Data, various years. Also Population Projections for Canada, Provinces and Territories 1989-2011. 91-520

the job market to support them. While population growth soared at 3 per cent a year at the height of the baby boom in the 1950s and into the 1960s, the growth is now roughly 1 per cent a year. Our fertility rate (the number of children each woman of child-bearing age has) is running at 1.66, which is below the replacement rate of 2.1 and less than half the 3.63 fertility rate that Canada averaged in 1945–66. Although the number of children is currently growing because the large number of baby boomers are having children, this so-called echo effect will have run its course by the early part of the next century so that, in the absence of much higher immigration, Canada's population will begin to decline.

According to Statistics Canada, our population will stabilize at 31 million in 2026 if we maintain the current fertility rate and accept 140,000 immigrants a year, and it will then begin to decline. If immigration is raised to 200,000 a year, the population will stabilize nine years later, in 2035, at 34 million people, before it starts to decline. In the interim, based on a figure of 140,000 immigrants a year, the population will rise to 28.9 million in 2001 and to 30.3 million in 2011; based on 200,000 immigrants a year, it would rise to 29.5 million in 2001 and to 31.7 million in 2011. Canada's population in 1990 was 26.5 million.[18] According to other federal calculations, if there was zero immigration, Canadians would eventually disappear altogether, the last of them dying in the year 2786![19]

Behind these numbers are key trends that will have an important impact on Canada's future:

- The number of young new workers entering the labour force will decline. The number of Canadians between the ages of 15 and 24 peaked in 1981 at 4.7 million, and by 1990 it was down nearly 1 million to 3.7 million. The number of potential new workers will remain at roughly this level for the next two decades; however, a rising participation rate for women in the workforce will stimulate additional growth in the labour force. In 1990–2000 the labour force will grow by about 2.2 million; in 2000–2010, by about 1.2 million. This means that employers will have to compete harder for young workers. No longer will we have the "luxury" of complacently accepting a 30 per cent high school dropout rate, and business will have a much greater incentive to automate and a greater need to retrain and upgrade its employees. Human capital will be an invaluable business asset.

- Companies will have to change their hiring practices. They will have to find ways of bringing into the workforce people they once screened out — for example, disabled people, older workers, minorities, and women. This also means that companies will have to devote greater efforts to recruiting and training new employees. This will be a major challenge for small business, which relies on young workers fresh out of school. Companies may find themselves paying bonuses to employees who help find new workers, as some did at the height of the 1980s economic boom. But because companies will have to offer better wages and working conditions, they will also have to learn how to use workers more productively.

- With the workforce aging, companies will have to find ways to motivate and retrain older workers and to offset the loss of flexibility that young workers bring with them. In 1986, just over 30 per cent of Canadians in the workforce were aged 45 or older; by the year 2000, the 45-plus workers could constitute nearly 40 per cent of the workforce, and by 2025 they could reach 45 per cent. The number of workers aged 20 to 29 would decline from just over 30 per cent of the 20-to-64 age group in 1986 to just over 20 per cent by 2025.[20] At the same time, governments will be forced to spend greater efforts retraining unemployed older workers so that these people can return to the workforce. Just as we can no longer afford the waste of high school dropouts, we shall not be able to afford the waste of older workers who drop out of the workforce.

- With more of our wealth being generated by capital instead of by large numbers of assembly-line workers, we shall have to rethink our tax system. We have been shifting the tax burden away from capital and onto individuals through income taxes and through consumption taxes such as the goods and services tax. But if more of our future wealth is to be generated by highly automated systems of production for both goods and services, much of it owned outside Canada though located here, we shall have to find some way of capturing part of that higher productivity for federal and provincial tax collectors. The money will be needed to help finance an aging society.

There will be other changes as well. It seems likely that the housing boom is over and that Canadians can no longer count on rapidly rising housing prices as an automatic form of savings; old-fashioned savings habits will become more important. Regional and urban shifts will probably continue as at present, with Ontario, British Columbia, and Alberta leading Canada in growth and with Toronto, Vancouver, and Montreal the largest population centres. As more women join the workforce, there will be pressures for more and better child care and for flexible hours, and as the proportion of two-spouse working families grows, there will be greater pressure for benefits connected with care of the elderly, such as time off and flexible time to attend to aging parents.

The prospect of an aging Canada has raised fears that we will not be able to afford the health-care and pension needs of tomorrow's senior citizens. This will not be a major issue during the next 20 years, when the proportion of seniors of 65 and over will rise from just over 11 per cent to just over 14 per cent; and it should not be a major problem after that, starting in 2012 as the baby boomers reach retirement age. But there is one big "if" — that is, there need not be a problem *if* we develop a more productive economy. Research by Frank Denton and Byron Spencer of McMaster University for the federal demographic review concluded that population size will make little difference to per capita gross domestic product (GDP) or income per household, two measures of economic well-being. "Whether the Canadian population in 2036 is 27 million, 30 million, 34 million or 41 million makes little difference to income per person or per household," the two economists say. "These explorations indicate that it is not so much the numbers of people that will affect Canadians' economic well-being as their skills and the effective deployment of those skills."[21] With falling birth rates, productivity can be maintained and even accelerated by substituting capital for labour while at the same time providing job opportunities for many Canadians who have been marginalized in the past.

But as the Economic Council of Canada pointed out in its 1989 annual review, the key issue is how well we do in raising productivity. Unless the growth of productivity is greater than it has been in the past 10 to 15 years, the incomes of Canadians will stagnate, because the needs of an aging society will (through higher taxes, for example) cut into the income gains that even modest productivity growth would otherwise provide. But "if, with the unfolding of the electronic age, productivity growth should rebound to over 2 per cent per annum, there would be no difficulty in ensuring rising living standards for both workers and retirees, particularly over the next several decades."[22]

Moreover, substantial increases in immigration are not needed to slow the aging of Canadian society. According to a study by the Economic Council of Canada, a higher rate of immigration would cushion the higher fiscal burden of an aging society, but only very slightly. With immigration levels above 200,000 a year, the per capita cost of health, education, and social programs would be only $109 lower by the year 2015 — and this would be offset by the higher social and language-training costs associated with the increased level of immigration.[23]

Nonetheless, in the late 1980s the federal government embarked on an expansionary immigration policy. In 1985 immigration quotas had been set at 85,000–90,000, and they were raised to 105,000–115,000 in 1986. By 1989 the quota level was up to 165,000–175,000. In 1990 the government set out a five-year immigration plan, by which the number of immigrants was to rise to 250,000 a year in the period 1992–95.

The Economic Council criticized the federal move as being too fast, arguing that the sharp increase "runs the risk of provoking social problems, creating temporary increases in unemployment, and perhaps overstretching the capacity of the institutions that handle the arrival and settlement of immigrants."[24] Other population experts, such as David Foot of the University of Toronto and Shirley Seward then of the Institute for Research on Public Policy, also raised concerns. They noted that, on the one hand, the age group of the new immigrants would be the same as the tail end of the baby boom, creating employment difficulties for Canadians in that age group, while, on the other hand, a large proportion of the immigrants (at least 70 per cent) would come from developing countries and would lack the language or skills to fit quickly into the Canadian job market. Even without a big increase in immigration levels, immigrants are likely to account for close to half of all new workers by the end of the 1990s, compared with just 25 per cent at the start of the decade.[25] David Foot argues that instead of aggravating employment problems for today's baby boomers by a policy of higher immigration, Canada should be attracting younger immigrants to offset the labour shortages that will follow the baby boom era. In the year 2000, for example, immigration should favour those in the 14-to-32 age group in an age-directed immigration policy;[26] under the Economic Council's gradualist approach, immigration would reach 340,000 by 2015.

While the strengthening of the Canadian economy does not depend on sharply higher rates of immigration, we shall come under growing pressure to accept more immigrants because of the population explosion taking place in the developing world. This will be a moral issue, not just an economic or demographic issue; and we shall be bound to play a bigger role in helping to solve the world's population problems. This means that Canada will need to have a coherent population policy as we move into the next century.

A combination of the aging baby boomers and increased life expectancy means that the number of seniors will soar in the early part of the next century. The first boomers, those born in 1947, will reach 65 in the year 2012, and by 2031 the tail end of the baby boom, those born in 1966, will turn 65. Thus, the number of seniors is expected to climb from 3.1 million in 1990 to 3.8 million in 2000 and to 7.1 million by 2025; and the number of seniors aged 80 and over — who are much more likely to need expensive health and institutional care than seniors aged 65 to 74 — will grow from 640,000 in 1990 to 930,000 in 2000 and to 1.7 million in 2025.[27]

But while there will be additional costs (for example, employer and employee premiums to sustain Canada Pension Plan benefits will be raised from the current 4.4 per cent of the average industrial wage to 7.6 per cent by 2011), population aging need not be a reason for "prognoses of doom and gloom," says Michael Wolfson, director general of analytical studies for Statistics Canada. He points out that "European countries with significantly larger shares of older individuals in their populations are managing successfully to provide reasonable health care services and pensions and, at the same time, are maintaining successful profiles of economic growth. Aging populations have not led to economic ruin, contrary to some forecasts of demographic doom."[28]

One reason why Canada should be able to cope is that the size of its labour force will increase as the participation rate of women continues to grow, and consequently there will be a growing labour force to support our aging society. But we shall need better productivity performance as well. Moreover, says Wolfson, while there have been many forces driving up health-care costs in Canada, an aging population has not been the major one; and as we learn more about the limits to health care, we shall turn to other determinants of health that are more important, such as diet, sanitation, wealth, friends, and coping skills. More Canadians staying in the workforce after the age of 65 and new forms of housing and care for seniors could also reduce overall costs.

On the other hand, the aging of the workforce could affect our ability to compete. Young people are fast learners, and they bring energy and new thinking to their work. This will be an advantage for developing countries. Because of the large number of young and, increasingly, educated workers in developing countries, exciting new centres of innovation could emerge in São Paulo, Mexico City, Seoul, Bangkok, Singapore, Taipei, or Jakarta; and young Canadian entrepreneurs, finding their own society too conservative, might well be attracted to these centres in a reverse flow of migration. So one of our challenges will be to invigorate and motivate an aging workforce and to provide an encouraging climate for entrepreneurial innovation and youthful optimism.

This will not be easy because the normal incentive of a job promotion will not be there. "Huge numbers of baby boomers are now reaching their early and middle-management ages and there simply are not enough management positions to go around," David Foot says. "Employers can continue to promise baby boomers that if they work hard, they will get promoted, but there are few promotional opportunities for people over the age of 30."[29] So there are very real dangers that middle-aged baby boomers will tune out, attaching less importance to work. This will not help plans for higher productivity.

As labour markets tighten in the 1990s and beyond, business organizations will have to pay more attention to how they treat and reward skilled employees if they want to keep them. Lateral moves will have to replace up-the-ladder promotions for middle-aged baby boomers, says Foot. "In the 1990s they will have to come to grips with the basic fact that the whole idea of rewarding people by promotion will no longer be an effective human resources tool." There will not be enough executive offices to promote them to or enough underlings for them all to boss. Employees will be moved around organizations, with pay increases, instead of being promoted upward; and companies will have to spend more time meeting their employees' need for greater independence — for example, with an expanded use of flextime and with clearer negotiation of responsibilities, rewards, and benefit programs — as well as addressing employee rights on privacy, job security, and severance. Unless baby boomers can be stimulated in their middle-management years, Canada will lose much of its potential productivity gains.

Another possibility is that Canada's aging workforce, faced with few prospects to move up the corporate ladder, will generate a boom in small business startups. Firms employing less than five people generated about half of all new jobs in 1979–87, and the importance of small business will expand in the future, according to DRI/McGraw Hill, an economic consulting firm. [30] "The typical small business is started by people in their forties. Significantly, the beginning edges of the baby boom have started to enter the age of peak small business formation," says economist Robert Fairholm. "To date, the propensity to form a new business by age group has remained at its historical average. But in the future, as the corridors of power become clogged, a greater portion of those in the middle to tail end of the baby boom will see self-employment as a far greener pasture." [31] Starting your own business will be seen as a way out of a corporate dead end; and for those who succeed, earnings will be higher than if they had stayed in a large organization.

There is another reason why we shall have to find innovative ways to ensure that there are opportunities for highly educated workers. Sitting right next to us is the United States, which is worrying about its own future shortages of skilled workers and scientific and engineering manpower. The United States has changed its immigration rules to make it easier for U.S. companies and universities to bring in talented manpower from the rest of the world. Under the revised 1990 Immigration Act, annual quotas for professional and skilled workers have been tripled to about 140,000, and the Canada–U.S. free trade agreement will facilitate this kind of movement. U.S. companies already recruit at Canadian universities for highly trained people; Microsoft's Bill Gates, for example, says that the largest single source of computer programmers for his huge software company is the University of Waterloo in Canada. U.S. headhunting firms are also tapping the Canadian market. In fact, the United States is counting on highly educated foreign workers to meet its own shortages.

The *Economic Report of the President* in 1990 made clear that immigration was certainly one way that the U.S. would deal with its skills shortages. "With projections of a rising demand for skilled workers in coming years," the report said, the U.S. could achieve greater benefits from immigration "with policies designed to increase the number of skilled immigrants." Immigrants with more education or training "will likely make the greatest contributions to the U.S. economy."[32] Christine Keen, issues manager for the U.S. Society for Human Resources Management, says, "Employers may step up dramatically their importation of skilled workers because the domestic work force cannot meet the demands for quantity or quality. Canada, for example, which currently has a higher national unemployment rate than the U.S., could be one pool to tap in the '90s." She adds that "Canadians tend to be well educated, speak English and free movement of labor may be encouraged by the U.S.–Canada free trade agreement."[33]

This pressure will not come from the United States alone. Japan and Europe also will intensify the global search for talented people. For example, "by the year 2010, Japan will face a shortage of about 100,000 software engineers," says Masayuki Sumi, managing director of personnel at Meitec Corp., a Japanese software engineering firm.[34] This may explain why Queen's University and other Canadian universities received faxes from Toshiba Corporation's Canadian subsidiary offering three- to five-year contracts in Tokyo for 15 university graduates in computer science and engineering, with no experience needed, and why a Japanese software company recruited several of the top computer science postgraduate students at the University of British Columbia.

There is no escape from the pressures of demographic change. The enormous growth in population and the demand for jobs in the developing world will create strong competition for many of Canada's traditional industries, will precipitate major changes in world flows of trade and investment, and will intensify the competition for the world's pool of savings. If these opportunities are blocked, then, as Mexican president Carlos Salinas has warned, developing countries will flood the industrial world with economic refugees. Conversely, if the growth opportunities of the developing world are unleashed, great opportunities will exist for Canadian exports and jobs — but only if we succeed in creating new high-value industries and high-skill jobs, and move our trade horizons beyond the United States to the rest of the world. In the process, a more productive Canadian economy will be better prepared to respond to the needs of an aging society.

3

The New Economy and the Environment

THE SCARE IN THE WINTER OF 1992 that the ozone layer over Canada was deteriorating faster than scientists had projected provided a stark symbol of the way in which the health of the planet is directly affecting our daily lives. It was also a reminder that environmental deterioration can spring nasty surprises and that we are less in control than we like to think. Federal and provincial governments responded by agreeing to eliminate the production of ozone-threatening gases by 1995, and the federal government began issuing regular reports to warn Canadians about threats from exposure to the sun's rays. The ozone depletion scare was also a reminder that the world should move faster to deal with the threat of global warming, the continuing decline in the planet's genetic pool, and other threats to human existence.

In many ways, we are already in the midst of an ecological revolution. We use the familiar blue boxes to separate garbage for recycling. Communities are concerned about the transportation and disposal of toxic wastes. Power utilities and metals companies are spending hundreds of millions of dollars to curb acid rain. Consumer goods companies are being pressured to reduce the waste from packaging. Fishing quotas are being imposed on Canada's Atlantic coast to halt the decline in fish stocks. The planned shutdown of roughly 2000 service stations by Petro-Canada and Imperial Oil is as much as anything the result of higher fuel-efficiency standards for automobiles. Municipalities across North America are mandating the use of recycled newsprint and forcing great adjustment problems on Canada's forest industry. The number of "green" products on supermarket shelves is growing. And Ontario Hydro plans to spend $6 billion this decade on energy conservation and efficiency measures in industry, offices, and homes. In 1989, medium-sized and large organizations invested $916 million in retrofit facilities and equipment for pollution abatement and control, according to Statistics Canada.[1]

Yet these developments are only the beginning of a new industrial revolution — the eco-revolution — as the world moves to a new, sustainable form of economic growth and development. This revolution will have much greater consequences for the world than the breakup of the Soviet Union and the end of the Cold War. It will truly transform the lives of people everywhere by creating a global partnership in which decisions in China, Africa, or Brazil will profoundly affect the future of Canadians. As we grapple to save the health of the planet while also expanding the global economy to meet the urgent needs of a fast-growing population, there will have to be new breakthroughs in science and technology, new international rules and institutions, and major transfers of money and technology from rich countries such as Canada to the developing world.

At the same time, the environmental challenge will create exciting new opportunities for Canadians. Some countries are already regarding the challenge of a green "economy" as the way to gain a competitive advantage in the next generation of jobs and technologies. Science and technology will be of fundamental importance in this process. If sustainable ways of creating wealth cannot be found, the future of life on the planet will be put at risk. Today, Canada's economy requires more energy per unit of output than that of any of the other major industrial economies; unless we move to greater energy-efficient and materials-saving forms of production, our competitiveness will decline. And if Canada does not set high environmental standards at home, as well as investing more in science and technology, Canadians will lose out on the opportunities in the transition to a green economy. What Canada needs, but does not have, is a strategy to make sure that Canadian companies and Canadian workers are full participants in this technological transformation.

The new economy is to be built on the principle of sustainable development, which was set out in the 1987 report of the World Commission on Environment and Development, *Our Common Future.* The commission, headed by Norwegian Prime Minister Gro Harlem Brundtland, pointed to two ominous trends that were unsustainable. In the first place, existing patterns of economic activity in the industrial countries (for example, gas-guzzling automobiles, coal-burning electric power plants, the use of chlorofluorocarbons in refrigeration and insulation, the disposal of wastes into oceans, the erosion of the productive capacity of agricultural land, and the use of energy-wasteful and materials-wasteful methods of production) were using up resources and generating wastes that exceeded the productive and absorptive capacity of the planet. Changes had to be made if ecological disaster was to be averted.

Making this even more urgent, the Brundtland commission warned, was another alarming trend — the rapid growth in population (and aspirations for a better life) in the developing world, where most of the human population lives. In the developing world, the standard of living is only a fraction of that enjoyed by typical Canadians, and more than 1.1 billion people live in abject poverty. Moreover, the world's population is growing by nearly one billion people a decade, and almost all of these people are being born in developing countries. It is inconceivable that the world's environment could accommodate four to six billion more people driving cars, using electricity, and producing steel, chemicals, food, and minerals in the same way Canadians do today. The pressure on resources and on agricultural and forest lands would be unprecedented, and the capacity of the earth's natural systems in the atmosphere and its water systems would be overwhelmed. The World Bank estimates that world output will be 3.5 times what it is today by 2030. But "if environmental pollution and degradation were to rise in step with such a rise in output, the result would be appalling environmental pollution and damage," the World Bank said in its 1992 *World Development Report.* "Tens of millions more people would become sick or die each year from environmental causes. Water shortages would be intolerable, and tropical forests and other natural habitats would decline to a fraction of their current size."[2] A new kind of economy has to be devised for the twenty-first century if ecological disaster, massive movement of refugees, widespread poverty, and international instability are to be avoided, said the Brundtland commission.

The sustainable development that is envisaged as the basis of this new economy was defined by the commission as "development that meets the needs of the present without compromising the ability of future generations to meet their own needs."[3] In fact, the concept was not entirely new. The Science Council of Canada had come up with a similar warning a decade earlier in a report on what it called the conserver society, in which it said that Canadians had to find the means of building concern for the future environment into today's decisions on investment and on the ways we spend our household dollars. "Economists used to say that the market would look after everything," the Science Council report said, but "we have only to remember our present concern regarding the probable effect on the ozone layer in the upper atmosphere 30 to 50 years hence of fluoro-carbon aerosols used today to realize that continuing to discount the future (waiting for economic effects to show in the market before we act) cannot be regarded as responsible behaviour."[4] The conserver society, the council said, would be a "smart society," using the latest ideas from science and technology to put the economy on a more sustainable footing. The council stressed the urgency of developing renewable sources of energy such as solar energy, of including the costs of environmental cleanup in the price of products, and of increasing energy conservation, recycling, and agricultural practices that maintain the productivity of the soil. Unfortunately, Canada did not pay attention to the Science Council report, losing out on the opportunity to gain a head start in developing the technologies and institutions for a sustainable society.

The concept of sustainable development is more than a new model of economic development; it is a new ethic, one that forces society to pay much greater attention to the needs of future genera-tions and to recognize that there are intergenerational obligations. Decisions made today must make tradeoffs that take into account the lives of the future children of today's kindergarten toddlers.

Not surprisingly, sustainable development has triggered consider-able debate. For example, there is controversy over how to calculate tradeoffs that affect future generations, since this forces us to consider sacrifices today for benefits perhaps 50 years from now. There is disagreement about what it is that should be sustained. Should we minimize our use of natural resources so that future generations will have a larger supply to pick from, or should we focus on advancing human knowledge so that substitutes can be found? Jean-Philippe Barde of the OECD argues that heritage, or patrimony, must include both artificial capital (such as human knowledge and infrastructure) and natural capital (such as the productivity capacity of soil and the biosphere itself). Artificial capital or technology can provide fuel cells and solar energy to replace oil and gas, fibre optics to replace copper wiring, and plastics instead of metals; but there are no substitutes for the ozone layer.[5] There is also controversy over how to determine how much human activity will in fact lead to the degradation or overburdening of the carrying capacity of the planet.

We do, however, know enough to know that changes are essential. Maurice Strong, the Canadian who chaired both the 1972 Stockholm conference on the environment and the 1992 Rio conference on environment and development, warns, "It has become increasingly evident that the patterns of growth that have produced such unprecedented levels of wealth in industrialized countries are not sustainable in either environmental or economic terms. 'No growth' is not an acceptable option. But 'no growth' is precisely what we will get if current wasteful and environmentally destructive growth practices persist."[6] The move to sustainable development implies much more than using blue boxes to recycle garbage and putting more insulation in homes. It would be "a modification of society comparable in scale to only two other changes: the agricultural revolution of the late Neolithic and the Industrial Revolution of the past two centuries," says William Ruckelhaus, a former head of the U.S. Environmental Protection Agency and a member of the Brundtland commission. "Those revolutions were gradual, spontaneous and largely unconscious. This one will have to be a fully conscious operation, guided by the best foresight that science can provide — foresight pushed to its limit. If we actually do it, the undertaking will be absolutely unique in humanity's stay on earth."[7]

The global nature of the environmental challenge can be seen in two threats to the future of mankind: the threat to the ozone layer, which shields us from the harmful effects of the sun's ultraviolet rays; and the threat to the world's climate as a result of greenhouse gases in the atmosphere, which affect food production, water supplies, and ecosystems. Both threats stem from our industrial way of life, and both could worsen if developing countries have economic growth that is not accompanied by new technologies and international agreements.

The threat to the ozone layer comes mainly from chlorofluorocarbons (CFCs), which are used in refrigerators, air-conditioners, and insulation materials; and halons, which are used in chemical fire extinguishers. Chlorine atoms from CFCs attach themselves to ozone in the atmosphere, eliminating our shield against the sun's ultraviolet rays. These rays can lead to various forms of skin cancer, cataracts, and a weakening of the immune system, affecting, for example, the spread of AIDS and other infectious diseases, as well as causing lower crop yields and a decline in marine life. CFCs are also a source of greenhouse gases and so contribute to global warming.

The 1987 Montreal Protocol on Substances that Deplete the Ozone Layer, which came into force at the beginning of 1989, committed signatory nations to cut CFC production to 50 per cent of 1986 levels by 1998. However, the ozone layer was deteriorating faster than scientists had expected, and consequently, in 1990, the Montreal protocol was amended in London, incorporating new targets: to eliminate five CFCs altogether in industrial countries by the year 2000 and in developing countries by 2010; to establish a US$240 million fund to help developing countries adapt; and to adopt trade penalties to be used against countries that do not take action to preserve the ozone layer. A number of industrial countries, including Canada, agreed to end CFC production by 1997. But early in 1992, the U.S. National Aeronautics and Space Administration warned of a weakening of the ozone layer over the Northern Hemisphere. Now Canada, the United States, the European Community, and others are moving to eliminate CFC production by the end of 1995. Yet even if all these goals are met, the accumulation of CFCs already in the atmosphere will threaten the ozone layer well into the next century.

Much less progress has been made in dealing with global warming, because an ambitious strategy to curb the emission of greenhouse gases would have far-reaching implications for the industrial systems and way of life in countries around the world (whereas dealing with the ozone layer was mainly a question of using science to develop a substitute for CFCs and halons). Yet something has to be done. Greenhouse gases — carbon dioxide, nitrous oxide, methane, and CFCs — trap radiated heat from the sun within the earth's atmosphere, preventing it from returning to space. The effect is to raise the temperature of the earth. The largest man-made source of greenhouse gases is the fossil fuel energy on which our modern societies are built: coal, oil, and natural gas, which account for about 75 per cent of man-made greenhouse gases. About half of all man-made greenhouse gases come from carbon dioxide, with methane and CFCs each contributing another 15 per cent and nitrous oxide 9 per cent.

In the great sweep of history, the planet has experienced swings in temperature that have included both very warm periods and ice ages; but for the past 160,000 years carbon dioxide concentrations have always fluctuated between 190 and 290 parts per million. Today they exceed 350 ppm, and a report for Environment Canada warns that they could rise to 450 ppm by the end of the next century, even with intensive energy conservation and efficiency programs.[8] According to the International Panel on Climate Change, the earth's temperature is rising at ten times the rate observed after the last ice age. The world's climatologists are largely in agreement that the earth's surface temperature could rise between 1.5° and 4.5°C between the years 2030 and 2050 unless there are strong efforts to curb the emission of greenhouse gases. Projections by the International Energy Agency show that energy-related emissions of carbon dioxide yielded 5895 million metric tonnes of carbon in 1989, compared with 4345 million in 1973; by 2005 the world can expect 9060 million metric tonnes of carbon from this source. While the industrial countries accounted for 60 per cent of this carbon in 1973, they will account for only about 40 per cent in 2005, when the main growth will come from developing countries such as China and India.[9] A report from the International Panel on Climate Change warns that because of the long life of greenhouse gases, we would need "immediate reductions in emissions from human activities of over 60 per cent to stabilize their concentrations at today's levels."[10]

The World Conference on the Changing Atmosphere, held in Toronto in 1988, called on Canada and other industrial countries to reduce their carbon dioxide emissions by 20 per cent by the year

2005, and 50 per cent by 2050. Without this kind of strong effort, the Environment Canada report warned, "human societies would be faced with physical, social and economic dislocation that could equal or surpass any the world has yet experienced."[11] For its part, the International Panel on Climate Change in its 1990 report predicted that without major new emission-reducing programs, the earth's temperature would rise 0.2° to 0.5°C per decade over the next century. To slow down the rate to 0.1°C per decade would require cutting greenhouse gas emissions by half from current levels.

Global warming would lead to a partial melting of the polar ice caps, raising ocean levels and flooding parts of Prince Edward Island, British Columbia, and the Arctic. Other effects would include serious drought and soil erosion on the prairies, lower water levels in the Great Lakes, a change in growing conditions in Canada's forests, and the spread into Canada of insects and plant diseases from southern regions. Globally, it could have far-reaching implications for the world's ability to feed itself, and it could cause havoc in low-lying countries such as Bangladesh, forcing millions to flee the developing world and seek refuge in the rich industrial countries.

TABLE 13

Carbon Dioxide Emissions from Energy Use

million tonnes of carbon

Country	1975	1980	1989	1989 Per Capita
CANADA	113.6	130.0	135.5	4.8
U.S.	1274.7	1410.0	1480.0	5.8
Japan	261.8	272.0	288.0	2.2
France	130.7	144.0	110.8	1.8
W.Germany	279.6	304.5	281.9	3.2
Italy	102.4	112.0	117.3	1.9
Britain	171.7	169.0	164.0	2.9
Sweden	26.9	25.0	21.4	2.5
WORLD	4811.5	5528.4	6255.9*	

*1988

SOURCE: *OECD Environmental Data: Compendium 1991* (Paris: OECD, 1991).

The Intergovernmental Negotiating Committee on the Framework Convention for Climate Change has yet to negotiate a document that agrees on the overall objective of holding greenhouse gases to a safe level; but once it does, individual countries will have to commit themselves to per capita targets. This will put significant pressure on countries such as Canada. With less than 1 per cent of the world's population, Canada accounts for about 2.1 per cent of the world's carbon dioxide emissions; in 1988 Canada released 123.5 million tonnes of carbon into the atmosphere from energy-related activities (and like CFCs, greenhouse gases remain in the atmosphere for decades). To stabilize emissions at 350 ppm would require a 50–80 per cent cut in carbon dioxide emissions.

The level of pollution in the world is a combination of the size of the world's population, the rate of world economic growth, and the amount of pollution that is generated for each unit of gross world product. We know that the world's population will continue to grow for decades and that the developing countries must achieve high rates of economic growth to end their severe poverty and produce a higher standard of living. That means we have to use all the capabilities of science and technology to reduce the amount of pollution that is generated for each unit of production, and to provide the financial and human resources to make sure that the developing countries, as well as ourselves, are able to move to sustainable forms of production.

We experienced a taste of things to come in the 1970s. Two oil price shocks made much of the world's industrial capacity obsolete, because it consumed too much energy when oil prices were high. Many industries began moving to energy-efficient methods of production, and there was a surge of investment in home insulation and fuel-efficient cars. This transition slowed in the 1980s as oil prices declined, but it is now on the increase again — for environmental reasons.

This time, the transition has to be much greater. Many of the industrial processes that produce the goods and services we consume must be redesigned. We must find ways of husbanding our resources and of recycling. And instead of dealing with pollution after it has happened, we must invent systems of production that prevent it from occurring in the first place. There will have to be new spending and investment on the development of new technologies, including biotechnology, as well as on information systems to regulate and monitor the production systems. None of this will be cheap. The United States estimates that it is spending 2 per cent of its gross domestic product (GDP) for anti-pollution measures, and this is expected to rise to 3 per cent later in the decade. With a Canadian GDP of about $700 billion, this would be the same as Canada spending $14 billion a year now (or roughly half the federal deficit) and $21 billion if 3 per cent of the GDP were spent.

Some Canadian companies, government agencies, and university research teams are already working towards a sustainable economy, though their numbers are small compared with those in many countries. In Vancouver, Ballard Power Systems is developing high-tech batteries that one day may power motor vehicles. In Toronto, Electrolyser Corporation is pursuing the use of hydrogen as a non-polluting successor to hydrocarbons. Experco of Drummondville is helping Mexico and other countries tackle water pollution. Loblaws is expanding its line of green products. Canada's chemical producers are implementing a new code of environmental behaviour, and Canada's packaging industry is working to halve the amount of packaging that ends up in the garbage by the year 2000. A growing number of companies are conducting environmental audits. Northern Telecom has eliminated ozone-depleting solvents from its 42 manufacturing plants, the first electronics company in the world to do so.

Nevertheless, Canada lacks a strategy to bring the new jobs and new forms of wealth creation that should be involved in building a new sustainable society. In 1990 the federal government at last unveiled its own Green Plan, but although the plan moves Canada in the right direction, it fails to provide the bold measures that are needed to play a leading role in the coming technological transformation to a new economy. And there are reasons to doubt that even its modest commitments will be met. Within three months of unveiling the plan, the government in its 1991 budget announced that its spending of $3 billion over five years under the Green Plan would be spread over six years instead. The Green Plan failed to meet its first year's targets, and in the 1992 budget another $150 million of spending was deferred into the future.

In moving from environmental policies that emphasize the clean-up of pollution to a society that develops totally new ways of doing things, we will need to draw on the knowledge gained from better science and innovation. Some of the transition costs will be painful (for example, jobs will be lost and communities affected) but new companies and new jobs will emerge. These will be found in a wide range of areas: electric cars; new recycling technologies; biotechnology to deal with hazardous wastes; fuel cells; solar energy systems; the design of products for easier recycling; new processes to reduce waste in resource upgrading and manufacturing; the application of information technologies to improve our monitoring of the environment; and new systems of home insulation and building efficiency. Germany's new recycling laws provide a view of what lies ahead. Under German law, manufacturers are being required to take responsibility both for their products and for what happens to them when they are discarded. Packaging is the first target, but laws will require industry to take back cars, refrigerators, photocopiers, tires, electronic components, batteries, and many other products and to recycle them.

The move to sustainable development will put enormous pressure on countries such as Canada. Maurice Strong states the position clearly: "Our patterns of production and consumption have brought the whole human community to the threshold of risks to our survival and well-being which rich and poor alike must share. We must reduce our impacts on these thresholds and make room for the growth of developing countries." This, Strong says, "requires a transition to lifestyles that are less wasteful and indulgent, more modest in their use of resources and the pressures they exert on the environment."[12] The challenge is thus not only to our science and technology; it is also to our culture and values.

It is the environmental challenge, in fact, that is the real force for globalization, since it will impel the rich industrial countries to make drastic changes in their economies and lifestyles in order to make room for growth in the developing world. Although the rich countries account for less than 25 per cent of the world's population, they consume 80 per cent of the world's goods, including 75 per cent of the world's energy, 72 per cent of the world's steel production, and more than 85 per cent of the world's wood products; in the process, they generate 90 per cent of the world's hazardous wastes, nearly 100 per cent of CFCs, and 74 per cent of carbon dioxide. As Norwegian Prime Minister Gro Harlem Brundtland says, "the industrialized countries have been developing for decades without having to pay for the damage done to the environment. Our economies have been built on cheap and abundant fuels as if there were no tomorrow. That is one of the main reasons why we have to pay extra. We cannot say to the developing world: Sorry, we have filled the wastebasket, there is no room left for you."[13]

Estimates by the Brundtland commission showed that with the world's population expected to double over the next 50 years to more than 10 billion people, world output would have to increase five to ten times its current levels to meet even modest aspirations for a better life in the developing countries. The number of motor vehicles is expected to increase from 500 million today to more than 2 billion over the next 20 years. Likewise, developing countries are expected to spend more than US$100 billion a year building new power plants. That is why it is crucial that developing countries should be able to leap-frog the technologies that are the source of today's environmental problems.

This will mean, among other things, that the wealthy countries will have to increase their financial transfers to the developing world. Work carried out for the 1992 Earth Summit by staff of the United Nations Conference on Environment and Development indicates that in order to implement an action plan for sustainable development, international financial aid would have to be increased from the US$55 billion annual transfer provided today to an annual transfer of US$125 billion. (This would mean an increase in Canada's foreign assistance budget of about 70 per cent — from about 0.44 per cent of GDP to more than 0.7 per cent.) The total costs would be four to five times this amount, with developing country governments and their private sectors accounting for most of the required spending.

As the U.N. document warned, the cost of inaction will be high. Without changes, it said, "we can expect serious problems ahead in many areas. Often the costs of inaction will have serious implications as in the case of increased health care costs resulting from higher skin cancer rates and more respiratory problems; the higher costs of cleaning up as opposed to the prevention of pollution and wastes; and the major costs anticipated to accommodate the sea level rise. In some cases inaction will narrow the choices for future generations. It is important in considering the financial resources issue to be very clear about the costs of inaction."[14]

Sustainable development cannot be achieved through easy targets. Jim MacNeill, Canada's leading expert on the subject (he was executive secretary to the Brundtland commission) warns that "a transition to sustainable forms of development will require a fundamental reorientation of dominant modes of decision-making in government and industry and on the part of individuals who buy, consume and dispose of the world's goods. It will also involve significant changes — many of them politically very difficult — in economic, fiscal and energy policies which guide national, corporate and private behaviour."[15] As well, there will need to be new international institutions and a surrender of sovereignty. The urgency of this was spelled out at the 1988 World Conference on the Changing Atmosphere, when scientists warned that human and industrial activity constituted "an unintended, uncontrolled, globally pervasive experiment whose ultimate consequences could be second only to a global nuclear war" unless the importance of the environment was built into all our decisions and actions.[16]

While the concept of sustainable development has been accepted almost universally, the implications and necessary follow-throughs have not. The United Nations Conference on Environment and Development, held in Brazil in June 1992, was organized as a follow-up to the Brundtland commission to try to persuade world leaders to adopt ambitious plans to implement sustainable development. Its plans for an Earth Charter, setting out basic principles of conduct for individuals and nations, and Agenda 21, an action plan, represented just the first steps to a new world agenda for a sustainable planet. But while the Rio summit was a step forward, it also revealed that great differences remain on how and when the world should move to sustainable development.

In Canada's own Green Plan, the Mulroney government announced that "sustainable development is what we want to achieve" and that "the Green Plan sets out how we are going to achieve it."[17] But the plan also falls far short of what is needed, although it does make positive commitments to improve the management of our forests, fisheries, soils, and water, and our methods of dealing with toxic waste and abandoned mine sites, as well as reducing smog levels.

Although $175 million is to be spent under the Green Plan to address the problems of global warming, there is no strategy to bring Canada's energy efficiency and conservation levels anywhere close to those of countries such as Japan and Sweden or to curb Canada's high per capita consumption of fossil fuels. Since the mid-1980s, energy policy has been left to the free play of market forces, even though Prime Minister Mulroney told the World Conference on the Changing Atmosphere that "Canada is committed to applying the principles of sustainable development to our energy future."[18]

There is also the question whether Canadians themselves are prepared to take the necessary steps even when they know they should. A 1990 poll conducted by the Angus Reid Group for the Federation of Canadian Municipalities found that nearly 75 per cent of Canadians opposed taxing the use of cars in cities to reduce downtown pollution, more than half opposed charges for garbage pick-up based on how much people threw away, and more than half opposed a tax on packaging to reduce packaging garbage.[19]

As noted earlier, moving to sustainable development will cost money and some jobs. The use of recycled paper will put some pulp mills in jeopardy and some people out of work. The packaging industry's pledge to halve the amount of packaging ending up as garbage may also cost jobs and could close some packaging plants. The use of fuel-efficient cars has meant lower gasoline sales and fewer gasoline stations. Carl Sonnen, a vice-president of the economic consulting firm Informetrica Ltd., has estimated that about $46 billion would have to be spent by business, consumers, and all levels of government in the 1990s and another $25 billion in 2001–2010, in 1989 dollars, just to meet the identifiable costs of implementing the government's Green Plan. This is equivalent to about 15–20 per cent of average net investment in Canada; and it does not include the costs of such things as new packaging standards, measures to deal with solid non-toxic wastes, changes in agriculture and forestry practices, nuclear waste disposal, and much-increased assistance for developing countries.

Moreover, additional measures will be needed before the end of the 1990s, so spending in the first decade of the next century will be even higher. Sonnen proposes that Canada introduce a $50-per-tonne carbon tax by 1993, hitting coal the hardest, then oil and then natural gas; this would generate an additional $13 billion in revenue in 1993, increasing to more than $17 billion by 2000. This, he says, could be offset by a reduction in the GST or other taxes or by government debt reduction. There would also be benefits from a green economy — for example, a healthier environment and more competitive industry. Sonnen believes that the transition to sustainable development could result in relatively "modest" costs.[20]

It is not clear, however, that even the modest goals of the Green Plan will be implemented, says analyst Bruce Doern in a study for the C. D. Howe Institute. He predicts that there will be growing opposition from business. "Business has tended to greet the Green Plan with a sigh of relief. A more interventionist approach, including environmental taxes, was avoided," he points out.[21] The aim of business has been to slow down the environmental movement; some members of the oil industry are fighting the idea that there is a problem at all. Imperial Oil Ltd.'s senior economist, J.W. Chuckman, even questions the existence of global warming. "The answer is that we do not know," he says. And he argues that even if a long-term trend in global warming were detected, "how would we know that that was anything more than part of one of the many natural, long-term cycles of heating and cooling?"[22] Even before the Green Plan was unveiled, the Canadian Petroleum Association had stated that Canada's pledge, at the 1990 World Climate Conference, to stabilize greenhouse gas emissions in 2000 at their 1990 levels was premature.[23] Yet as the Science Council of Canada has pointed out, if Canada wants to influence the behaviour of other countries, it must set a good example at home. Otherwise, "who will pay attention to us when we broach problems that can only be solved through international collaboration?"[24]

The go-slow approach also ignores a crucial point made by Michael Porter, the Harvard Business School expert on competitiveness strategy; namely, that "tough regulatory standards are not a hindrance but an opportunity to move early to upgrade products and processes." As he explains, "they pressure firms to improve quality, upgrade technology and provide features in areas of important customer and social concerns. They also encourage the start-up of specialized manufacturing and service firms to help address them."[25] This is why companies in Sweden, Japan, Germany, and Denmark are ahead of the United States and Canada in serving world markets with sustainable technologies. It is also why, unless Canada acts soon, it could end up having to import much of the technology it needs for sustainable development.

It is not surprising, then, that Canada's environmental performance ranks below that of other leading countries. "While there have been some instances of success…the total quantity of pollution entering the environment each year has not been significantly reduced; in fact, it may well have increased, due to increases in population and economic activity, since the present regulatory system was established in the late 1960s," says Doug Macdonald, former executive director of the Canadian Environmental Law Research Foundation.[26]

The problem, says Macdonald, is that Canada cannot transform itself into a non-polluting society without paying a significant price, "a price measured in public and private spending, job dislocations, and the availability of many goods and services deemed essential." So far, we have not been willing to pay this price, so we keep on polluting. Even Canada's auditor general, in his 1991 report to Parliament, was strongly critical of Environment Canada's lax enforcement of our environmental laws.[27]

The forest industry provides a good example. Faced with the threat of pulp mill shutdowns, provincial governments have backed away from enforcing regulations. As a result, there have been repeated delays in meeting even weak pollution standards; in 1985, some 60 per cent of direct discharge mills in Canada were out of compliance with even minimum federal standards. William Sinclair of Environment Canada says that even when profits are high, the industry has been unwilling to invest in pollution control.[28] In the 1987 boom year, for example, figures from the Canadian Pulp and Paper Association show that only 5 per cent of planned capital investment was designated for pollution control. Yet U.S. mills have succeeded in meeting U.S. standards, which on traditional mill effluent "are significantly more stringent than the existing Canadian federal limits on

Biochemical Oxygen Demand and more stringent than even the proposed Canadian standards for 1994."[29] Today, Canadian companies are paying a price because, aside from a new Howe Sound pulp and paper mill on the West Coast, they do not have the chlorine-free systems to produce the unbleached paper that customers in Europe and the United States are now demanding.

On a per capita basis, Canada has one of the poorest environmental records in the industrial world. In 1987, its per capita emissions of sulphur dioxide totalled 148.3 kilograms — much higher than 83.6 kilograms by the Americans, 31.6 by the Germans, 23.2 by the French, and 6.9 by the Japanese. Canadian per capita emission of carbon monoxide totalled 428.4 kilograms, compared with 290.9 by the Americans, 145.7 by the Germans, and 115.0 by the French. And Canadian per capita emissions of nitrous oxide totalled 77.8 kilograms, compared with 82.7 by the Americans, 48.5 by the Germans, 28.6 by the French, and 11.5 by the Japanese.[30]

Canadians are also profligate users of energy. In 1988, primary energy demand in Canada totalled 335 gigajoules per capita, compared

TABLE 14

Man-made Emissions of Air Pollutants: Late 1980s

	kilograms per US$1000 of GDP			
Country	*Sulphur Oxides*	*Nitrous Oxides*	*Particulates*	*Carbon Monoxide*
CANADA	9.7	4.9	4.3	27.4
United States	4.7	4.5	1.6	13.8
Japan	0.6	0.8	0.1	—
France	2.4	3.1	0.5	11.0
W. Germany	1.9	4.3	0.8	13.0
Italy	4.4	3.4	0.9	11.9
Britain	7.0	4.9	1.0	10.7
Netherlands	1.9	4.2	0.7	7.9
Norway	1.0	3.6	0.4	9.6
Sweden	1.8	2.9	1.6	16.2
OECD	4.1	3.8	1.3	12.8
WORLD	7.3	5.0	4.2	13.1

SOURCE: OECD, *The State of the Environment* (Paris: OECD, 1991).

TABLE 15
Energy Consumption Per Capita (kilograms of oil equivalent)

Country	1965	1989
India	100	226
China	178	591
Mexico	605	1288
Brazil	286	897
South Korea	238	1832
Hong Kong	413	1629
Australia	3287	5291
Britain	3481	3624
Italy	1568	2721
France	2468	3778
Germany	3197	4383
Japan	1474	3484
United States	6535	7794
CANADA	6007	9959
Netherlands	3134	4948
Sweden	4162	6228
Switzerland	2501	3913
Low-income economies	125	330
Middle-income economies	663	1242
High-income economies	3641	4867
OECD	3748	5182

SOURCE: *World Development Report 1991* (Washington: World Bank, 1991).

with 322 in the United States, 231 in Sweden, 185 in Germany, 148 in France, and 132 in Japan. In other words, a typical Canadian used 2.5 times as much energy as a typical Japanese and about 1.5 times as much as a typical Swede.[31] This helps explain why the Canadian per capita emission of carbon into the atmosphere was 4.8 tonnes in 1988, compared with 5.8 in the United States, 3.2 in Germany, 2.4 in Sweden, 2.2 in Japan, 1.9 in Switzerland, and 1.8 in France.

How much energy we use as well as the kinds we use are key issues in the move to a sustainable economy. The design of our homes, office towers, industrial plants, and shopping malls will be affected, as will the kinds of cars we drive, the appliances we use, and the packaging on all the products we consume. Our farms, fisheries, forest and mining companies, chemicals producers, steel-makers, food processors, oil and gas companies, and a wide range of manufacturers will all have to change the ways they do business. Cities will be forced to adopt new pricing systems for water, to review their land zoning and density rules, and to find new solutions to the growing mountains of garbage. Our systems of taxation, pricing, and other incentives will change as prices come to reflect the full life cycle cost of a product, including its environmental cost.

Various economic instruments will have to be used so that the right market signals are sent. These could include charges on the emission of pollutants, user charges for the costs of cleanups, taxes on harmful products, fines, and incentives such as tradable permits that would allocate quotas on polluting emissions and allow low polluters to sell their unused quotas to higher polluters. As well, deposit-refund systems like those on pop bottles could be extended to big products such as automobiles and refrigerators. And as mentioned earlier, a carbon tax could be used to discourage fossil-fuel consumption at home and to generate revenue for what Maurice Strong calls an Earth Increment to assist developing countries build economies based on sustainable development. Likewise, tradable permits could be allocated globally, the majority going to developing countries, which could then sell them to high polluters such as Canada and the United States.

The suggested tax on the carbon content of energy to discourage the use of oil and coal and, eventually, natural gas would be the most important green tax. This kind of tax helps achieve full cost pricing by including the environmental damage in the price of the energy. The highest rate would be for coal, the next highest for oil, and the least for natural gas. Although gasoline is taxed by virtually all countries, coal and natural gas are rarely taxed. The European Economic Community is planning a carbon tax; much of the revenue from this will be used to help European companies devise new environmental technologies, and part may be used to help developing countries adopt these technologies.

For Canada, the move to a carbon tax is complicated by the unwillingness of the United States to put high taxes on energy. Taxes account for 40.3 per cent of the price of gasoline in Canada but only 24.2 per cent in the United States, and already our tourism industry and border communities are complaining that our higher gasoline prices are causing a loss of business. In most European countries taxes account for 60 to 70 per cent of the price of gasoline, and this will of course increase with the new carbon tax.[32] Research by the OECD suggests that Canada's gasoline tax is equivalent to a carbon tax of US$108 per ton of carbon on oil alone and US$52 on all fossil fuels (coal, oil, and natural gas). By comparison, the implicit carbon tax on all fossil fuels amounts to US$28 in the United States, US$79 in Japan, US$95 in Germany, US$198 in Switzerland, and US$214 in Sweden. A US$100 carbon tax could reduce carbon emissions by 25 per cent in the industrial world, the OECD research suggests.[33] So if we are serious about combatting global warming, we should see that Canada, too, brings in a carbon tax.

Although the threat to the planet comes mainly from rich countries, global poverty, which is spreading, is also causing damage to the environment. With about 1.1 billion people living in absolute poverty today, and with the number expected to increase to 1.5 billion by the end of the century, there is enormous strain on croplands, forests, and water supplies.[34] Without financial help, many developing countries will not to able to cope with environmental problems and move to sustainable development. This is one reason why the developing countries' US$1.3 trillion debt remains an unresolved issue, despite the progress that has been made. If these countries are to help the world deal with environmental threats, they will need further debt relief as well as added flows of financial and technological help.[35] Without an attack on world poverty, sustainable development is not possible.

In its 1990 Green Plan, the federal government said that its goal was to hold carbon dioxide emissions in the year 2000 to the same level as those in 1990. But the plan admitted that without new policies, carbon dioxide emissions in the year 2000 would be 17 per cent higher than in 1990. How Canadians are to achieve this goal has yet to be spelled out. In 1991, a National Energy Board forecast reported that carbon dioxide emissions from energy use alone (even after

TABLE 16
Per Capita Consumption of Fossil Fuels

	Oil		Natural Gas		Coal	
(million tonnes per capita)						
	1979	*1989*	*1979*	*1989*	*1979*	*1989*
CANADA	3.8	2.9	2.1	2.0	0.8	1.3
United States	3.9	3.2	2.3	2.0	1.7	1.9
Japan	2.3	1.8	0.2	0.3	0.4	0.6
Germany	2.4	1.7	0.8	0.7	1.3	1.2
Britain	1.7	1.4	0.8	1.3	1.4	1.1
France	2.2	1.6	0.4	0.4	0.5	0.3
Italy	1.8	1.6	0.4	0.6	0.2	0.2

SOURCE: Energy, Mines & Resources, *BP Statistical Review*, June 1990.

making some assumptions for energy efficiency and conservation) would rise 14 per cent between 1990 and 2000, from 518,000 to 590,000 kilotonnes; and emissions could reach 675,000 kilotonnes by the year 2010 — a 30 per cent increase over 1990. The board said that without stringent new building codes and energy-restricting measures, Canada's appetite for coal, oil, and natural gas would continue to grow.

A Task Force on the Environment appointed by Canada's energy ministers reported in 1989 that Canada could make progress towards a 20 per cent reduction in carbon dioxide emissions by the year 2005 through intensive energy-efficiency and conservation measures. But a full 20 per cent reduction would mean a net reduction of 40 per cent from the currently projected emission levels, and that "would be difficult to achieve."[36] The federal and provincial energy ministers took the easy way out, concluding that more research was needed before Canada took additional steps. A report by the Canadian Climate Board notes that Canada will be under strong international pressure to lower the amount of energy used to produce a unit of GDP. Canada currently uses more than twice as much energy per unit of GDP as Japan and about 20 per cent more than the United States. If Canada is to do its share, "this will require a vigorous energy efficiency and conservation program, a gradual move away from fossil fuel energy sources, and major efforts at reforestation."[37]

Meanwhile, Canada is missing out on the new businesses and jobs that will emerge from the transition to a sustainable economy. One of the first acts of the Mulroney government in 1984 was to close down the National Research Council's renewable energy division, saving $60 million a year but seriously weakening Canada's emerging companies in solar energy and other renewable sources of power. Through the second half of the 1980s the government slashed research and conservation programs. According to the Department of Energy, Mines and Resources, its research and development spending on energy efficiency declined from $33.8 million in 1984–85 to $14.9 million in 1990–91, a 55 per cent cut. Similarly, its R & D spending on renewable energy fell from $39.7 million in 1984–85 to $11.2 million in 1990–91, a 72 per cent cut.[38]

At the same time that the federal government was slashing programs that would improve energy efficiency and find alternatives to fossil fuels, it offered huge subsidies to develop additional oil and gas supplies (which, of course, add greenhouse gases to the atmosphere and smog to city streets). These subsidies included $675 million towards the Lloydminster heavy oil upgrader, $2.7 billion towards Hibernia ($1 billion in grants and $1.7 billion in loan guarantees), and a promised $1.3 billion for the OSLO tar sands project. In 1990, for budget reasons, the federal government limited the OSLO offer to the funding of engineering plans. But during a visit to Alberta in late 1991, Prime Minister Brian Mulroney said that his government would reconsider the project.

Some scientists, such as David Suzuki, contend that we should limit economic growth itself to save the environment.[39] Suzuki questions the ability of scientists to come up with solutions, as well as the ability of politicians to create new institutions. In response, economist Richard Lipsey argues that "to try to stop growth by freezing technology at its existing levels is to condemn much of the world's population to unnecessary suffering, and many less developed countries to perpetual poverty. Technological developments, and the economic growth that comes in their wake, are the main hope for reducing pollution, and saving the environment, as well as raising living standards of the less developed countries to levels near those currently found in the developed nations."[40]

Clearly, if the standard of living of all of the world's 5.4 billion people were raised to the level enjoyed by a typical Canadian, we would face environmental disaster. But halting economic growth and redistributing the world's income — even if it could be done — would not work either. The world's GDP in 1990 was about US$22.3 trillion when the world's population was 5.3 billion, according to the World Bank. So dividing the economic pie evenly would give everyone in the world a per capita GDP of US$4220, causing incomes in countries such as Canada to drop far below the current poverty level.

This shows why technology is so important. Technology is the way to provide room for economic growth without putting the environment under extreme stress. Energy efficiency and conservation can bring great financial savings as well. As Canadian environmental expert Jim MacNeill states, "the gains in human welfare over the past few decades have been breathtaking and, if we continue to avoid world-scale conflict, the potential for future gains is even more awesome." MacNeill points out that "many new and emerging technologies in biology, materials, construction, satellite monitoring, and other fields offer great promise for increasing the production of food, developing more benign forms of energy, raising industrial productivity, conserving the earth's basic stocks of natural capital, and managing the environment."[41]

Richard Lipsey suggests that critics of technological progress should go back 100 years and look at how life has changed since then: "Victorian Canadians could not have imagined the modern dentist's office, doctor services, penicillin, pain killers, bypass operations...washing machines, vacuum cleaners, disposable nappies, and a host of other new products that their grandchildren take for granted."[42] Technology is crucial to sustainable development.

Technological solutions call for long-term strategic investments in research and development. Canada has achieved impressive accomplishments in monitoring the state of the world's atmosphere, as well as in a few other areas, such as waste management, the treatment of waste water, and the development of new batteries, but the overall level of research and development that is necessary to achieve sustainable development has been seriously underfunded and given a low priority in Canada. Although the Green Plan admits the need for "a significant increase in support," additional funding has been slow to materialize, and now the Science Council of Canada, which has studied environmental technologies, has been abolished by the Mulroney government.

Meanwhile, the United States is giving active support to its environmental industries. The 1990 Clean Air Act is spurring new technologies, and "a number of new laws and initiatives regarding oil pollution, ozone layer depletion, climate change, federal facility cleanup, reforestation, ecosystem restoration and education will have the same effect," says Michael Deland, chairman of the Council on Environmental Quality in the White House. U.S. government R & D spending for environmental technologies has been raised. In fiscal 1992, funds for federal R & D for surface transportation rose 60 per cent; for new transportation fuels, they rose 20 per cent; for efficient buildings and industrial processes, 22 per cent; and for cleaner, more efficient electrical technologies, 28 per cent. "The growing size of the world market for environmental technologies (one preliminary estimate places it in the range of US$228 billion and growing 5 to 6 per cent a year) indicates that thousands of jobs and a global strategic niche are at stake," says Deland.[43] In 1991 President George Bush announced that the U.S. government would fund half the US$260 million cost of a four-year project to make electric cars competitive by the year 2000. The money will go to the U.S. Advanced Battery Consortium formed by the "big three" U.S. automakers to develop new batteries.

The Science Council of Canada has urged us to seize the opportunity presented by sustainable development and double our efforts to build an economy based on science and ideas. It said that many of the new technologies will make Canadian industry more competitive; for example, the thermo-chemical pulping process that is replacing the sulphite process in paper mills to conserve energy and wood supply. The process has increased the recovery from raw wood from 50 per cent to more than 90 per cent.

"Some new technologies can be readily identified as important building blocks of a sustainable economy," the Science Council said. "The information technologies, the most developed and diffused of the emerging technologies, have already shown a great capacity to increase the efficiency with which all industries use energy and resources through, for example, computerized product design and computerized control during manufacturing. New materials also conserve energy and resources because less energy is used in their manufacture and, being lighter, they contain less matter than conventional materials. Examples include advanced coatings for industrial tools, advanced wear-resistant bearing alloys, and cobalt-free alloy systems for the hard facings of engine exhaust valves."[44] Biotechnology — whether used to develop new high-yield, pest-resistant crop varieties or to deal with toxic wastes — could also help achieve a sustainable society. But to realize the potential, Canada needs a green industrial strategy.

Japan is a good example of a country that has a serious energy policy designed to make significant gains in energy efficiency and to find alternatives to coal and oil. The International Energy Agency reported in 1991 that "consistent efforts in conservation and effi-

TABLE 17
Total Final Consumption of Energy Per Unit of GDP
(1981 = 100)

Country	1970	1975	1980	1985	1989	TOE/US$1000*	
						1980	1989
CANADA	110	100	100	84	79	0.46	0.36
United States	120	110	100	84	80	0.38	0.30
Japan	125	118	100	85	81	0.21	0.17
France	116	106	100	89	82	0.24	0.20
W.Germany	115	107	100	92	81	0.28	0.23
Italy	119	115	100	91	90	0.18	0.16
Britain	128	113	100	92	84	0.24	0.20
Sweden	119	112	100	89	80	0.36	0.29
Switzerland	98	96	100	101	93	0.20	0.19
Finland	118	105	100	88	86	0.40	0.34
Norway	124	106	100	92	87	0.34	0.30

*Tonnes of oil equivalent per US$1000 of GDP at 1985 prices and PPS.

SOURCE: *OECD Environmental Data: Compendium 1991* (Paris: OECD, 1991).

ciency, especially in industry, has made Japan one of the world's most energy-efficient economies, with one of the lowest ratios of total primary energy supply per unit of GDP."[45] While Canada used the equivalent of 0.46 tonnes of oil to produce US$1000 of GDP, Japan used less than half, 0.21 tonnes.

In October 1990, the Japanese cabinet adopted energy supply targets to the year 2010, boosting the role of renewable energy. The Japan Development Bank will provide low-interest loans to utilities exploiting hydro or co-generation opportunities. The Solar System Development Association will make loans to utilize solar systems. The New Energy Foundation will make loans for geothermal waste-heat and waste-utilization systems. The Japanese government will also fund model projects that use new energy sources to help share the risk of new energy systems. For example, its Agency of Natural Resources and Energy is working with electric power utilities, gas companies, and electrical equipment manufacturers in what is probably the world's biggest effort to develop fuel cells.

The Japanese government has also adopted an Action Program to Avert Global Warming for 1991–2010 to achieve "an environmentally sound society, compatible with stable economic development and international coordination." Japan is looking to the development of new technologies, including solar, hydrogen, and fusion power, and is also stressing energy-efficient buildings, electric cars, and improvements in automobile efficiency. It has had energy R & D programs since the early 1970s. The Sunshine Project, launched in 1973, funds government R & D programs in solar energy, geothermal energy, hydrogen production, coal liquefaction, and gasification as well as research in other renewables, including wind energy. In 1978 Japan launched its Moonlight Project, which funds R & D in energy conservation and energy-efficiency technologies. And the New Energy and Industrial Technology Development Organization (a joint venture between government and industry organized by the Ministry of International Trade and Industry) promotes the development of new energy and conservation technologies; it constructs and operates large-scale demonstration projects, such as those featuring photovoltaic power generation, fuel cells, and electric battery storage. One priority is to commercialize solar power in the 1990s.

As the International Energy Agency points out, Japan has been at the forefront of efforts to combat environmental degradation, and government policy has been a major factor. "The leading position of its industry in the development of environmental protection and control technology is largely the result of legislation introduced since the early 1960s to control industrial pollution. Thus, Japan has known for some time that environmental and energy policy goals can be coordinated and pursued to mutual benefit."[46] It is no accident that a Japanese company, Mitsui, is providing coal-burning technology for a new coal-burning plant in Nova Scotia.

Other countries, too, have found that when they take the initiative and institute new regulatory standards, they give their own industries an advantage in developing the products and services to meet these new demands. In Sweden, early regulations on acid rain caused Swedish companies to devise scrubbers and other technologies that are now exported around the world. Californian companies are hoping to cash in on tough new rules that give California some of the most demanding environmental standards in North America. The state already leads North America in the development of solar and wind technologies, water treatment, and air quality. Its Silicon Valley entrepreneurs hope to increase the spread of solar energy and environmental services, and the use of biotechnology-based super-bugs to eat up toxic wastes.

Canada needs a similar push. Geraldine Kenney-Wallace, the president of McMaster University and former chairman of the Science Council of Canada, has proposed that we mount a project that will be as large as the U.S. Strategic Defense Initiative ("Star Wars") but will be concerned with technology to protect the environment; she calls it the Environmental Defence Initiative.[47] A small start has been made with the federal Green Plan, which is providing $100 million over an unspecified number of years to help companies launch or demonstrate new products and services that will help clean up the environment. But Canada needs a policy of identifying and then targeting technologies that will be the source of new companies and jobs in the sustainable economy. Canada's electric power utilities, for example, have an opportunity to develop businesses in energy efficiency and conservation by strategically handling their demand management programs so that they encourage homeown-

TABLE 18
Environmental Indicators

	Greenhouse Gases (tonnes/person)	Municipal Waste (kg/person)	Population Served by Wastewater Treatment Plants (%)
CANADA	9.2	632	66
United States	10.0	864	74
Japan	3.3	394	39
Germany	5.3	331	90
France	4.0	304	52
Britain	3.8	353	84
Italy	5.4	301	60
Sweden	4.0	317	95

SOURCE: *OECD State of the Environment* (Paris: OECD, 1991).

ers and businesses to use energy more efficiently. The $6 billion that Ontario Hydro plans to spend on energy conservation programs could be used strategically to help develop Canadian technologies and companies. Without strategies and government-industry partnerships, we shall be lucky to develop and capitalize on new technologies and jobs.

The federal Department of Industry, Science and Technology launched the Environmental Industries Sector Initiative in 1989, and it estimates a Canadian market of $12 billion a year by 2000, compared with just under $2 billion now. But the study found that Canada's environmental industry faced serious barriers that could "significantly" limit Canada's share of the growing global environmental market. "The industry," it said, "is composed of a large number of small firms with limited financial support and marketing experience." It is "fragmented, lacks identity and needs cohesion.... Research and expertise is scattered across industry, government agencies, universities and other institutions."[48]

In 1991, the federal government published a study on the environmental services industry: environmental consultants and specialists (including consulting engineers, waste management operators, and recyclers), private laboratories and research establishments, and public-sector agencies that provide services for a fee. The study estimated that in 1987 just over 90,000 Canadians were employed in the industry. About half the jobs were in some 3500 companies and the remainder were in government agencies. The main areas of expertise were remote sensing and the environmental application of geographic information systems, wastewater treatment, computer modelling and control systems, environmental engineering and auditing, and instrumentation for monitoring and detection systems.[49] Like the manufacturers, the service companies suffer a competitive disadvantage because of their small size.

What we need is a bold and determined strategy to capture the economic benefits of sustainable development. This strategy will need to employ all the tools of public policy, including R & D support, the setting of tough standards, the use of government purchasing to accelerate the development of new technologies, risk sharing in their development, and support of our educational system to produce the suitably qualified people who will become the environmental entrepreneurs establishing the new business enterprises. Canada's move to a sustainable society could play the same unifying role that building the transcontinental railroad did in the nineteenth century and establishing the modern welfare and health-care state did in the twentieth.

The move to a new sustainable society and to environmentally sound economic behaviour is a challenge we cannot escape. Maurice Strong holds that "if our diagnosis is right, it represents a fundamental transition in human affairs which is already well underway and will be seen in the perspective of history as the main source of the forces which are shaping our future in the 21st century and beyond. It is, of course, inexorably linked with the unprecedented political, economic and technological changes that are transforming our world into a single, interdependent planetary society."[50]

4

Our Competitors
Try Harder

IN THE UNITED STATES, proposals from competitiveness councils proliferate as the U.S. government moves closer and closer to
an industrial strategy. In the European Community, the new
treaty preparing for economic, monetary, and political union makes
clear that improved competitiveness through science and technology
is one of the fundamental goals of the new Europe. In Japan, future
"visions" from the Ministry of International Trade and Industry
state that the nation's goal is to become a science superpower in the
twenty-first century. Likewise, emerging industrial competitors such
as South Korea, Taiwan, and Singapore are pursuing science and
innovation strategies to move up the value-added ladder of economic progress. Since ideas and innovation are the foundation of future
economic growth, Canada cannot afford to fall behind its competitors in this area; but it is in danger of doing just that.

In this contest for future prosperity, the real race is to establish
the policies and institutions that can develop the big ideas for future
technologies and to find the most effective instruments and incentives to convert these big ideas into a wide range of new products,
services, and processes. As the nations of the world move towards
this ideas-driven economy, they are engaged in an intensely competitive race to gain advantage in the next generation of technologies:
information systems, high-speed computers, powerful semiconductors, new materials, biotechnology, and new forms of energy. These
technologies will transform almost everything we produce and use,

while new technologies that we have yet to imagine will create possibilities that we have yet to dream of. Although this contest for the economy of the future will be waged mainly by corporations and their employees, governments will make a difference through their own policies and through the partnerships they develop with industry and research universities.

With the collapse of the Soviet Union and the adoption of market reforms in China, Latin America, and elsewhere, it is beyond dispute that we live in a world of markets. But successful countries recognize that markets alone cannot deliver winning economies. For most areas of fundamental research, only governments can afford to pay the cost — an investment that is clearly justified because of the widespread benefits that accrue to society at large. Increasingly, precompetitive research and development and the production of new technologies is proving too risky for many companies as well. So here, too, there is a role for government to play. Markets alone, cannot "assess or anticipate many of the future social costs and benefits of technical change," say analysts Christopher Freeman and Geoffrey Oldham. Public policies do influence technological development. For example, "technologies which improve the quality of life, which protect the environment and which are energy- or material-saving may well become the cutting edge of world technological development. But this will not happen automatically. It will require active regulatory policies for the environment and new policies for R & D."[1]

Although we live in an era of globalization, what individual countries do or don't do still matters. Nation states remain the places where key decisions are made and key policies set. Each country's history and culture, as well as its knowledge base, shapes its competitiveness. Swedish and Finnish forest and mining companies developed close ties with machinery companies and customers that built world-competitive machinery and other supplies, as well as developing high-value products; Canadian forest and mining companies did not do so, because Canadians had a different attitude to innovation. "The concept of a 'national system of innovation' is much wider than a network of R & D and other scientific and technical institutions," Freeman and Oldham contend. "It also involves the production system and a continuous process of learning by doing. For a whole variety of cultural, linguistic, historical, economic, geographical and institutional reasons, a great deal of this learning by doing and by using is conditioned by national and local circumstances."

Pari Patel and Keith Pavitt, world experts on science and technology, argue that there are two kinds of national systems of innovation: myopic and dynamic. Britain and Canada are examples of myopic systems; Japan, Germany, Sweden, France, Switzerland — and, increasingly, the United States — are examples of dynamic systems. "Myopic systems treat investments in technological activities just like any conventional investment; they are undertaken in response to a well-defined market demand and include a strong discount for risk and time," explain Patel and Pavitt. "Dynamic systems, on the other hand, recognize that technological activities are not the same as any other investment. In addition to tangible outcomes in the form of products and profit, they also entail important but intangible by-products in the form of cumulative and irreversible processes of technological, organizational and market learning that enable them to undertake subsequent investments."[2] These different national systems may help explain why Canada ranked seventeenth out of 23 countries in science and technology in the 1991 *World Competitiveness Report*, well behind Japan, the United States, Switzerland, Germany, Finland, and Sweden, the high-ranking countries.

To achieve success, industrial policy must combine cooperation and competition, argues economist Michael Best in his important book, *The New Competition*.[3] Cooperation is essential to build up the long-term infrastructure of the sector, and competition is necessary to ensure that individual businesses remain innovative and respond to new challenges. While English-speaking countries such as the United States, Britain, and Canada often associate industrial policy with bailouts for dying companies, Japan and other countries use it as a productive way of enhancing competitiveness.

In Japan, with its families of businesses, or *keiretsu*, and in Italy, with its regional agglomerations or clusters of small and medium-sized businesses, industrial policy has been based on three critical principles, according to Best. First, it shapes and uses the market. Second, it promotes the production, not the distribution, of wealth by encouraging the "new competition" of entrepreneurial firms, by promoting consultative relations between companies and their suppliers, and by encouraging cooperation among firms to facilitate new technologies. Third, it is strategically focused to increase economic growth by moving into new sectors ahead of the competition, and to increase value-added through superior organization and knowledge-intensive processes.

No country has demonstrated a more successful industrial strategy than Japan. Devastated by World War II, Japan has clearly caught up with the United States and with other leaders in technology, and is now moving ahead in many areas. Its economy is already 60 per cent that of the United States and, says Kenneth Courtis, the Canadian-born strategist and senior economist for the Deutsche Bank Group in Asia, "on the basis of its long-term potential the Japanese economy could well be 85 to 90 per cent the size of that of the United States within a decade." Yet Japan has only half the population of the U.S. In 1991, for the fourth consecutive year, Japan invested more in new plant and equipment than the United States did. Its actual spending on civilian R & D in 1990 was US$110 billion, which was not only more than that of the United States but also more than that of all the member states of the European Community. Over the 1990s, Courtis predicts, "Japan will move to play increasingly the role of new product laboratory for the world economy."[4]

This Japanese success, as U.S. analyst Lawrence Krause says, has required "a strong state and a strong sense of national identity.... The Japanese model depends on an activist government, not laissez faire."[5] Regulation, informal direction through consensus-building "visions" of the future, the strategic use of government procurement, the provision of low-cost capital through public-sector financial institutions, and strong public support for research and development through public-private research consortia to raise Japan's capacities in key technologies have all played major roles.

The goal of Japanese industrial strategy has been to help its people and industries to absorb, adapt, and advance technology and to create new technology. This is easier to do in Japan than in Canada. Lifelong job security in the major Japanese firms makes workers readier to accept change as well as giving them a long-term interest in the health of their employer; business and government cooperate closely and reach consensus on strategy through "vision" documents; major companies and suppliers have long-term relationships that build confidence; and because of the *keiretsu,* the interlocking families of corporations, big business can concentrate on long-term strategies rather than on quarterly earnings.

Japanese government programs have emphasized science and engineering in education, have provided the finance to create industries that can master the new technologies, have helped companies access the best technologies from the rest of the world through licensing and other means, have blocked foreign takeovers, and have used government procurement in telecommunications, transportation, and other sectors to encourage new technology in industry. Not least, the government has supported major programs in research and development, first of all to catch up with other countries and then to try to get ahead. Meanwhile, its aims have changed. Today, Japan's priority is to become a science superpower and a world leader in the information economy.

Underlying its approach has been a distinctly Japanese view of the market economy. "Although capitalism is considered to be the best economic system yet devised, its imperfections are clearly understood," says Daniel Okimoto, an expert on Japanese industrial policy. He says that officials at the Ministry of International Trade and Industry (MITI) "realize that the market mechanism cannot be expected to generate economic outcomes that are always in the nation's best interests. To further the collective good, unfettered market forces need to be harnessed and guided by the visible hand of the state."[6]

The centrepoint in Japanese industrial strategy is the fabled MITI, a government department that is sometimes, if exaggeratedly, credited with single-handedly achieving the Japanese miracle. MITI is advised by an Industrial Technology Council of private-sector experts, and today it operates its industrial strategy through the Agency of Industrial Science and Technology, the New Energy Development Organization, and (with the Ministry of Posts and Telecommunications) the Japan Key Technology Centre. Other agencies also are important. Nippon Telephone and Telegraph (NTT), the giant Japanese telephone company that was 100 per cent government-owned until it embarked on a program of privatization in the 1980s, continues to play a major role by using its huge research and development budget and its procurement market to facilitate the growth of Japan's computer and telecommunications suppliers. The Ministry of Education, Science and Culture, which has its own Science Council, also plays a key role in science education and basic research.

Overseeing the entire enterprise is the Prime Minister's Office itself. The Prime Minister's Council for Science and Technology, which is composed of leading business and scientific figures and is based in the Prime Minister's Office, sets the overall direction for the country. Reporting to the Prime Minister's Office as well is the Science and Technology Agency, which works with the Science Council of Japan and directs the country's many national research institutes and public research corporations. The government-owned Japan Development Bank provides low-cost financing to commercialize important industrial technologies and to construct research facilities and demonstration plants or assembly lines.

There are no detailed "blueprints" spelling out Japan's industrial future. Instead, Japan develops "visions" for the future through MITI and other agencies. These "visions" set the directions in which the economy should grow and pinpoint which industries should be stressed; thus, they provide a frame of reference for individual business decisions throughout the economy, says Richard Nelson, an international expert on technology policies. To follow the directions set out in its "visions," MITI employs whatever policies are necessary to get R & D support for the high-technology industries it is promoting. "Perhaps more important than any particular instrument," says Nelson, "has been the general agreement among the Japanese, including Japanese businessmen, that government leadership is not only legitimate but desirable and even necessary if Japan is to prosper, although there is occasional strong resistance."[7]

MITI's intervention, according to Okimoto, is forceful but selective, and is based on extensive prior consultation with the private sector. "Areas in which MITI has actively intervened include: (1) consensus building and the articulation of a long-term 'vision' for those industries under its jurisdiction; (2) the setting of sectoral policies; (3) the allocation of subsidies and facilitation of financial flows to priority sectors; (4) adjustments of industrial structure; (5) infant industry protection; (6) investment guidance in certain industries and under certain conditions; (7) regulation of excessive competition; (8) downside risk reduction and cost diffusion; and (9) export promotion and mediation of trade disputes."[8]

To accelerate the development of technology, MITI has made significant use of precompetitive research associations or consortia among major Japanese companies, funding about 50 per cent of the costs. Between 1971 and 1983, some 59 of these consortia were formed, including 25 in the 1981–83 period alone. Today, these arrangements remain extremely important as MITI pushes industry to the next technological frontier in such areas as semiconductors, telecommunications, software, information systems, and next-generation computers, as well as new forms of energy, new materials, and biotechnology. Early examples of research consortia include the Computer Basic Technology Research Association, the Super High-Performance Computer Project, the New Series Project, and the Very Large Scale Integrated Circuit Project (VLSI). In less than four years, the VLSI project, with a budget of US$320 million (of which 42 per cent was in interest-free loans from MITI), generated hundreds of patents and positioned Fujitsu, Hitachi, Mitsubishi, NEC, and Toshiba of Japan to capture a growing share of the world market for semiconductors and to close the technology gap with the United States.[9]

During the 1980s, Japan embarked on three major new research consortia to advance the competitiveness of its computer industry: the Optoelectronics Applied Systems Project; the Scientific Computer Project, which is seeking to develop the components for a new supercomputer system; and the Fifth Generation Computer Project, which, with 50 billion yen ($454 million) of government funding from 1981 to 1992, advanced Japanese skills in parallel processing, artificial intelligence, and advanced software. Now Japan has embarked on the sixth-generation computer project, the New Information Processing Technology project. The goal is to make computers into thinking machines that have the capacity to learn, just as the human brain does.

Japan makes effective use of corporate associations to enter new areas of technology on favourable terms. One goal is to gain a greater presence in the world aviation industry. With MITI support, the Japan Aircraft Development Corporation (JADC) has been established, consisting of airframe and component manufacturers who identify aerospace projects that will help develop Japan's aerospace industry. In 1991, for example, the corporation signed a contract with Boeing for a 21 per cent share of the new 777 passenger aircraft program; the Japanese companies will participate in the detailed design and development work, as well as in production. MITI is also funding feasibility and early design work by JADC for a 75-to-100-passenger regional jet. Meanwhile, another Japanese research company, Japan Aero Engines Corporation, is working with other countries to develop Japan's capacity in aircraft engines.[10]

Now that Japan has caught up in many areas with the United States and Europe, it is moving more strongly into basic research, an area in which it has been weak. One example is the Japan Key Technology Centre, which provides up to 70 per cent of the capital for joint research firms set up by Japanese corporations; the financing is done through low-interest loans, with repayment based on commercial success, and by funding basic infrastructure. In 1989, when seven major projects in electronics, large-scale communications networks, and information systems were approved, the centre provided 9000 million yen ($82 million) — about two-thirds of the total budget of 13,307.7 million yen ($121 million) for the seven projects.[11]

Japan's ambition to become a science superpower is also supported by MITI's Research Program on Basic Technologies for Future Industries. This program was established in 1981, and its projects run to the year 2000. As MITI explains, its purpose is "to set forth a basic framework for the formulation and implementation of national industrial policy." Looking to the future, Japan had to find ways to maintain its economic vitality, and "for Japan, which is poor in natural resources, the most effective means of solving these problems is to pursue technological development with a view to establishing itself as a country founded on the basis of technology."[12]

Projects funded under the program must accelerate the development of basic technologies that could influence a wide range of industries and require 10 years or more of research and investment risk. Projects are screened by the Next-Generation Technology Development Committee of MITI's Industrial Technology Council and by the Planning Office for Basic Technologies for Future

Industries in the Agency of Industrial Science and Technologies. By 1991 some 59 corporations, 12 national research institutes, and 46 universities had linked up in 361 projects, and 66.8 billion yen ($607 million) had been allocated under the program's budget, of which 52 per cent was for new materials, 19 per cent for electronics, and 16 per cent for biotechnology.

MITI runs yet another long-term R & D program, the National Research and Development Program, known as the Large-Scale Project. It was started in 1966, and since then 29 projects have been launched, eight of which were still underway in May 1991. On average, a new project is launched every year, and each lasts five to ten years. Projects must pioneer large-scale industrial technology that is "essential and urgent for the national economy," that requires considerable funds, has long lead times and high risks, and is in areas where private-sector R & D is too risky.[13] About 390 billion yen ($3.5 billion) has been funded since 1966 for projects on advanced robotics, high-speed computing, laser technology, jet engines for aircraft, electric car technologies, advanced materials processing and machining systems, and advanced chemical processing technologies, among others. The latest project is for micromachine technologies.

The driving force behind all these measures is the careful exercise in information gathering, analysis, and consensus building that goes into Japan's "visions" for the future. The MITI vision for the 1990s says that the challenges "include creating a vital industrial structure that can respond flexibly to changes in the values and needs of the people" and "developing new industries, rationalizing or converting low-productivity industries and fostering small and medium size companies — the source of energy which drives the Japanese economy." . . . "Science and technology and information will be keys to Japan's success. Work must be done now to promote science and technology and to expand Japan's information capabilities."[14]

Having caught up with other nations, Japan "must now begin cultivating its own future," says the MITI vision. Biotechnology, new materials, solar energy, and the next generation of information technologies are key areas. This will involve going beyond the traditional business boundaries and will require greater investment in Japan's basic research and knowledge base, in infrastructure, and in the use of foreign investment to help make the Asia-Pacific region a centre for global growth.

While there will be a continuing shift to services, centring on the increasing role of information and other services for manufacturing, the interdependence of services and manufacturing is deepening, the MITI report says.[15] Manufacturing is of prime importance "in supporting the technological innovation that is essential for driving Japan's progress."

The report states that the Japanese government itself has to play a much bigger role in science and technology, increasing its support from about 0.6 per cent of GDP to 1 per cent, a near doubling; for Japan's ability to achieve its science goals depends on how well it overcomes its lag in basic research and graduates a sufficient number of high-quality research scientists. The MITI vision calls for the creation of new research institutions to facilitate cooperation in basic research between industry, government, and the universities. Large-scale basic research facilities also need the support of government because they are too expensive for companies alone. The report stresses that government spending on research and investment in intellectual property should be seen as investment in that it creates national assets that deliver benefits over long periods. Japan seems assured of success in its goal to become a science superpower and an ideas-driven economy.

Europe 1992, the ambitious plan to create a single internal market of the 12 nations of the European Community by the end of 1992, shows that the Europeans, too, are determined to create a new economy for the twenty-first century. A major factor underlying this agreement was the conviction by Europe's leading industrialists that radical changes were necessary to overcome economic stagnation and the Europessimism that went with it, and to make European business more innovative.

This objective is spelled out in the Single European Act of 1987, which states: "The Community's aim shall be to strengthen the scientific and technological base of European industry and to encourage it to become more competitive at an international level." This emphasis on developing competitive industry is even stronger in the 1992 Treaty on European Union, signed at Maastricht in the

Netherlands. This treaty, which is, in effect, the European constitution for economic, monetary, and political union, includes among its goals "the strengthening of the competitiveness of Community industry" as well as "the encouragement of research and technological development."

The idea of bringing European industry together in a single market to create a stronger economic base had some successful precedents: the satellite-launching capacity of the Ariane rocket program of the European Space Agency, and the Airbus consortium's emergence as number two in the world's civil aviation industry. The Europeans wanted to extend these examples of technological success into intensely competitive areas such as information technologies and telecommunications, in which they feared they were heavily overshadowed by American and Japanese corporations.

The European Space Agency, created in 1975 and funded by European governments, successfully spun off a company, Arianespace, with government and private-sector owners. It is now the world's leading player in civilian satellite launching (Canada's Telesat is among its customers) and is involved in three ambitious but costly space projects: the Columbus manned space station, the Ariane-5 rocket, and the Hermes space shuttle. Similarly, the Airbus Industrie partnership of European aircraft companies has become a technologically advanced global competitor — albeit with generous support from governments. Set up in the 1960s to counter the U.S. domination of the industry, Airbus delivered its first A-300 aircraft in 1975, and by 1990 — only 15 years later — it had captured one-third of the world's US$40 billion of jet aircraft sales and was the world's second-largest civil aircraft manufacturer after Boeing. The space and Airbus programs allowed Europe to accumulate significant technology and engineering expertise, to create well-paying jobs in these activities, and to support hundreds of high-tech suppliers in electronics, new materials, manufacturing technologies, and sub-assemblies.

Since the mid-1980s, the European Community itself has embarked on a far-reaching series of collaborative programs to build up the technological capability of European companies and research institutes. Its programs target precompetitive R & D in civilian technologies and provide roughly 50 per cent of the cost of research projects; every project has to include companies or research institutes from at least two different member countries. The Community carries out its science and technology programs through research and technology framework agreements spanning up to five years. These lay down the key scientific objectives, define priorities, and fix the funding level. The framework agreement is then implemented through specific programs, such as the Esprit program for information technology.[16]

The Community has now embarked on the third of its framework programs. The first ran from 1984 to 1987 with 3.7 billion ecu ($5.7 billion) in funding, the second from 1987 to 1991 with 5.4 billion ecu ($8.3 billion) in funding, and the third, adopted in April 1990, runs from 1990 to 1994 with 5.7 billion ecu ($8.7 billion) in funding. In Canadian dollars this amounts to a total of $22.7 billion. In a number of the programs in this overall budget, Community spending represents just half the total amount spent, with industry putting up the other half.

The Community's funding for R & D — about 2.6 billion ecu ($4 billion) in 1992 — is less than 5 per cent of total publicly funded R & D in the Community, but its programs are strategically significant because they identify the priorities for Europe and facilitate cooperation between companies and research institutes to build European strengths. The framework program for 1990–94, for example, is targeting 39 per cent of its spending for information and communications technologies, 16 per cent for industrial technologies and new materials, 14 per cent for energy, 13 per cent for life sciences and technology, including biotechnology, 9 per cent for environmental technologies, and 9 per cent for human capital and mobility.[17]

The Community works through a busy alphabet of programs to implement its science and technology strategy. The best known is Esprit, modelled on Japan's VLSI project of the 1970s that launched Japan as a major producer of semiconductors. Esprit was initiated in 1984, and its goal was to stimulate Europe's weak information technologies industries by facilitating R & D in microelectronics, information processing systems, and application technologies in the face of strong competition from the United States and Japan. Esprit II, which runs from 1988 to 1993, has 1.6 billion ecu ($2.5 billion) in Community funding, double that of Esprit I, and participants are expected to put up the other 1.6 billion ecu. This has meant that, with matching industry funds, there has been $7.4 billion in pre-competitive R & D spending for information technologies at the Community level in 1984–93.

The Race program (R & D in Advanced Communications Technologies for Europe) is working in tandem with Esprit to bring Europe into the Information Age. With 460 million ecu ($705 million) in funding in 1988–92, it is helping European telecommunications companies develop the equipment, standards, and technology necessary for Europe's proposed Integrated Broadband Communications System, the next generation of telecommunications infrastructure.

Another important Community program is Brite/Euram, which funds precompetitive R & D in manufacturing technologies and new materials. Its 1990–94 funding is set at 670 million ecu (about $1 billion); it will generate an equal amount of participant spending for about $2 billion in precompetitive R & D on the factory of the future, automation systems, and new materials. There are many other programs, dealing with everything from food processing and biotechnology to database networks, environmental technologies, aquaculture, biomedicine, health technologies, and renewable energies such as solar and fuel cells.

One of the major benefits of the Community programs, according to analyst Margaret Sharp, is that European companies have been forced to rethink their strategies and undertake sweeping reorganizations, with a significant increase in joint ventures, strategic alliances, and mergers and acquisitions. The result has been the emergence of stronger European companies that are global players. Sharp points to Alcatel, which in 1975 was a modest French telecommunications company and is now the second-largest telecommunications company in the world; Thomson, a French consumer electronics company, which is now the world's largest manufacturer of television sets; and Siemens, which is now one of the world's top technology companies.[18]

As European industry moves from precompetitive R & D to commercialization, one of Europe's other ambitious initiatives kicks in support. This is Eureka, a program first conceived by French President François Mitterrand in 1983 after U.S. President Ronald

Reagan unveiled his plans for "Star Wars," or the Strategic Defense Initiative (SDI). Mitterrand and his advisers recognized that SDI could bring huge research and development opportunities for American companies in computer systems, semiconductors, software, lasers, new materials, satellite systems, and aerospace, and could draw away European scientific talent because of the billions of dollars that would be spent on R & D, even if Star Wars itself did not work.

The Europeans unveiled the Eureka program in 1985. It linked together the 12 member states of the European Community and the five members of the European Free Trade Area. Since then, Turkey and Iceland have joined. A key meeting of Eureka ministers, held in Hanover later in 1985, set out a seven-page statement of principles. "The objective of Eureka," the statement said, "is to raise, through closer cooperation among enterprises and research institutes in the field of advanced technologies, the productivity and competitiveness of Europe's industries and national economies on the world market" so that "Eureka will enable Europe to master and exploit the technologies that are important for its future, and to build up its capability in crucial areas." This will be achieved, it said, "by encouraging and facilitating increased industrial, technological and scientific cooperation on projects directed at developing products, processes and services having a worldwide market potential and based on advanced technologies."

Eureka has no budget of its own; its small secretariat works as a technology broker with governments, companies, and research institutions to encourage collaborative projects. The funds come from the participants themselves and their own governments and, in some instances, from the science and technology programs of the European Community. The program appears to have been a boon to many European businesses and research groups, both large and small. In its first five years, Eureka fostered more than 500 projects, bringing together more than 3000 companies and research institutes, with a total investment of more than 8 billion ecu ($12.3 billion). Another 200 projects were to be approved by the end of 1991. The projects covered many different industrial sectors, including information technologies, computers, lasers, new materials, transportation, energy, biotechnology, robotics and automation, environmental technologies, and communications.

Canadian companies had the opportunity to participate in Eureka projects, and the federal government set aside $20 million under the short-lived Technology Opportunities in Europe Program to help fund participation. The program was launched in September 1986, but under its sunset clause, no applications were accepted after 31 March 1989. Spending of $16.1 million for 58 projects was authorized, but it is not yet known how much was actually spent.

Eureka is providing the financial means to support some of Europe's strategic high-technology targets. One example is the bid to create a European standard for high-definition television (HDTV). Although the future of HDTV is uncertain, the Europeans were deter-

---

TABLE 19

Research and Development

	US$ million (PPP)	% of GDP	No. of Researchers*
Belgium	2059.5 (1988)	1.61	8.9
Denmark	1147.8 (89)	1.53	8.5
France	18,987.7 (89)	2.32	11.0
West Germany	26,743.5 (89)	2.88	11.9
Greece	339.1 (89)	0.47	2.4
Ireland	248.5 (88)	0.87	6.6
Italy	10,335.5 (89)	1.29	5.8
Netherlands	4263.0 (88)	2.26	9.9
Portugal	328.3 (88)	0.50	2.4
Spain	2859.9 (89)	0.72	3.7
Britain	17,002.0 (88)	2.20	10.0
Luxembourg	—	—	—
EEC total	78,064.7		
United States	157,196.0(91)	2.75	n.a.
Japan	57,984.0(89)	3.04	13.8
Canada	7192.0(90)	1.35	8.1
Sweden	3647.1	2.76 (89)	11.1
Switzerland	3403.1	2.86 (89)	14.2

*Per 1,000 labour force

SOURCE: *OECD Main Science and Technology Indicators 1991:1* (Paris: OECD, 1991).

mined not to let the Japanese dominate what could be the next generation in consumer electronics. The Eureka ministers have approved funding for the second phase of HDTV development. Costing nearly US$600 million, it is led by Philips of Holland and includes Bosch of Germany, Thomson of France, and Oy Nokia of Finland. Experimental systems were produced for test broadcasting at the 1992 winter Olympics in France and at the world's fair in Spain, and the Europeans hope to be marketing HDTV sets, VCRs, and laser disc players by the mid-1990s.

Eureka is also behind Europe's ambitious eight-year plan to establish a stronger position in the semiconductor industry. Known as Jessi (the Joint European Submicron Silicon Initiative), the project was launched in 1989 by 14 European companies and research institutes, with a total funding of 3.8 billion ecu ($5.8 billion), which was provided 50:50 by government and industry. Today, there are more than 50 Jessi projects in the four key areas: design and production of semiconductors; machines and materials needed for chip production; applications of chips; and basic research and long-term development of semiconductors. More than 150 companies and research organizations are involved in the project. But major European companies such as Siemens are also having to link up with overseas companies such as IBM to overcome their technology gap.

Alongside Europe's determination to develop competitive, technology-based industry, there is a wide-ranging debate on how far governments should intervene. A European Community statement on industrial policy adopted in November 1990 stated that, rather than adopting defensive policies to protect weak and declining industries, "the role of public authorities" should be to act as "a catalyst and pathbreaker for innovation"; the Community and its member states should adopt measures "designed to strengthen the industrial and technological base."[19]

While the Community has rejected the French call for a European version of MITI, it is nonetheless committed to promoting science and technology. In its industrial policy statement, it stressed that global competition "requires staying ahead of technological competition, producing large productivity gains, sufficiently investing in human capital and especially accepting a high pace of structural change. There is no alternative to such an industrial strategy for the

European Community to preserve and improve on a high standard of living."

The key role of industrial strategy is to accelerate the process of innovation and change, the statement stressed. This means developing technological capacity. "The impact of technology is not limited to a few high technology sectors but affects the whole economy, both in terms of products and production methods. Thus, the mastery of generic technologies such as flexible manufacturing systems and information technologies, new materials and biotechnology possess great importance for the competitiveness of European firms."[20]

It is in electronics that the Europeans feel they must push the hardest. They are driven by the fear of losing out to Japan and the United States. Konrad Seitz, chief of the German foreign ministry's policy-planning staff and author of *The Japanese-American Challenge: Germany's High-Tech Industries Fight for Survival,* warns that Europe could experience the same fate as Britain, losing out on the next industrial revolution and facing a long period of decline, with the result that it becomes "a technological colony of Japan's and America's global companies."[21]

Seitz argues that the mainstream economics belief that government should stay out of the market is a recipe for economic decline. Europe "must set ambitious goals and bring together, as Japan's MITI does, industry consortia for developing new technologies," he says. "It must apply an innovative procurement policy to build the infrastructure of the 21st century: a European-wide optical fibre network that carries HDTV-pictures and high-speed data transmissions between supercomputers; an intelligent vehicles-and-highway systems; and magnetic-levitation trains. Megaprojects will drive Europe's high-tech industries into global leadership."[22]

The concern to develop a strong European electronics and information technology industry was spelled out in a major 1991 Community report, which predicted that electronics, which was then just over 5 per cent of GDP, could grow to 10 per cent by the year 2000. The report warned that because of the pervasive role of electronics in so many other industries, the electronics and information technology industries "also form an infrastructure which plays a major part in economic competitiveness, employment and social development."[23] Trans-European networks should therefore be strengthened; for example, computerized telecommunications links between governments and government agencies in the Community, and infrastructure in distance learning, transport, and other areas. There should also be a second generation of Community research and technology development, whose projects could include software, computer-integrated manufacturing, microelectronics, high-performance computing, and telecommunications.

The European Commission is now devising a new five-year framework for the period to 1997, which will concentrate R & D spending on fewer projects and ones that industry can quickly exploit. Commission president Jacques Delors stresses that improving the competitiveness of European industry must be a priority for the next five years: "With industry facing keener competition and needing to digest scientific and technological progress, the Community as such must support the efforts of its people, its workers and the Member States to relieve the tensions and overcome the disruption caused by these changes." Delors has asked the Community to increase spending on competitiveness so that spending levels in 1997 will be 3.5 billion ecu ($5.4 billion) higher than in 1992. He points out that in the new treaty for European union, industrial competitiveness is, for the first time, set out as a key goal of the Community. This means that science and technology programs must be "better adapted to the needs of industry" and that intervention must be concentrated "on a few key, multisectoral technologies" targeted on major industrial priorities.[24] The commission subsequently agreed to redirect its research and technological development strategy for 1993–97, putting more emphasis on "priority technology projects more directly linked to key generic technologies on which the competitiveness of European industry depends."[25] Projects, to be submitted by industry, could include microelectronics, advanced technologies for the auto industry, high-performance computing, flat screens, environment-friendly industrial technologies, and advanced molecular biology, the commission said.

In their bid to gain new industries based on ideas, the Europeans are planning to extend the "Europe of science and technology" to Eastern Europe, where countries such as Czechoslovakia and Hungary were once centres of industrial technology, and to the new

Russian republic, with its high level of science literacy and its vast military-industrial complex that can now be redirected to peaceful technologies.

While Canada faces intensified competition from a surging Japan and a resurgent Europe, it also faces the prospect of competing with a United States that is adopting a much more targeted policy to strengthen its industry and increase its ability to come up with new ideas for the economy of the twenty-first century — in particular, by accelerating large-scale and commercially relevant research and development. As the United States headed into the 1992 election year, the Bush administration kicked off its National Technology Initiative and boosted funding proposals for precompetitive R & D. Meanwhile, the leading Democratic contenders outlined their own strategies to make America competitive again.

Reflecting this more assertive mood, the bipartisan Competitiveness Policy Council (created by the U.S. Congress in a 1990 amendment to the 1988 Omnibus Trade and Competitiveness Act) said in its first report, "The time has come for the United States to establish a serious 'competitiveness strategy' through both sector-specific and generic policies." Referring to similar efforts in the past, the report said that "the results have sometimes been spectacularly successful: the world's most competitive farms and commercial aircraft, a robust computer industry and many more."[26]

While there has always been ideological uneasiness in the United States over industrial policy, there is no doubt that the strong U.S. position in computers, semiconductors, aerospace, biotechnology, and pharmaceuticals is due in large part to government support for research and development and to government procurement, much of it military. For example, IBM's first computers were built under contract to the U.S. government, and "large-scale federal support for IBM research and development continued well after the first business-oriented models began to roll out of the doors in the mid-1950s," according to one history of the computer industry.[27] Two large-scale government programs provided more than half of IBM computer revenues in the 1950s when the company was establishing its dominant position in the industry. From the mid-1950s to the mid-1970s, the federal government funded more than half of all R &

D in the United States, and even in the early 1990s it was funding nearly half.

In his study of the U.S. computer industry, Kenneth Flamm points out that "between 1945 and 1955 the U.S. government dominated computer development. All major computer technology projects in the United States were supported by government and military users." It was only after this that the commercial computer and semiconductor industries developed. But even then the U.S. government continued to play a key role, and it still does. The U.S. semiconductor industry was the creation of the U.S. military, which funded basic research at key U.S. universities, helped finance the start-up of semiconductor companies, and created a market with huge contracts to these companies. Flamm's study, which was published in 1987, pointed out that "a new generation of advanced computer products focussed on so-called 'artificial intelligence' concepts based on government-funded research and development of the 1970s and early 1980s has just come to market. And a new round of heavy investment by the military in advanced computer technology promises future returns."[28]

Despite the slowdown in military spending, the U.S. Department of Defense is expected to continue to play a key role in technology policy; this includes providing support for the top research universities in the United States and the use of procurement to accelerate the development of new technologies and even new industries. In fiscal 1992, the Pentagon had a US$40 billion R & D budget, just over half the government's total R & D budget of US$74.6 billion; and in its fiscal 1993 budget proposals, the Bush administration sought US$40.5 billion for defence R & D, out of a total R & D budget of US$76.6 billion, despite overall plans to scale back defence spending.

The Pentagon is now putting greater emphasis on what it calls "dual-use" technologies — those that have both military and civilian application. Key funding for U.S. R & D continues to be sourced by the Air Force Office of Scientific Research, the Army Research Center, the Office of Naval Research, the Office of Naval Technology, and the Defense Advanced Research Projects Agency (Darpa).[29] U.S. military procurement also remains important — as AT & T could testify after it was awarded a contract worth nearly US$5 billion to supply the Pentagon with 20,000 minicomputers.

The Department of Energy, with a proposed us$6.6 billion R & D budget for 1993, is responsible for nuclear weapons programs, but it is shifting to a key role in super-computing and new materials as well as in energy research. It also manages a huge network of government research laboratories, which employ many of the most talented scientists and mathematicians in the United States. These are being redirected to deal with civilian problems that have commercial potential. Likewise, the National Aeronautics and Space Administration, with a proposed 1993 R & D budget of us$8.7 billion, is a major funding source for new technology. While military spending no longer spins off the same commercial benefits as it did 25 to 30 years ago, there is no question that benefits still exist. In Massachusetts, much of the spending awarded by the Pentagon for large-scale research and testing goes to research universities and non-profit research institutes, where it operates in an environment that is constantly seeking spinoffs, according to research at the Federal Reserve Bank of Boston.[30]

One of the most active agencies in promoting U.S. high technology is the Defense Advanced Research Projects Agency (Darpa). A small operation in the Department of Defense, it scans the United States for challenging research projects and funds U.S. companies and universities to carry out high-risk R & D that is at the leading edge of new technology. Set up in 1958, after the Soviet Union surprised the world with its Sputnik satellite, the agency operates with a budget of about us$1.5 billion a year. Darpa is credited with pioneering work in time-sharing or computer data networks, computers and advanced computer architecture, computer graphics, artificial intelligence, advanced microelectronics, lasers, composite materials, and high-temperature metals (all of which have widespread commercial applications), as well as cruise missiles and Stealth aircraft.

However, it is now in civilian R & D that U.S. government spending is on the rise — and in areas that specifically focus on the needs of industry. While welcoming this trend, the Council on Competitiveness, a private-sector group of leading U.S. industrial, labour, and academic figures, points out that the United States still has a long way to go. The government's civilian R & D spending in the Bush 1993 budget proposals are equivalent to just 0.5 per cent of

GDP, compared with 0.6 per cent at the beginning of the 1980s and a high of more than 1 per cent in the mid-1960s.

Nonetheless, the budget proposes an 8 per cent increase in federal spending on basic research to US$14 billion. The Council on Competitiveness notes that this will be extremely important in training talented researchers, and it points out that basic research is "especially valuable" in areas where it can quickly be translated into useful products, such as pharmaceuticals, chemicals, and software. At the same time, the budget proposes that spending on civilian applied research be increased 6 per cent to US$17 billion to support applications of science and technology in industry. As the council states, "The budget affirms that support of generic or enabling technologies at the pre-competitive stage of R & D is an appropriate federal role"[31]

In some sectors, the United States is moving much more aggressively. For example, the National Science Foundation, which provides 25 per cent of all federal support for university research and plays a vital role in promoting better science and math education in the schools, is to have its after-inflation budget doubled between 1987 and 1994. For 1993, the Bush administration sought an 18 per cent increase in funding to US$3 billion. It also approved the establishment of a Critical Technologies Institute in the science foundation, which will track key technologies and assess U.S. performance and that of its industrial competitors.

Since 1987, the National Science Foundation has been helping set up science and technology centres at major universities to pursue long-term projects that link universities and industry. In fiscal 1992 it planned to spend US$162 million in support of these centres. A typical example is the Science and Technology Center for Computer Graphics and Scientific Visualization, which in 1991 was awarded nearly US$15 million by the National Science Foundation and Darpa to develop interactive computer graphic tools for the design of parts for aircraft, automobiles, and computer chips, and to "work with U.S. companies to enhance the country's lead in computer graphics."[32] Other centres are promoting mathematics and computing science, new materials, microelectronics, high-temperature superconductivity, parallel computing, and microbes research.

The National Science Foundation launched a similar program in the mid-1980s to support engineering research centres at major U.S.

universities. "The increasing severity of economic rivalry in the world makes it imperative that we make every effort to develop basic knowledge in engineering fields," said Erich Bloc, then director of the National Science Foundation.[33] The engineering research centres receive support from state governments and industry as well as from NSF. So far they have been established for hazardous substance control, optoelectronic computing systems, advanced combustion, engineering design, robotics systems, composites manufacturing science and engineering, systems research, biotechnology process engineering, and intelligent manufacturing systems.

There is growing pressure in the United States to move beyond basic research to generic or precompetitive research that will help industry develop new products and production processes. In a major report in 1991, the Council on Competitiveness warned that "in today's highly competitive world markets, government support for basic science and military technology programs is no longer sufficient to ensure a strong U.S. technology base"; it called on the government to provide strong support for "the generic enabling technologies that will drive national economic performance in the decade ahead" and to make such research "a national R & D priority."[34] The council analysed the critical technologies for U.S. competitiveness, and it found that the areas where the United States was "strong" or "competitive" were those that were strongly supported by government investment in basic research, defence procurement, or environmental regulations, and by high levels of private-sector R & D.

The United States is, in fact, moving in this direction. One example is Sematech, the industry consortium that was set up in 1987 to regain lost ground in semiconductor manufacturing technologies. Through Darpa, the government committed US$500 million over a five-year period, with matching funds from industry. The Sematech project has already brought U.S. gains in chip-manufacturing technologies, in which Japan had been moving into an overwhelmingly dominant position. Now the Sematech consortium is seeking from the government another five-year commitment of US$500 million to develop computer-integrated manufacturing software for automated chip plants, as well as other technologies for chip production.

Another indicator of the U.S. move to industrial policy is the Office of Technology Policy, which was created in the U.S.

Department of Commerce by the 1988 Omnibus Trade and Competitiveness Act to develop strategic partnerships among U.S. companies in large-scale emerging technologies and to fund the development and diffusion of new technologies. Its National Institute of Standards and Technology, with a proposed 1993 budget of US$311 million, operates a number of programs that directly benefit industry. One is the Advanced Technology Program, which helps fund government-industry consortia to develop advanced, precompetitive, and generic technologies that have significant commercial promise. In 1991 it funded 11 such consortia. Funding started slowly, reaching just US$36 million in 1991; but the legislation envisages annual funding of between US$100 million and US$250 million a year. The Bush administration proposed US$68 million for 1993. Participants range from large blue-chip companies such as Du Pont and AT & T's Bell Labs to a wide range of high-tech up-and-comers.

Much of the shift in thinking in the Bush administration appears to be due to the top science adviser, Canadian-born Allan Bromley, who heads the Office of Science and Technology Policy in the White House. In 1990 he won approval from the White House to present a statement to Congress on "the Administration's technology policy," the first time the Bush administration had acknowledged that it had such a policy. While emphasizing that market forces are best at allocating technological resources, Bromley acknowledged that "government can nonetheless play an important role in supplementing and complementing those forces." Listing the federal government's R & D responsibilities, he said these included increasing federal investment in support of basic research and participating in research with the private sector in technologies with commercial application. He said that they should take advantage of opportunities for technology transfer and research cooperation, especially with small and medium businesses, and should build on state and regional technology initiatives; many U.S. state governments run major technology programs.[35]

Bromley also said that the United States was speeding up technology transfers. This included the creation of the Precision Manufacturing Technology Program by the Department of Energy to give U.S. companies access to formerly secret manufacturing technology, expertise, and facilities in the defence weapons complex; formation of the Biotechnology Research and Development

Corporation with the Department of Agriculture, two key universities, and six U.S. corporations; and formation of a high-temperature superconducting materials and applications joint venture by Du Pont, Hewlett-Packard, and the Los Alamos National Laboratory.

Bromley's message was followed up by Bush, in a speech to the American Academy for the Advancement of Science, in which he stressed that his proposed 13 per cent increase in R & D spending for fiscal 1992 was "proof of our determination to make the investments needed to ensure this country's continued leadership." Bush added, "We face a crucial challenge in developing the generic technologies that are important to both the public and private sectors. And that's why this budget supports work in high performance computing and communications, in energy research and development, in aeronautics, in biotechnology — the basis for some of the most promising industries of the 21st century."[36]

This message was repeated in the 1993 budget proposals, which included US$1.8 billion for advanced materials and processing, US$4 billion for biotechnology, US$914 million for energy technology R & D, US$803 million for the high-performance computing and communications project, and US$321 million for non-defence advanced manufacturing R & D.

As the major industrial powers press ahead with industrial strategies to compete in the ideas-driven economy, developing countries may not be far behind. It may have been a sign of things to come when in 1990 Trigem Corporation of South Korea became the first company in the world to bring a laptop engineering workstation to market. Following the example of Japan, South Korea is investing heavily in education, science, and technology. In a 1991 speech to his country's scientists and engineers, President Roh Tae Woo said, "Our science and technology must catch up to the levels of the G-7 countries by the year 2000. I am convinced of our capability to accomplish such a task."[37] Roh outlined plans for a major increase in scientific and engineering education, with new science and technology institutes, upgraded equipment and facilities, and sector programs to boost the science and technology capacities of industry, as South Korea approaches possible reunification with North Korea, which would create a country of more than 70 million people. The president promised that R & D spending, which was 2.5 per cent of GDP in 1990, would rise to 3.4 per cent by 1993 and to 5 per cent by the year 2000.

South Korea is not alone. Taiwan, Singapore, Brazil, and Mexico will all be pushing industrial programs to become more competitive. The world technology race is large enough to provide prizes for all, but only those that enter the race can win prizes. While other countries are off and running, Canada still seems uncertain whether it wants to be in the race at all. If it does not join in, its economy will be too weak to create the wealth and opportunity needed for future prosperity.

5

Losing the Canadian Team

UNDER CANADIAN OWNERSHIP and control, the pulp and
paper giant Consolidated-Bathurst became a powerful multinational whose operations spread beyond North America with
major paper companies in Britain and Germany. It also had a working relationship with China, including a joint venture with Chinese
interests in British Columbia, and it was contemplating a major pulp
and paper facility in the huge forests of Siberia. The company ran its
global strategy out of an active head office in Montreal and enjoyed a
reputation as a supporter of universities and the arts in Canada.

In 1989 all this changed. The company was sold to Stone
Containers of Chicago in a takeover that was quickly approved by
Investment Canada. Paul Labbé, then president of Investment
Canada, assured a parliamentary committee that "Consolidated-
Bathurst will remain as a separate company, with a Canadian identi-
ty, with its headquarters in Montreal and with Canadian manage-
ment."[1] Canadians were promised that Consolidated-Bathurst would
be responsible for some world product mandates under Stone
Container's ownership.

But the Montreal head office now exists in name only. The staff
has been reduced from the more than 400 employed before the
takeover to about 150 today. The functions of chief executive officer
and chief financial officer and the key decision-making have been
transferred to Chicago. The Canadian president is now responsible
only for managing the company's Canadian mills and handling

labour and government relations. The European operations are run out of Chicago, and the strategic operations of the renamed company — Stone-Consolidated — are now run out of Chicago as a division of the U.S. parent. "The mill superintendent will not lose his job because somebody still has to run the mill. But the young people who came out of school in the past 15 or 20 years with a bachelor of commerce or MBA in accounting, finance or marketing are being cut out," says Brian Neysmith, president of the Canadian Bond Rating Service. As for world product mandates, Canada gets the low value-added commodity mandates while the high value-added products are in the United States. This should not be surprising, says University of Toronto business professor Joseph D'Cruz. "Most U.S. parents will not assign a world product mandate in a product line that is important to them. Canadian (subsidiaries) end up with mandates that are either trivial or marginal to the corporation."[2]

As with so many Investment Canada approvals that are supposed to meet a test of "net benefit" for Canada, it is hard to see what Canada gained from the sale of Consolidated-Bathurst. But it is easy to see what Canada lost — a major global player in the pulp and paper industry with its decision-making centred in Canada and an ownership group that was much more sensitive to Canadian interests. If Consolidated-Bathurst was an isolated case, it might not matter so much. But from the time Investment Canada opened for business in mid-1985 up to the end of 1991, it approved the foreign takeover of 839 Canadian-controlled corporations with assets of $62.5 billion — and did not reject a single takeover. Another 2678 Canadian-controlled companies with assets of $6.3 billion were also acquired, but these were below the threshold level requiring Investment Canada approval.

While there is no reason to block every foreign takeover, the fact is that every time a promising Canadian company with good technology and marketing is acquired by a multinational, it no longer has the prospect of becoming a future Canadian multinational and joining the ranks of companies such as Bombardier, McCain, and Northern Telecom — Canadian multinationals that will be the vital foundations of a strong economy for the twenty-first century. As the Ontario Premier's Council reported in 1988, Canadian-based multinationals enhance the stability of the economy, provide high value-added jobs, and are more likely to create spinoff companies, as well as creating jobs in business services such as accounting, law, advertising, and management consulting. "Large indigenous firms are therefore well-equipped to sustain the environment required for economic growth. They develop the skills and mentality and provide an industrial base which nurtures new ventures and emerging industries. Through contracts with smaller companies close to home, they also provide the seeds of growth for sophisticated supplier and spin-off industries."[3]

When promising Canadian companies are the target of foreign takeovers, they lose the potential to grow into Canadian-based multinationals, exporting around the world and entering strategic alliances with companies in Japan, Europe, and the United States, or in industrial newcomers such as South Korea, Mexico, and Brazil. Although Connaught BioSciences will not disappear because it is now owned by Institut Mérieux of France, and although Lumonics will continue to develop laser technology under the ownership of Sumitomo Heavy Industries of Japan, neither of these companies (nor the hundreds of others of their size that have been taken over) any longer has the prospect of becoming a Canadian-based multinational. Their future is as divisions of other countries' multinationals, and it will depend on decisions made in the corporate boardrooms of other countries.

Foreign investment has played a major role for much of our history, bringing us jobs, technology, and new and better ways of doing things. But Canada has made itself so dependent on foreign corporations for economic development that it lacks the domestic corporations and capacities it needs to compete in the new global economy — to develop innovative new products, pursue far-flung export markets, and form strategic alliances with dynamic companies around the world. In the process, much of the decision-making power over the Canadian economy (including future investment, export, and science and technology plans affecting Canada's future jobs and prosperity) resides in corporate boardrooms in the United States, Europe, and Japan. When most of these decisions affecting Canada's future are made, there will be no Canadian sitting at the boardroom table. Although globalization is the buzzword, in fact most transnational corporations have a strong national identity and ownership. Few of those with major investments in Canada have a Canadian on the board of directors; nor do they permit the head of the Canadian subsidiary to deal directly with the board of directors or even with the chief executive officer of the parent. Most presidents of foreign subsidiaries in Canada report to regional or divisional vice-presidents in the foreign parent company.

Statistics show that foreign control of the Canadian economy has been growing since 1985, when Investment Canada was established as part of the new Conservative government's "open for business" policies. According to Statistics Canada, foreign-owned companies at the end of 1990 controlled 52 per cent of the capital employed in Canadian manufacturing, compared with 48 per cent at the end of 1984; and they controlled 43 per cent of the capital employed in the Canadian resource industries, compared with 36 per cent in 1984.[4] This means that corporate boardrooms in other countries exercise enormous power over Canada's economic future; their decisions concern not only investments in new technology, support of research and development, the pursuit of export markets, and so on, but also such diverse matters as the use of Canadian service industries, donations to Canadian universities, the level of skills training that Canadian workers will receive, and whether the Canadian subsidiary will support or oppose federal or provincial policies such as those on the environment, on labour law, and on workplace health and safety. Canadians are extremely vulnerable to the strategies and calculations of people in other parts of the world, and as foreign ownership increases, so does that vulnerability.

Today, many sectors of the economy that are critical to Canada's future are dominated by transnational corporations. In 1988, according to Statistics Canada, foreign-controlled companies accounted for 86.3 per cent of the revenues in our huge automobile and other transportation equipment industry, 83.2 per cent of the tire and other rubber products industry, 76.7 per cent of the chemicals industry, 57.5 per cent of the electrical products industry, and 50.6 per cent of the machinery industry, all of which are key sectors for the future economy. The highest levels of Canadian control, conversely, are in sectors that are likely to decline. Canadians control 92.2 per cent of the knitting-mill industry, 90.8 per cent of the clothing industry, 85.6 per cent of the furniture industry, 85.5 per cent of the shoe and leather industry, and 82.7 per cent of the steel and other primary metals industry, all of which face intensified international competition from developing countries.[5]

Our foreign-controlled industrial economy has created jobs but has failed to provide the science and technology, distribution networks, or human skills in marketing, exporting, finance, and top management that are so essential for Canada's future. The Canada–U.S. free trade agreement and the worldwide breakdown of trade barriers are rapidly making our branch-plant industrial structure obsolete, leaving even less decision making in the hands of the Canadian subsidiaries. Canadian "head offices" are being cut back and Canadian operations are being consolidated into North American divisions, with a loss of business service jobs in Canada that ranges from marketing and management consulting to packaging design and graphics. In 1991, General Motors, Canada's largest manufacturing company, moved its Canadian purchasing operations to the United States, joining Chrysler and Ford. More recently, another multinational Giant, IBM Canada, has seen responsibility for sales, service, and marketing shifted to the United States.

At the same time, foreign nationals are filling more of the top executive positions in Canada. Companies such as General Motors of Canada, Ford Canada, Xerox Canada, Honeywell Canada, Coca-Cola Canada, General Electric Canada, Amoco Canada, Mobil Canada, and Maple Leaf Foods, as well as the major Japanese companies operating in Canada, are all headed by foreign nationals rather than Canadians. As a result, governments pursuing ways to increase technology, training, and research investment often find themselves dealing with foreign executives who are passing through Canada as a stage in their career and have little capacity to make decisions, but who nonetheless are responsible for major segments of Canada's industrial economy. No other major industrial country faces a similar situation. These same executives are active in Canadian business organizations, where they protect the interests of their parent companies and can discourage these Canadian organizations from taking a strong stand in favour of policies that would strengthen Canadian-owned businesses.

Technology and other global changes also are shrinking the role of Canadian "head offices" and their "chief executive officers." An

Investment Canada report on globalization found that "organizational structures are moving away from accountability based on regional or product divisions, to more complex structures involving shared responsibility between the divisions. This often leads to a decrease in the autonomy of foreign subsidiaries, as they are more closely linked with head office strategy."[6] This is clearly happening in Canada where, increasingly, a separate "head office" is just a legal formality. Even in major subsidiaries, such as General Electric Canada, the function of the Canadian-based chief executive (beyond labour and government relations) is hard to see, since the line or product managers in the various GE divisions in Canada report to counterpart vice-presidents in the United States.

At the same time, as Investment Canada found, "the need for greater efficiency is encouraging greater centralization of upstream activities (that is, those activities which are less closely linked to the consumer). Upstream activities generally include production, research and development, and fiscal planning." As this happens, it means that foreign subsidiaries in Canada develop fewer opportunities for Canadians to acquire skills in financial management, marketing, production engineering, product development, research and development, export sales development, and computer systems design. These are the same concerns that were raised in the so-called Gray Report on foreign ownership published by the Trudeau government in 1972, which led to the establishment in the 1970s of the Foreign Investment Review Agency (which was replaced by Investment Canada in 1985). In view of the new information technologies, it is not hard to see why some Canadians fear that Canada could become a country of warehouses and assembly lines operating at the end of computer terminals that are linked to foreign head offices around the world.

While foreign control of the Canadian economy is growing, little of the increase in foreign ownership represents an inflow of new funds to Canada. Of the increase in the stock of foreign direct investment from $61.7 billion in 1980 to $126.6 billion in 1990, 80 per cent was financed out of the reinvested profits of foreign corporations that were operating in Canada; not quite 20 per cent represented new inflows of capital, according to Investment Canada. Foreign subsidiaries have been able to establish themselves in

Canada with an initial investment from their parent corporations but have relied on access to Canadian savings through Canada's banking system and, when up and running, have used profits from their Canadian operations to expand in Canada by investment or by the takeover of other Canadian companies. Retained earnings are another good measure of the strength of foreign-owned companies in Canada. At the end of 1987, retained earnings on the balance sheets of foreign-controlled manufacturing companies amounted to $32.7 billion; Canadian-controlled manufacturing companies had retained earnings of just $14.2 billion. For all non-financial corporations, foreign-controlled companies had retained earnings of $49.8 billion, compared with retained earnings of $36.3 billion for Canadian-controlled companies.[7]

A high level of foreign ownership means a significant outflow of capital from Canada each year. "Foreign ownership of Canadian firms and, even more importantly, foreign ownership of Canadian debt, are sucking huge amounts of capital out of the country on an annual basis and it's getting worse," investment banker Scotia McLeod has warned. Foreign ownership of Canadian industry, for example, means "steadily rising profit repatriation. That hits in two places. First in the investment income balance and second in 'business services,' which includes patents, trademarks, fees and other handy accounting concepts."[8] In the six years 1986–91, foreign-owned subsidiaries in Canada paid out $35.6 billion in dividends and interest to their parent companies.[9] In the four-year period 1986-89 Canadian subsidiaries paid their foreign parents $22.4 billion in royalties, management fees, advertising, licence costs, research and development payments, computer services, and other head office charges.[10]

Moreover, much of the growth in foreign investment is not to create new business enterprises in Canada or to turn Canadian branch plants into Canadian home-based enterprises with a complete world product mandate. In the period from mid-1985 to the end of September 1991, most of the activity that came under Investment Canada's umbrella was for takeovers rather than for new resource projects, new factories, or new commercial activities. Of the $106.7 billion of investments subject to the Investment Canada Act, only 8.3 per cent represented new businesses; 91.7 per cent represented takeovers.

Yet there is no doubt that foreign investment will continue to play an important role in Canada. For one thing, its presence is so large that it is hard to contemplate a restructuring of the Canadian economy in which foreign subsidiaries do not play a major role. For another, foreign multinationals can bring needed technologies, distribution systems, and management skills. But Canada will have to pay much greater attention to the kind of foreign investment it wants to attract; and, even more important, it will have to consider how it can foster the emergence and growth of new Canadian-controlled multinational corporations. In the new global economy, Canada must field its own team of players.

In his trail-blazing book, *The Competitive Advantage of Nations*, Harvard business expert Michael Porter ranked the four types of investment that can take place in Canada, from the most attractive to the least attractive. The best investment, he said, consists of Canadian-controlled companies that make Canada their home base — companies such as CAE Industries, one of the world's leading suppliers of flight simulators, or Bombardier, a global supplier of rail, urban transit, and aircraft transportation systems. The second-best investment comes from foreign multinationals that make Canada their home base for a world product line and allow the Canadian operation full autonomy to operate — subsidiaries such as Pratt & Whitney's turboprop aircraft engine operation in Canada or ICI's explosives company in Canada. The third-best investment consists of Canadian-controlled companies that make another country their home base; and although Northern Telecom maintains its core research and development in Canada, there are grounds for fearing that it could move into this category. The least attractive investment consists of foreign-controlled companies that maintain their home base for all products outside Canada, leaving Canadians with only assembly and local sales jobs; and as Porter acknowledges, most subsidiaries fall into this category.

Porter argues that a high level of foreign investment is a clear sign that Canadians have problems with their own industry: "Except when it is largely passive, widespread foreign investment usually indicates that the process of competitive upgrading in an economy is not entirely healthy because domestic firms in many industries lack the capabilities to defend their market positions against foreign firms."[11] Despite the large pools of investment in Canada, there were no Canadian businessmen who felt they could successfully run Canada Packers, Connaught BioSciences, Lumonics, Polysar's huge rubber operations, or the many other Canadian companies that were sold to foreign multinationals through the 1980s and into the 1990s. But as Porter stresses, "inbound foreign investment is never the solution to a nation's competitive problems." While he argues that simply blocking foreign takeovers is counterproductive, "widespread foreign investment is a sign that policy initiatives toward industry must receive high priority."[12]

Porter found, in his study on Canada, that most foreign investment had located here either to gain access to Canadian natural resources or to get behind tariff walls to serve the Canadian market, leaving Canada with a large number of branch-plant operations that make little sense in today's global economy. Most of these companies did the minimum necessary to operate in Canada, and the existing pattern of foreign activity, he argues, "reflects weaknesses that are a cause for concern." One of these is the lack of sophisticated machinery, component, and business service suppliers in Canada. Foreign subsidiaries themselves have contributed to this problem. When they came to Canada, "foreign firms, particularly those based in the U.S., had existing supplier relationships," observes Porter. "Depending upon the transportability of the input or service, many firms maintained their existing outside-of-Canada supplier relationships. Overall, there has been relatively little attention given to developing indigenous supplier relationships."[13] This is true not only in manufacturing but also in resource industries, such as oil and gas, where foreign firms have continued to use foreign service companies.

A series of sector studies carried out by the then Department of Regional Industrial Expansion during the Canada–U.S. free trade negotiations in the late 1980s spelled out how Canadian economic development has been held back because of the high level of foreign ownership and control. In the automotive industry, Canada's largest manufacturing sector, "virtually no research and development is done in Canada," the government study said;[14] and "major management decisions with respect to investment and plant improvements in Canada are made by the U.S. parents. These decisions may not always be based entirely on economic factors." The specialty chemicals industry is dominated by multinational corporations, "which serve the domestic market primarily, and have limited scope for export." The computer and office equipment industry also is dominated by a small number of foreign multinationals, which "centralize R & D and marketing at corporate headquarters, usually in the U.S. Consequently, the levels of R & D and marketing employment in Canada are lower than might be expected in a situation where these Canadian firms were Canadian-owned and based." Canada has a rising trade deficit in this sector because "multinational investment has not been commensurate with the size of the Canadian market, nor has it been growing as rapidly."

In the pulp and paper equipment industry, which is about 75 per cent foreign-controlled, "most of the subsidiaries have been relying heavily on the parent company to provide the technical support required to remain competitive and have done very little if any R & D in Canada." While the industry needs to make strategic commitments to R & D and access foreign technology through joint ventures, "due to the large segment of foreign ownership in the industry, mainly from the U.S.A., the lack of freedom to deal directly with European and Scandinavian firms will severely curtail Canadian opportunities in this sector."

The government's analysts found that the same was true across Canada's industrial landscape. For example, they reported that the major household appliance industry was dominated by three U.S.-based companies: they "operate as branch plants producing mainly for the domestic market and making products similar to those made by the parent companies in the U.S. plants." The construction machinery and materials handling industry, too, is largely foreign-controlled. "Rationalized subsidiary plants of U.S. multinationals have only a production mandate, rather than a product development mandate, and have limited autonomy for independent research and development, and rarely conduct R & D here"; and because their U.S. parents are having trouble competing against Japanese and European companies, they are shifting activities to low-cost developing countries, which brings the risk that they may not make investment in Canada to keep their Canadian plants competitive.

In the high-tech instrumentation industry, which supplies process controls, medical electronics, automation controls, measuring equipment, scientific instruments, and remote-sensing devices, "the majority of foreign-owned corporations have only a limited mandate to supply export markets from their Canadian operations." Moreover, a number of these companies have been cutting back manufacturing in Canada, shifting "from branch plants to regional sales and systems integration and service and maintenance centres." The disposable paper products industry, which makes everything from paper napkins and towels to diapers and facial and toilet tissues, also is largely foreign-controlled. "Corporate policies developed in headquarters outside Canada often prevent Canadian subsidiaries from exporting." The paint and industrial coatings industry is another that is largely foreign-controlled and is weak in R & D in Canada. "Most work is carried out at the parents' headquarter facilities. This has deprived Canada of the availability of exportable, specialized coatings," reported the government sector analysts.

Other studies came to similar conclusions. In a report to Prime Minister Brian Mulroney, the National Advisory Board on Science and Technology (NABST) stated that many foreign-owned subsidiaries were underperforming in research and development in Canada compared with Canadian-controlled companies in the same industries. Spending on R & D by Canadian-controlled companies in industries such as telecommunications, computers, office equipment, and scientific and professional equipment was comparable to levels spent by their U.S.-based counterparts, but "most foreign-owned companies in Canada, on the other hand, exhibit a very weak propensity to conduct R & D in this country," the report said.[15]

The report cited the example of the auto industry, Canada's largest manufacturing industry. Canadian-controlled auto parts companies accounted for just 17 per cent of auto parts industry shipments in 1986 but performed 46 per cent of the R & D in the automotive sector, which included both the parts producers and the big assembly companies. This illustrates how "the branch plant nature of many Canadian manufacturers is one of the primary factors responsible for the feeble R & D statistics for the economy as a whole," the NABST report said. It pointed to the chemicals industry as another in which the existing structure of foreign ownership worked against Canada's future interests. Although Canada's chemical industry has grown significantly over the past 15 years under foreign ownership, it remains primarily a producer of basic feedstocks rather than high-value intensive specialty chemicals. "Most Canadian producers have been prevented from making major investments in world-scale specialty chemicals facilities by their foreign-parent enterprises, which typically have established plants in the United States to serve the North American market." This "lack of strategic autonomy has diminished the ability of Canadian industry to expand export markets and to make the investments in R & D needed to be internationally competitive in higher value-added products," the NABST report stated.

Today, foreign ownership is high in Canada compared with that in other industrial countries. In 1988 foreign-controlled companies accounted for 55.7 per cent of the revenues in the oil and gas industry, 48.1 per cent in the manufacturing sector, and 28.2 per cent in the wholesale-distribution industry. Of the 100 largest non-financial enterprises in Canada, 48 were foreign-controlled, compared with 43 in 1987; and of the 1000 largest non-financial enterprises, 439 were foreign-controlled. Statistics Canada records that in the four years 1987–1990, there were 799 Canadian-controlled companies with assets of $44.3 billion that were sold to non-resident corporations. Foreign multinationals also account for about 75 per cent of Canada's manufacturing exports. As the world economy restructures, Canada is in an extremely vulnerable position, as Michael Porter argues: "Many of the strategic decisions in important Canadian sectors are made outside Canada, based on the overall global strategies of parent companies." How these companies allocate home base activities is "a critical issue for the Canadian economy."

For Porter, the key concept is the home base. Despite all the focus on globalization, Porter strongly believes that the nation-state still matters and that it plays a crucial role in shaping the competitiveness of industries. The home base matters, fundamentally, because that is where the highest-value activities take place: "Typically, a company's home base is where the best jobs reside, where core research and development is undertaken, and where strategic control lies. Home bases are important to an economy because they support high productivity and productivity growth." As Porter explains, "the home base is where the firm normally contributes the most to the local economy in a particular industry, by establishing the most productive jobs, investing in specialized factor production, acting as a sophisticated buyer for other local industries as well as a sophisticated related and supporting firm for other industries, and helping to create a vibrant local competitive milieu."[16]

Canada's priority must be to build up more of its own business enterprises, with their headquarters here — and with all the power and expertise and business spinoffs that go with a headquarters. But this means finding alternatives to foreign takeovers. In the United States, Fred Bergsten, a former U.S. Treasury official who now heads the Institute for International Economics in Washington, has argued that the United States needs a better capacity to preserve U.S. ownership of firms whose output, technology, or production processes are critical. The U.S. government, he told a congressional committee, should encourage corporate rescues like that mounted by IBM to prevent a Japanese company from acquiring the high-tech Perkin-Elmer corporation. The government could also provide loans, purchase guarantees, extend R & D grants, and even bail the company out. Failing this, Bergsten said, the United States should impose performance requirements for R & D and on U.S. production.[17] This is the challenge for Canada. If we want our threshold companies to move up from the junior league and become world-champion players in the global economy, we will have to find ways of making sure that there are new sources of capital so that these companies are not put on the auction block — and inevitably snapped up by foreign buyers. Unless we do so, Canada will become nothing more than a greenhouse of new technologies and businesses whose long-term benefits will be captured by foreign multinationals.

Canada will have to stand its ground in developing more Canadian-based multinationals, since the United States in particular will oppose intervention. The Canada–U.S. free trade agreement already severely restricts Canada's options by limiting Investment Canada's scope to block U.S. takeovers of Canadian companies to the very largest enterprises. The free trade deal also prevents Canada from requiring U.S.-controlled subsidiaries to sell shares to Canadians and from imposing the sale of shares as a condition for a takeover.

It is obvious why the United States pushes the interests of its multinationals. As the State Department explained in a briefing document on free trade with Mexico, "the U.S. government has a strong interest in encouraging favorable conditions for new and expanded investments in Mexico. U.S. firms investing there tend to use U.S. suppliers and U.S. designing and managerial talent."[18] During the Canada–U.S. free trade negotiations, the United States publicly challenged the Mulroney government not to block Amoco Canada's takeover of Dome Petroleum, with its huge natural gas reserves. "With barriers that could prevent that kind of takeover, you couldn't have a free trade agreement," Bruce Smart of the U.S. Commerce Department bluntly warned Ottawa.[19] It was not hard to figure out why Amoco enlisted the support of the Reagan administration. Amoco executives told U.S. financial analysts, "The reserves acquired with Dome have positioned us as the largest private holder of natural gas in North America."[20]

Without Canadian businesses to provide jobs for future scientists, engineers, skilled workers, financial strategists, product designers, marketing experts, and other productive skills, talented Canadians will head south, leaving behind a poorer Canada. Although some foreign subsidiaries will provide the variety of jobs and activities that will be required, Canadian multinationals will have to play the key role.

Now that transnational corporations are increasingly determining where much of the world's productive investment will take place, what the level and priorities of research and development will be, and what patterns of trade and kinds of job each country has, Canada has to respond by creating its own opportunities. This is doubly important because global networks of strategic alliances, distribution systems, and technology-sharing activities are of growing influence. "Export competitiveness cannot in fact be achieved by an industrial strategy simply through low production costs, an undervalued exchange rate or other forms of export subsidy; it depends above all on the ability of the industry in that system to participate actively in the international network of new industrial alliances and partnerships," says Carlo De Bendetti, chairman of Italy's Olivetti & Co.[21] But Canadian-based foreign subsidiaries are not going to be the vehicles that link Canada to global markets through strategic alliances. If we want to participate in the world economy, we must have our own corporate players.

Other countries, such as Sweden, Switzerland, Germany, France, and Japan, recognize the strategic importance of developing their own major corporations, and they have pursued policies that ensure that most of the key business decisions affecting their economies are made at home by their own businesses. Even today, it is much harder for a foreign multinational to make an acquisition in these countries than to do so in Canada.

In today's world, foreign investment is outpacing international trade as transnational corporations extend their manufacturing, distribution, and service activities to almost every corner of the globe. By 1989, according to a major United Nations report, the worldwide stock of foreign direct investment totalled a massive US$1.5 trillion; and in that year alone, the flow of new foreign direct investment reached US$196 billion. In the process, transnational corporations have been developing the power to challenge national governments on their tax, workplace, environmental, and social policies.[22]

In fact, about 600 transnational corporations now account for about 25 per cent of production in the world's market economies and for a growing portion of international trade, since an increasing share of trade is now between affiliates of the same transnational corporations operating in countries around the world. Many of the names of these corporations are household words: General Motors, IBM, Coca-Cola, American Express, Exxon, General Electric, Kodak, and Xerox from the United States; Sony, Honda, Toyota, Fujitsu, Fuji, NEC, and Canon from Japan; and Siemens, Bayer, British Petroleum, Olivetti, Reuters, and Volkswagen from Europe. So, rather than moving to a world market of intensifying competition, we could see a movement towards global oligopoly with a handful of companies dominating many of the world's industries.

While many of the biggest transnational corporations come from the countries with the biggest economies, such as the United States, Japan, and Germany, countries much smaller than Canada have succeeded in creating some of the most important global businesses, based on advanced technologies, sophisticated marketing, and high skills that pay good wages and salaries. Sweden, with a population that is one-third that of Canada, is home to Volvo in cars and trucks,

Electrolux in household appliances, Alfa-Laval in machinery, Saab-Scania in industrial products, SKF in ball bearings, and Ericsson in telecommmunications. Switzerland, with just one-quarter Canada's population, has Nestlé in food, Asea Brown Boveri in engineering, and Ciba-Geigy, Sandoz, and Hoffmann-La Roche in pharmaceuticals and chemicals. Canada's relatively small size, compared with the United States, Japan, or Germany, is no excuse for a lack of international industry. On the Fortune Global 500 list in 1991, there were 17 Swedish companies, 12 Canadian companies, and 11 Swiss companies.

In the past, foreign investors targeted our natural resources and manufacturing. Today, they are shifting to high technology and into service industries: entertainment, hotels, retail stores, fast-food franchises, and business services such as banking, insurance, temporary employment, training, airlines, marketing, and engineering. According to a U.N. report on transnational corporations, "all indications are that the internationalization of service industries through foreign direct investment is in its early stages and that the momentum in the growth of services through foreign direct investment will be maintained or even increased during the 1990s."[23]

The growing role of foreign service companies is already evident in Canada; for example, Sears, Woolco, K-Mart, Ikea, A & P, and Safeway are key players in retailing; American Express in credit cards and travel; UPS, Federal Express, and American Airlines in transportation; WPP Group and Interpublic Group in advertising; Trans Union and Equifax in credit bureaus; Cargill in commodity trading; William Mercer, Towers Perrin, Booz Allen, Arthur Andersen, Hewitt Associates, and McKinsey in business services; Pinkerton, Wells Fargo, and Burns in security services; McDonald's, Burger King, Pizza Hut, and Dunkin Donuts in fast foods; Sheraton, Westin, Hilton, and Holiday Inn in hotels; Budget and Avis in car rentals; Manpower in temporary services; Bechtel, Fluor, and Swan Wooster in engineering; and Century 21 and Remax in real estate.

Franchising is one of the newest forms of foreign investment in services. In 1985 some 342 U.S. franchising companies operated 30,188 outlets in foreign countries, including more than 9000 outlets in Canada. The Canadian outlets included 1542 restaurants, 714 auto and truck rental services, 1599 non-food retailers, 695 construction, home improvement, maintenance, and cleaning services, 276 hotels and motels, 112 laundry and dry-cleaning services, and 767 other outlets in such areas as educational and training services and equipment rental services.[24]

Canada has some important service transnationals of its own, including the major banks and some life insurance companies, as well as a variety of other companies such as Four Seasons Hotels, SNC Engineering, and Laidlaw Waste Management. But as Michael Porter found in his study on Canadian competitiveness, "relatively few industries in the Canadian services sector have reached international standing and Canada's service exports as a percentage of total exports are the lowest in the G-7." This is a critical matter, since services represent nearly 70 per cent of Canada's gross domestic product (GDP). In 1981–85 only 31 per cent of Canada's direct investment abroad was made in service activities, compared with 62 per cent of Japanese investment and 53 per cent of U.S. investment. During the 1980s, 70 per cent of foreign investment flows into Canada went into service industries, according to the U.N. study.

New information technologies and telecommunications networks will sharply increase transborder data flows and thus the ability to produce services in one country and deliver them in another (as can be seen from airline and hotel reservation systems). These technologies can only accelerate foreign investment in services. "The reason is that the use of transborder data flows makes it easier to establish service affiliates abroad which are linked to their parent corporations in an interactive manner via transnational computer communications systems," the U.N. study concluded. Most of the value-added activity — such as software development in an airline reservations system — will take place in the home country of the parent corporation. Foreign subsidiaries will be "mere outposts — in the extreme case, they are no more than offices with terminals."

The consulting firm Ernst & Young warns that something must be done to give Canada's software and other high-technology companies an alternative to foreign ownership, for they are at a financial dead end. "To make up for this lack of funds Canadian companies are increasingly seeking alliances with, or are selling their operations to, foreign companies. If this trend continues, Canada will not reap the benefits of technologies developed here."[25] While Canada's high-tech companies are struggling to survive, foreign high-tech companies are shopping the world for promising companies that will help them stay competitive. "The key question is this: will Canadian technology developers be strong enough to form alliances in their own interest, or will they be acquired to serve the interests of others? Should the latter scenario prevail, the change in Canada's future will be dramatic."[26]

In a confidential 1990 paper on Canada's competitiveness problems, federal government analysts warned that "the vulnerability of flagship Canadian-owned firms to foreign takeovers is a serious concern. Given the relatively small size by world standards of even our larger indigenous companies, Canadian firms seldom have the financial resources needed to obtain effective control in mergers, acquisitions and strategic partnerships. On the other hand, failing to participate in the globalization of business activity, even as a junior partner, could result in isolation, stagnation and decline over the longer term. This policy conundrum needs to be addressed to determine whether there are initiatives which could be taken to facilitate a greater number of Canadian companies becoming capable of building and sustaining a position in global markets."[27]

The case of Lumonics, the leading Canadian company in lasers and one of the most important in the world, illustrates the serious difficulties Canadian high-tech companies face and their vulnerability to foreign takeovers. The senior management of Lumonics spent more than a year seeking Canadian financing, without success, before turning to Sumitomo Heavy Industries of Japan, which purchased the entire company for $83.7 million in 1989. Lumonics had a major Canadian shareholder, Noranda, which was part of the huge corporate empire of Edgar and Peter Bronfman and which owned 31.5 per cent of Lumonics; but the Bronfman group lacked the vision, management skills, and shareholder patience and commitment to build a new Canadian multinational. "The landscape was changing in the laser business with a lot of companies consolidating," Doug Cameron of Noranda explained. "Whereas it once was a small group of independent companies, all of a sudden it was being controlled by either the Japanese or the Germans. It was becoming a land of giants who could wait for the return on their investment." Sumitomo Heavy Industries of Japan, a member of one of Japan's major *keiretsu* or corporate families, had the patient capital to make a long-term strategic investment. According to Noranda's Cameron, "they felt that lasers were going to be an industry of the future and they wanted to be positioned in it. Lumonics was one of the premier candidates to position Sumitomo in this industry." So when the Japanese found that neither Canadian business nor the Canadian government was prepared to do anything to maintain Canadian ownership in this future technology, they purchased the company, and Noranda picked up $27 million for what had been a $500,000 investment in 1973.

The Connaught story is not much different. In 1989 Connaught Laboratories Ltd. won the Canada Award for Business Excellence gold medal for innovation. But that was not enough to cause the Canadian investment community or the Canadian government to take steps to keep it Canadian. Although the federal government, in its 1989 Throne Speech, identified biotechnology as a "strategic technology," it readily agreed to the sale of Canada's largest domestic biotechnology company to the French government-controlled Institut Mérieux in 1989 for $942 million. Like Lumonics, Connaught needed new capital to finance its international expansion; and like Lumonics, it failed to find Canadian investment. Paul Labbé, president of Investment Canada, defended his agency's approval of the Connaught takeover by contending that the sale was "the only way to maintain Connaught and Canada as a global force in the world vaccine and human protein markets."[28] This implied that Canada was too small to support such a company on its own (despite the success of similar companies based in Switzerland, Denmark, and Sweden). Yet Quebec did not feel the same way. A Quebec-based subsidiary of Connaught, Bio-Research Laboratories, was sold to Quebec interests, with the province's pension fund manager, the Caisse de dépôt et placement, providing financial backing by buying 30 per cent of the company.

Not everyone agrees that ownership matters in the economy of the future. U.S. analyst Robert Reich of Harvard University is a leading exponent of a new world of stateless corporations, or cosmo-corps, which locate research and development, engineering, marketing, and other activities wherever the best combination of skills, infrastructure, and tax climate can be found.[29] According to Reich, the links between a corporation and its country have been broken, and the new global managers coolly pursue higher profits, greater market share, and improved stock prices with no regard for country or community. Some Canadian analysts share this view and its implication that national governments have, in effect, become powerless in directing economic activity.

There is considerable disagreement, however. Ethan Kapstein, co-director of the Economics and National Security Program at Harvard University, insists that "the power of the home country over the multinational has not diminished; if anything, it has continued to increase. Corporations have not become anational, multinational, or transnational; they remain wedded to their home governments for both political and economic reasons." In general, Kapstein argues, "large corporations are not only aware of the identity of their home country, they wish to maintain a close relationship with the government. Only the state can defend corporate interests in international negotiations over trade, investment and market access. Agreements over such things as airline routes, the opening of banking establishments, and the right to sell insurance are not decided by corporate actors who gather around a table; they are determined by diplomats and bureaucrats. Corporations must turn to governments when they have interests to protect or advance."[30]

Moreover, there is little mystery about the nationality of most multinationals. The top executives at General Motors, IBM, Exxon, American Express, Coca-Cola, and General Electric know that they are American, just as the top executives at Siemens, Volkswagen, Bayer, and Mercedes-Benz know they are German, and those at Sony, Mitsubishi, Honda, and Mitsui know they are Japanese, those at Dassault and Thomson know they are French, those at Volvo and Electrolux know they are Swedish, and those at Ciba-Geigy and Nestlé know they are Swiss.

Banking is often held out as the quintessential example of globalization, yet for virtually all banks, their home market is their real base of activity, and that activity is determined by the domestic banking laws and regulations. Citicorp thinks of itself as a U.S. bank, just as Deutsche Bank thinks of itself as a German bank, Industrial Bank of Japan thinks of itself as a Japanese bank, and the Royal Bank of Canada thinks of itself as a Canadian bank. Canada's strong banking system is the direct result of Canadian laws, which favoured a national banking system and blocked foreign ownership of our banks. As Kapstein points out, "corporations certainly recognize the importance of their home state as much as any other societal actor. In most cases, the home country provides the single largest source of employee talent, of earnings, and of investment opportunities. In negotiations over market access, the corporation must rely on the state to advance its interests. Firms retain a national identity because they must, even if that identity is kept hidden at times from their critics."[31]

What is happening is that the transnationals of the triad powers are locating activities to tap markets and skills. Robert Reich points to high value-added Japanese activities in the United States: "By 1990, more than 500 U.S. scientists and engineers worked for Honda, in Torrance, California; another 200 worked in Ohio. At Mazda's new US$23 million R & D centre in Irvine, California, hundreds of U.S. designers and engineers are undertaking long-term automotive research. Nissan employs 400 U.S. engineers at its engineering centre in Plymouth, Michigan; Toyota employs 140 at its technical research centre in Ann Arbor. Fujitsu is now constructing an $80 million telecommunications plant and research centre in Texas. NEC has opened a research laboratory in Princeton, New Jersey."[32] What this means, Reich argues, is that a Japanese company may be more important to the United States than a Texas Instruments or IBM if the latter are locating more activities in other countries.

But even Reich does not propose a free market approach to foreign investment. Instead, he has called for the creation of the Office of U.S. Investment Representative to negotiate with global corporations. This office would identify key sectors of the U.S. economy, such as high-technology or state-of-the-art auto plants, and would pursue these investments. It would bargain "only for the global investments that promised large beneficial spillovers or that would not come to [U.S.] shores automatically [and] it would be selecting certain technologies and industries as more critical than others," Reich says.[33]

"It is simple common sense that large nations that bargain as a whole with global managers — or groups of smaller nations that pool their bargaining strength behind a single agent — have much more clout than smaller nations or separate states and cities," Reich says. He cites the example of Japan's Ministry of International Trade and Industry (MITI), which, he claims, by preventing Japanese companies from competing for foreign technology and by acting as a single buying agency, obtained U.S. technology at bargain prices; Japan in 1956–87 paid US$9 billion to acquire American technology that cost between US$500 billion and US$1 trillion to develop.

Even though Reich's ideas may be relevant to the United States, they do not apply as easily to Canada. Reich points to the joint venture between General Motors and Suzuki to build the popular Chevrolet model, the Geo-Metro, in Ingersoll, Ontario, as an example of the new global enterprise. Canadian workers did end up with the assembly jobs, but the design and planning was done in Japan, the plant is managed by Suzuki, and many of the components come from Japan. The only role for Canadians is to weld and bolt the pieces together. Similarly, although U.S. automakers General Motors and Ford have European operations that design and build their own cars, their operations in Canada are simply divisions of their North American operations without design or engineering roles.

The difference in market size between Canada and the United States is a major factor, according to the National Advisory Board on Science and Technology. "When a foreign firm establishes a significant presence in the U.S., it is less likely to be configured as a branch plant than if it were being located in a much smaller market such as Canada's. Therefore, foreign ownership may interact with a small market to produce low R & D propensity in Canada but not in the U.S., Japan, Germany and other large and/or technologically sophisticated economies."[34]

So despite all the obeisance to globalization, the nation-state and national policies will continue to be important. Gilles Paquet, professor of administrative studies at the University of Ottawa, maintains that the nation-state will become more important as the global economy takes shape. "The nation state of the year 2000 will be much more important on a strategic level with new policy instruments, instruments of coordination and animation rather than the traditional instruments of spending and taxation. The strategic state will intervene, not in a heavy-handed way but in a very specific way only at particular moments with the objective not to choose winners but to make winners. A government should not suffer the inefficient to survive, but should allow those with the chance of surviving the possibility of becoming efficient by giving them support — some financial help, but mostly support in the form of a guarantee."[35]

Even in terms of people, the boards and executive headquarters of multinational corporations are largely representative of the country of ownership. Japanese corporations are led by Japanese executives, just as American and European companies are dominated by top executives and directors from the country of the parent corporation. Gunnar Hedlund, a professor at the Institute of International Business in the Stockholm School of Economics, contends that the notion of "supranational globality" is highly exaggerated. "Home countries," he says, "still dominate multinational corporations in terms of employment, R & D and the nationality of top management." Globalization, in particular, has not reached top management. "For example, in 34 of Sweden's largest multinational corporations, a study found only 14 companies with any non-Swedes reporting directly to the CEO. None of the companies has a foreigner as the CEO. Note that this is a tiny country of 8 million, and one-third of Swedish industrial companies' employment and an even bigger fraction of its sales are abroad."[36] The *Economist* has pointed out that although "books have marvelled about the coming global shopping centres, stateless corporations and so on for at least two decades,…progress towards that goal is slow." Corporations such as IBM, Sony, and Nestlé have spread their operations around the world, "but the firms' character and competitiveness remains American, Japanese and Swiss. World citizenship remains science fiction."[37]

This is why Canada's future depends on our ability to develop Canadian-owned companies that can pursue global strategies from Canadian headquarters, using the best research, engineering, financial, marketing, and production skills of Canadians and building up the capabilities of sophisticated Canadian suppliers of parts, components, and services. Foreign subsidiaries will continue to be an important part of our economy, but Canada should seek the kind of investment that will make this country the home base for autonomous foreign-controlled companies with full responsibility for world mandates. Canada must find an alternative to the foreign takeover of key Canadian companies that could become our own future multinationals. We cannot rely on foreign investment to do the job for us. We have to build our own economy that is capable of producing unique products and services for the rest of the world. It is mainly through Canadian-controlled companies that we will meet this challenge. In the world economy of the future, Canada will have to field its own team of strong players — and we will not develop this strong team if we keep selling off our prime candidates.

6

It All Begins in the Classroom

HEN ONE OF CANADA'S TOP consulting firms surveyed more than 400 major Canadian employers at the start of the 1990s, it found that close to 60 per cent were having difficulty recruiting new employees — and this at a time when the country was in the grip of recession and when more than 1.3 million Canadians were looking for work. Some Canadian companies in fact had to recruit abroad for specialized skills and trades at the same time that they were turning down unqualified Canadian workers.

But the kind of employees sought by companies surveyed in the Towers Perrin report were educated, knowledge workers, not high school dropouts or even high school graduates.[1] The workers the companies wanted included supervisory and managerial, professional, technical, and technical support employees, and workers with skilled trades. Finding these kinds of people was expected to get even more difficult in the future. Yet at the same time, these same companies reported that the biggest single reason for turning down job applicants was their inadequate writing and verbal skills — not, as might have been expected, a lack of experience. Our classrooms are not delivering the young people who will be capable of taking on the jobs that will be the source of Canada's future productivity and prosperity.

The ability of a country to maintain a high standard of living depends more than ever before on the quality of its workforce. In the global economy of the twenty-first century, countries that invest in quality education will attract investment, while those that do not will stagnate. Companies that were once drawn to countries with the cheapest workforce will now be drawn to those with the best workforce. This reality puts enormous pressure on Canada's educational system — from kindergarten to graduate school — but we really have no choice. The knowledge economy depends on new ideas and innovation and on the ability of large numbers of people to show initiative, to work in teams, and to participate in lifelong learning. These capacities depend ultimately on education.

During the late 1980s we had a hint of what the future might hold if we fail to ensure that our educational system can produce the workers we will need. As the economy reached its peak in 1989, the demand for skilled workers was so intense that in the Toronto area companies had to develop special techniques to outwit the headhunters who were scouring firms to find employees who could be targeted with job offers from competing firms. "In the counter-espionage field we've seen companies with software engineers who are very much sought after, and who are zealously raided by employment agencies, making it impossible for employment agencies to telephone inside the company," Neil Macdougall, president of the Technical Service Council, said.[2] Even spouses needed codes to call inside. One practice was for a headhunter to call company switchboards masquerading as a university professor who was planning a free software seminar and needed the names of software engineers so that he could mail them an invitation. Until companies caught on to this trick, they supplied lists of names, which the headhunting firms then targeted for competitors.

Other companies, such as Sun Life Assurance, had to offer employees bonuses of between $200 and $1000 to help recruit new employees. In its 1991 survey, Towers Perrin found that 23 per cent of major Canadian employers had some kind of program to pay employees for employee referrals and that another 6 per cent were considering a plan. And in 1990, Toronto's Hospital for Sick Children, faced with a nursing shortage, offered bonuses of up to $9000 a year for experienced nurses so that it could keep intensive-care beds open.

The great difference from the old economy is that, in the future, most jobs and industries will demand good education and skills, not only in the executive suite but on the production line and in the office. If our schools are weak, our economy will be weak. If Japan graduates more than 90 per cent of its students from high school and they all possess high literacy and numeracy skills, and if Canada graduates only 70 per cent of its high school students and they are weak in literacy and numeracy skills, then Japan will have more competitive production lines, more competitive offices, and more competitive research and development laboratories to make more competitive products for the future. The days when we could concentrate education on an elite and not worry about ordinary workers are over. The challenge confronting Canada is to raise the level of education for everyone. As the Economic Council of Canada warned in a report on Canada's schools, "Canadians face a painful choice: develop skills or accept low wages."[3]

But in a country that honours outstanding athletes more than outstanding students, we have our priorities wrong. "We still have millions of Canadians — the majority, we can reasonably assume — who are not motivated to ensure their children will have the education and training most likely to give them well-being and fulfilment in life," says Science Council of Canada chairperson Janet Halliwell. "What little we know of this mass indifference indicates a certain smug satisfaction with what education has achieved in Canada over the past few decades — justifiable perhaps, for we have achieved a great deal. But there is still a lamentable ignorance of what our new world will demand, not only of our children but of adults."[4]

How else can we explain the lack of public anger over a high school system in which nearly 30 per cent of students never graduate? That is equivalent to 100,000 dropouts a year, or 1 million over a decade — young people who face a lifetime of living at the margin of the economy and who represent a powerful loss of productive potential for society.

Even students who graduate from high school seem inadequately prepared for the new economy. Too many lack basic skills. International science and mathematics tests in 1991, conducted through the International Assessment of Educational Progress, showed that Canadian 13-year-olds ranked ninth out of students from 15 countries in science tests while their 9-year-old brothers and sisters ranked fourth out of 10 countries. In math, Canadian 13-

year-olds ranked ninth out of 15 countries while Canadian 9-year-olds ranked eighth out of 10 countries. Japanese and German students were not tested, but South Koreans came first in every group, demonstrating what enormous advances can be made in a generation. When the Korean War ended in 1953, South Korea was an agrarian society with few university or high school graduates and with a low level of literacy. What the tests showed, the Economic Council said, was that "Canadian children receive a good start, but from the age of 13 or 14, they begin gradually to fall behind children in other countries."[5]

Literacy and numeracy tests by Statistics Canada also show poor results among young Canadians. In its 1989 literacy survey, Statistics Canada found that 29 per cent of Canadians in the 16-to-24 age group could not read at a level that allowed them to meet relatively simple everyday demands, and 44 per cent of the same age group lacked the numeracy skills to meet most everyday demands involving the use of numbers. A 1991 survey of 10,000 teachers across Canada conducted by the Canadian Teachers' Federation, *Teachers and Literacy*, found that about 30 per cent of students were felt to have problems in reading, writing, and mathematics. Of these, 18 per cent had problems understanding even simple levels of reading, writing, and mathematics, and the other 12 per cent had serious problems analysing what they read or devising ways of solving mathematical problems. If these figures do not improve, Canada will produce more than one million illiterates during the 1990s, the Economic Council warns.

The most recent results of the Canadian Test of Basic Skills suggests that, in 1988, Grade 8 students were almost one full year behind their 1966 counterparts in mathematics, reading, and spelling. This is a profile of a system in decline. Community colleges, according to a report from the Ontario Ministry of Skills Development, say that 25 per cent of their students are functionally illiterate.[6] This is why some colleges and universities provide remedial classes for high school graduates entering college.

Our school system is also failing students who want to pursue technical careers. In Sweden, for example, after completion of compulsory schooling at age 16, students who are not planning to go to university have the opportunity to take highly specialized training in technological, commercial, or industrial skills or in care skills such as nursing and social services. These courses generally last another three years. They combine school and workplace education and training, and are conducted in close cooperation with local employers and unions. The Swedish experience shows that "the key to improving the school-to-work transition, decreasing the dropout rate and producing a work-ready workforce is creating an educational system with an explicit and gradually increasing work experience component," William Nothdurft argues in his study of how schools in Sweden, Germany, Britain, France, and the United States are preparing for the workforce of the twenty-first century.[7] But in Canada, as Mark Holmes of the Ontario Institute for Studies in Education complains, "there is little focus on exactly what the two-thirds of students who are not going to post-secondary education are supposed to be achieving in school." This is the reason, Holmes contends, why "many young people, particularly dropouts, are leaving school without skills, aspirations or prospects."[8] Vocational education in underfunded and treated as a dead-end, a place to park difficult students. While Sweden, Germany, and Japan have highly effective systems for helping young people make a smooth transition from school, "Canada is in the unenviable position of having one of the worst arrangements for making this transition," the Economic Council of Canada says.[9]

Our colleges and universities also face big changes as we approach the next century. While their role will become even more important than it already is, they face serious budget constraints and shortages of the faculty and equipment needed to teach the next generation of knowledge workers. Industry and government, for example, are demanding more scientists, engineers, and managers, but the funding for graduate students, through granting agencies such as the Natural Sciences and Engineering Research Council, the Medical Research Council, and the Social Sciences and Humanities Research Council, has been virtually flat (after inflation) since the mid-1980s, despite soaring demand. This means that if Canada tries to raise its level of research and development to that of major industrial countries and to become more innovative, it will not be able to find the scientists and engineers in our universities. That is why it is imperative that we adopt new measures to make it possible for more science and engineering students to pursue advanced degrees. At present, nearly half the applicants for NSERC programs are being turned down because of lack of funds.

Even if we make an aggressive effort to revitalize our educational system, the benefits will take years to pay off. So we have to start now. Today's preschoolers will not get their first full-time job before the year 2010, and most of today's elementary students are unlikely to have their first full-time job until the early part of the twenty-first century. Even many of today's high school students will spend most of their time in the classroom until the end of the 1990s, because a high school diploma in today's world is not enough if one wants to be part of the middle class. The same job horizon is true for first-year university students in computer science, biology, or engineering who intend to become Canada's next generation of top researchers by earning their PhDs.

The education that we give these students will be more important than anything else we do to shape our future, because the economy of the future will depend more than anything else on how well each country develops the potential of all its people. Unless we have highly productive and flexible workers who can earn high pay, we will be forced to compete for low-paying jobs with Mississippi or Mexico. In the global economy, the high-value and high-pay jobs will flow to the countries that can provide the best-educated workers and the most advanced educational institutions. It is our brainpower that will give us the organizational, scientific, creative, and process skills of the new economy. But as South Korea, Taiwan, and Singapore are showing, other countries can develop expertise very quickly.

Education has become so important to the future that the leading economic powers around the world are busy developing new curricula, setting new standards, investing in new classroom structures, exploiting new educational technologies, reviewing teacher education and retraining, and experimenting with new forms of teaching and even with new kinds of schools. In the United States, the Bush administration and the National Governors' Association have launched an ambitious plan to rejuvenate the U.S. education system by the year 2000. The goals include high school graduation by 90 per cent of all high school students, the achievement of high levels of competence in five core subjects (English, science, mathematics, history, and geography) based on high standards, nationwide testing in Grades 4, 8, and 12, and the expansion of Head Start and other preschool programs so that all children entering the school system are ready to learn. In addition, the private sector has promised to raise US$150–$200 million to fund the New American School Development Corporation, which is to finance research teams to "reinvent the public school," with 535 new-style schools in place by 1996. The research teams will look at everything from teaching methods and materials to the school calendar and classroom size. While it is too soon to determine how successful the U.S. efforts will be, there is no doubt that the United States is approaching its problems with a strong sense of urgency.

With a zeal that matches the U.S. sense of urgency after the Soviets stunned the world in 1957 by sending the Sputnik 1 manned satellite into orbit, Americans are now striving to restore and expand their educational system so that they can become more competitive against Japan, Europe, and the newly industrializing countries of Asia. The Office of Science and Technology Policy (OSTP) in the White House is pushing hard for cooperation between U.S. government laboratories, universities, and industry to produce a technically competent workforce. In a 1991 report, the OSTP said that federal agencies can play a major role in supporting state, local, and university education initiatives in science and technology.[10] The National Science Foundation budget is to be doubled over five years, and the agency is investing heavily in research on mathematics and science curricula and on teaching methods and materials for elementary and high schools, as well as on new methods of teacher education, awards for teaching excellence, and programs for women, minorities, and the handicapped.

In 1991 the U.S. National Academy of Sciences convened a National Summit on Mathematical Assessment to develop standards for math education. The National Council of Teachers of Mathematics has developed new curriculum and evaluation standards for school mathematics. Similar efforts are being made for science and other subjects in U.S. schools. The National Science Teachers' Association has developed a new course of study for Grades 7 to 12 that is being tested in a number of states. The American Association for the Advancement of Science, in its Project

2061, is developing alternative curriculum models to integrate science, math, and other key subjects. And the Natural Sciences Resources Center, a joint undertaking of the National Academy of Sciences and the Smithsonian Institution, is working with educators to develop teaching modules for science. The United States is also experimenting with changes in the school year and has a National Association for Year-Round Education, which predicts that by the year 2001 virtually all U.S. schools will operate on a year-round calendar. In 1992 the U.S. Secretary of Labor's Commission on Achieving Necessary Skills (SCANS) proposed sweeping changes in teaching methods through "applied learning," which would teach students to work in groups and to develop analytical and critical thinking skills.

Japan, which is widely regarded as having one of the world's most demanding school systems, also is planning major changes. It has established the Prime Minister's National Council on Educational Reform to overcome what the Japanese see as the limitations of their system of education — its excessive focus on memory work and competition for marks — and the problems of school bullying and violence, which are among the consequences of Japan's intensely competitive, conformist, and materialistic system. Professor Michio Okamato, chairman of the council, sees late-twentieth-century changes in Japan's educational system as the prerequisite of a twenty-first century in which, he says, "Japan would go out to meet the world." Japan's educational system will become more flexible and individualistic, but at the same time it will put more emphasis on science and languages as well as on university-level basic research.

One example is what the Japanese call *Seikatsuka* — a new approach that merges the teaching of science with social and environmental studies in elementary school. An OECD report on curriculum reform says that, overall, "a brave effort is being made to find a central place in the core for creativity, logical thinking, imagination, inspiration, motivation to learn, enjoyment of learning and pleasure of accomplishment in the face of the 'desolation' of contemporary Japanese education and society."[11] Japan has also created a Bureau of Lifelong Education to pursue reforms. This fits with the country's strategy of becoming an even richer knowledge-research economy as it transfers more of its assembly and production to overseas bases in Asia, North America, and Europe.

In fact, there is a strong effort throughout the industrial world to improve education, with the emphasis on an improved core curriculum and on standards and testing. From Italy, Sweden, and Switzerland to Germany, France, and Britain, educational systems are being re-evaluated and reformed in preparation for the knowledge-based economy of the twenty-first century. Britain, for example, has passed an Educational Reform Bill that enshrines "foundation" and "core" subjects in legislation. Core studies consist of English, mathematics, and science, while foundation studies include history, geography, art, music, technology, a second language for students when they reach the age of 12, and physical education. National tests in English, science, and mathematics have been made compulsory.

Developing countries, too, see education as the key to economic progress. For example, South Korea is investing heavily in education, especially in science and mathematics, as it moves into a high-technology economy. The South Koreans put strong emphasis on elementary and high school teacher training and provide scholarships for top teachers to study abroad as a form of recognition for those who excel. This helps to explain the high standing of Koreans in international science and math tests. Singapore and Taiwan also are putting strong emphasis on higher education; and in our hemisphere, Mexico, Brazil, and Argentina can be expected to follow suit.

These same imperatives exist in Canada. As the Economic Council has argued, Canada's success in a new economy based on information and knowledge depends on "its capacity to develop a first-rate work force; and that capacity must be put in place now."[12] In fact, our educational system — from preschool to graduate school — faces two imperatives. "The first is to ensure that basic levels of competency are universally held; all Canadians must have literacy and numeracy skills and, more generally, the analytical tools to 'navigate' in an information-based society," the council has warned. "The second imperative is to pursue a standard of excellence through the development of highly educated individuals."

If Canadians needed a lesson in the importance of education, the 1991 recession gave it. Statistics Canada reported that despite widespread layoffs and plant closings, "job opportunities remained bright in most white-collar occupations, especially those requiring at least some post-secondary education." But it added that "blue-collar jobs that needed fewer skills continued to be marginalized."[13] Canada's 1991 unemployment rate, which averaged 10.3 per cent, ranged from a low of 4.9 per cent for university graduates to a high of 15.4 per cent for those with less than nine years of schooling. Canadians with some high school education, including those with a high school diploma, had an unemployment rate of 12.6 per cent, those with some post-secondary education had an unemployment rate of 10.2 per cent, and those with a community college diploma or other post-secondary certificate had an unemployment rate of 8.2 per cent.

During the recession, as companies strove to raise productivity and lower costs in a more competitive world, there were clear implications for the type of worker they hired. "Broadly speaking," Statistics Canada said, "there was a direct correlation between employment changes and education levels in the past year — the more education and training, the better one's job prospects." In fact, while total employment declined in 1991, employment for Canadians with university degrees actually rose 4.1 per cent; the only other increase was a 3.8 per cent job gain for Canadians with some post-secondary education. Jobs for high school graduates fell 0.8 per cent, and jobs for those with less than a high school education fell 5.5 per cent.

TABLE 20			
Unemployment Rate According to Education Levels			
	1980	*1989*	*1991*
	(%)	*(%)*	*(%)*
Total	7.5	7.5	10.3
Less than 9 years	9.0	11.1	15.4
Some or complete high school	8.6	8.9	12.6
Some post-secondary	6.4	7.3	10.2
Post-secondary diploma, certificate	5.0	5.2	8.2
University degree	3.1	3.7	4.9

SOURCE: Statistics Canada, Labour Force Annual Averages, 11-220

TABLE 21
**Participation Rates of 17- and 21-year-olds in Formal Education
1987–88 School Year**

Country	Participation Rate	
	17-year-olds	*21-year-olds*
	(%)	*(%)*
Japan	89.3	n.a.
Germany	81.7	23.4
United States	89.0	29.8
Sweden	83.1	11.3
Switzerland	84.6	9.4
France	79.3	21.2
CANADA	75.7	26.1
Australia	74.3	n.a.
Britain	52.1	5.3

SOURCE: *Education in OECD Countries 1987–88* (Paris: OECD, 1991).

TABLE 22
Education and Jobs

	Age 16–54	*Labour Force*	*Jobs*	*Unemployed*
	(%)	*(%)*	*(%)*	*(%)*
Less than 9 years	14.4	7.3	6.9	10.9
Some high school	22.9	19.6	18.5	29.1
High school diploma	20.9	22.8	22.9	22.7
Some post-secondary	8.8	9.8	9.8	9.7
Post-secondary diploma, certificate	21.9	26.1	26.7	20.7
University degree	11.2	14.3	15.2	6.8
Total	100.0	100.0	100.0	100.0

SOURCE: Statistics Canada, Labour Force Annual Averages,1991, 11-220.

Fortunately, more young Canadians are getting the education message, as the figures from Statistics Canada show. In 1991, although the number of Canadians in the 15-to-24 age group declined by 25,000, university enrolment rose by about 35,000 in the fall of that year, and the total student population rose by about 100,000. In 1981, just 23 per cent of the Canadian workforce had a post-secondary certificate, diploma, or degree; by 1990, the figure was 40 per cent. In the 1989–90 school year, 16.7 per cent of Canadians in the 18-to-21 age group were enrolled in university, compared with 10.7 per cent a decade earlier, while another 11.6 per cent were enrolled in community colleges.[14] But not all the news is good. In 1986–87, only 76 per cent of 17-year-old Canadians were participating in a formal education or training program, compared with 89 per cent of Japanese and American, 85 per cent of Swiss, 83 per cent of Swedish, and 82 per cent of German 17-year-olds, according to the OECD.

Dave Gower, a StatsCan researcher, found further evidence of the importance of education in the job market when he divided all the main occupations in the booming 1989 economy into four groups, or quartiles. The first quartile, with the lowest unemployment rate at 3.9 per cent, consisted mainly of technical and professional occupations in management, health-care, engineering, and advanced skills. The fourth quartile, which consisted mainly of manual or low-education, low-skill jobs, had the highest unemployment rate: 14.0 per cent. Gower found that 42 per cent of the new jobs created between 1985 and 1990 were in the first quartile and that 60 per cent were in the first two quartiles. "Some occupations, particularly ones requiring high levels of education, continued to experience job growth even after the recession was in full swing," he discovered. "In most other occupations, however, employment dropped."[15]

In the new economy, our schools, colleges, and universities are far more important than our forests, mines, and oil wells. But we do not act as though we believe this. In the 1991 *World Competitiveness Report*, Canada ranked eleventh out of 23 nations in assessing whether the compulsory educational system met the demands of a competitive economy.[16] The front runners, not surprisingly, were Japan, Germany, and Switzerland. The same report indicated that Canada ranked fifteenth in the availability of skilled labour and ninth in the availability of skilled engineers. We spend more than $40 billion a year on our schools, colleges, and universities, and devote 6.2 per cent of our gross domestic product (GDP) to education, ranking fifth among OECD countries, behind the Scandinavian countries. On a per-student basis, we rank ninth. But our spending is not reflected in the quality of our workforce, in our ability to develop new industries, or in our productivity performance.

These pressures for better education will only intensify in the future. Employment and Immigration Canada estimates that 40 per cent of all new jobs between 1986 and 2000 will require 17 or more years of education and that another 17.4 per cent will require 13 to 16 years of education. Almost 60 per cent of all new jobs will require education beyond high school graduation, compared to 45 per cent of existing jobs in 1986. A high school education is no longer a ticket to a middle-class standard of living. Only 5.5 per cent of new jobs will be satisfied by a high school diploma alone, compared to 8.7 per cent of jobs in 1986. But the biggest threat from the new economy is

TABLE 23
What Countries Spend on Education

Country	% of GDP	Spending Per Student/GDP Per Capita (%)
Norway	7.2	31.4
Sweden	7.1	42.3
Denmark	7.0	34.0
Netherlands	6.5	28.4
CANADA	6.2	25.3
New Zealand	5.6	20.6
Austria	5.5	27.1
France	5.3	20.7
Britain	5.0	20.5
Switzerland	5.0	25.4
Italy	5.0	24.9
United States	4.8	19.3
Japan	4.7	21.4
Germany	4.1	19.9

SOURCE: Economic Council of Canada, *A Lot to Learn* (Ottawa: ECC, 1992).

to high school dropouts and immigrants with low skills. While 46.7 per cent of jobs in 1986 required less than a high school education, in 1986–2000 just 37.1 per cent of new jobs will be available with less than a high school education.[17]

Recent developments in the job market display trends that are likely to become even stronger in the future. Between 1984 and 1990, the number of Canadians with jobs increased by 1.6 million to 12.6 million. Almost half the new jobs were in managerial and professional occupations — managers and executives in industry and government, engineers and scientists, doctors and nurses, teachers and professors, economists and statisticians, artists and writers. While total employment increased 15 per cent, jobs in science, engineering, and mathematics increased 20 per cent and in managerial and administrative positions 40 per cent. According to Employment and Immigration Canada, in 1989–95 the fastest-growing occupations will include computer programmers and systems analysts, data-processing equipment operators, and technical salespersons, along with occupations in health care.[18] But as a study for the Chemical Institute of Canada warns, "as Canada moves into the 1990s, and unless changes are made, the country appears certain to run out of the skills it needs to succeed in the economic conditions of the 21st century." In its 1992 report on education, *A Lot to Learn,* the Economic Council came to much the same conclusion. "The performance of the education system in Canada is just not good enough to assure Canadians of an improving standard of living in coming decades," it said. "Overall, Canada seems to be accepting mediocrity as the norm, when it has the potential for excellence."

Our schools, colleges, and universities produce many excellent and even outstanding graduates, but too many graduates still lack the learning skills and the basic knowledge that will be needed in the workplace of the twenty-first century. At the same time, too many students are dropping out or are failing to pursue the scientific or technological skills that we need for an innovative economy. As the National Advisory Board on Science and Technology has observed, we are squandering the bottom one-third of the student population who drop out of school before graduation, and we are squandering the talents of the one-third at the top by not doing enough to raise their achievements.[19] While all members of the student population are important, our greatest educational challenge is to provide better education for the nearly two-thirds who have not been getting any post-secondary education, especially high school dropouts and low achievers. These are the Canadians who will be needed to operate the factory or office of the future. Consequently, the quality of high school education is of crucial importance.

The truth is that we cannot afford to waste any student. As the Economic Council of Canada warns in its report *Good Jobs, Bad Jobs,* "in the emerging economy, universal attainment of basic skills, the development of excellence through highly qualified personnel, and widespread access to retraining opportunities are becoming imperative. To meet the challenges of the global marketplace, Canada simply must be a world leader with respect to the quality of its workforce."[20] This means better education for all.

Yet we are still content, says Science Council chairperson Janet Halliwell, "to supply industry — and society as a whole — with a high school product of rather indifferent quality. We are spending billions on a secondary school system that produces as many dropouts as it does university entrants, and that even among its graduates includes a distressingly high proportion of functional illiterates and innumerates."[21] Moreover, Halliwell says, "we have the kinds of attitudes, policies and programs in the vital area of technological or technical training and apprenticeship — as well as in company workforce training and adult education generally — that you might expect to find in a less-developed country." No wonder she concluded that Canada seems to behave like "a semi-industrial state"!

To be a world leader in the quality of our workforce, we must reform the system from top to bottom. There is growing evidence that the preschool experience of children has a significant effect on their ability to cope and learn when they enter the school system, and this will lead to greater attention being given to preschool child care. Our school systems have to adapt to the information revolution, giving new priority to problem solving, critical thinking, how to analyse and synthesize, and how to communicate, as well as how to work in teams. Science and mathematics will have to have a much higher priority. And our schools will have to concentrate far more effort on the nearly one-third of students who drop out. For both economic and social reasons, says education expert George Papadopoulos, "in the 90s the quest for a more equal spreading of educational opportunities will reassert itself as a major goal." As well, "the criteria that establish quality will have to be more broadly defined than mere school achievement to consider the extent to which the education is relevant to the requirements of young people in preparing them to manage their personal lives and to function effectively in modern technology-permeated societies, not only as workers, but also as parents, citizens and in their other roles."[22]

Much of the debate on educational reform is focused on the need to have a core curriculum in the schools and to set standards of achievement, with tests to see how well students are actually performing. There are many different forces driving the reform movement in our school system. As well as widespread dissatisfaction with the skill levels and work attitudes of high school graduates, there is concern about the large number of high school dropouts, the demographic pressures of an aging society, the demands of technological change, and the intensification of global competition. Changing social and cultural forces are also important factors, according to an OECD report on curriculum reform.[23] These include a changing family structure, high divorce rates and a growing number of single parents, child poverty, the increased participation of women in the workplace, the demands of a more pluralistic or multicultural society, drugs, and the environment. What this means is that schools are being asked to cope with an array of social and economic problems. As Jo Oppenheimer writes, a substantial number of children and youths "are at risk because, in addition to mental health problems, they face poverty, abuse, broken families, use of drugs and alcohol, crime, pregnancy, sexually transmitted diseases, living on the street, discrimination, suicide and an array of school related problems."[24] The Quebec government has been forced to introduce a meals program in schools in low-income neighbourhoods because students are so malnourished that they are incapable of learning.

Television and part-time work are other factors affecting the school system and the achievement of students. In the 1991 science and math tests conducted by the International Assessment of Educational Progress, students who watched five hours or more of

TABLE 24

Annual Dropout Rate for Secondary School Students in Canada

Year	%
1978–79	38.0
1979–80	38.0
1980–81	36.2
1981–82	35.7
1982–83	33.1
1983–84	28.2
1984-85	29.3
1985–86	29.8
1986–87	30.4
1987–88	33.0

SOURCE: Education, Culture and Tourism Division, Statistics Canada. 1990. Quoted in "To Be Our Best: Learning for the Future," Corporate–Higher Education Forum, Montreal, 1990.

television each day scored 7 points lower on average than students who watched for one hour or less, and they scored 4 points lower than students who watched for between two and four hours. Similarly, students who had 25 or more books at home scored 8 points higher than students who had fewer than that. Students on average spend 900 hours a year in school and 1040 hours in front of a television set. In addition, they face pressure from the fast-food and other service industries to take part-time jobs. According to Statistics Canada, the number of full-time students in the 15-to-24 age group with part-time jobs rose from 31 per cent in 1980 to 39 per cent in 1990. One of the dangers in the debate on educational reform is a readiness to blame the schools for many of today's social and economic problems that originate beyond the schoolyard.

The "back to basics" or core curriculum movement is a reaction to the cafeteria-style approach that was introduced in the 1960s and is blamed for the disappointing skills levels of many high school graduates. However, it is also true that workplace requirements have changed enormously since the 1960s, so there is a risk of swinging too far the other way. As the OECD study on curriculum warns, "it is not clear how the national drive towards compulsory subjects and testing will avoid a stultifying rigidity in teaching and learning or achieve the flexibility, independence and adaptability sought in the modern workforce." Educational reform cannot become a nostalgic turning back to an idealized version of the little red schoolhouse that never was. Educational reform has to look to the future.

This is the challenge facing Canadians as we move towards national testing. The knowledge of 13- and 16-year-old Canadians in reading, writing, and mathematics will be tested in the 1993 School Achievement Indicators Program under the auspices of the Council of Ministers of Education. This is a controversial but important first step towards gaining a better understanding of the achievement levels of young Canadians and also to setting the stage for ongoing national testing.

Today's students and tomorrow's workers will, of course, need more math, science, and technology, as well as a broader understanding of world history, geography, and languages. They will also need to become better critical thinkers, problem solvers, team players, researchers, and information handlers. The danger is that in the rush to reform our schools, too much focus will be on "back to basics" and too little attention will be paid to the knowledge and skills needed for the twenty-first century or to devising how these can best be learned by the entire student body. As the OECD study observes, making learning successful for all students "remains one of the great unfinished tasks in education."

Nor does the rush to reform pay sufficient attention to other vital issues: teacher education, teacher support, teaching materials, the role and quality of vocational guidance and counselling, classroom and school organization, the school calendar and the length of the school year, the freedom for teachers to use their own judgement, the role of specialized or experimental schools and classes, and the increasingly powerful role for multimedia technology and distance-learning systems such as those developed in British Columbia and Ontario. In all these areas more research and more experimentation will be essential, as has been done in Alberta with respect to science education.

While the use of computers in the classroom has produced disappointing results so far, new multimedia technologies offer great potential for education, combining computer software, TV screens, video discs, teleconferencing, and other technologies. Lewis Perelman of the Hudson Institute in the United States contends that Nintendo and other video games may already be doing more to cultivate skills and challenge students for the Information Age than most classroom exercises do. "The first nation not to 'reform' its education and training institutions but to replace them with brand-new, high-tech electronic schools learning systems will be the dominant economic leader in the 21st century," he contends, in an exaggeration which nonetheless contains more than a grain of truth.[25] An important challenge for Canada as we move to greater use of information systems in our schools will be to make sure that Canadian teaching materials are available — just as we have had to fight for Canadian textbooks. Fortunately, there are some enterprising Canadian companies at the elementary and secondary school levels. But in May 1989, the only major producer of instructional software for community colleges and universities in Canada, the Manitoba Computer Assisted Learning Consortium, was forced to close its doors for lack of funding, even though it focused on Canadian content in a market which, as the Association of Colleges and Universities in Canada said, was "otherwise dominated by American sources."

However, "ensuring the continued supply of good-quality teaching staff may prove to be one of the major educational policy challenges of the 1990s," says education researcher David Istance. "Even maintaining existing numbers will, in some countries," require "recruitment rates significantly higher than those at present — at a time when good candidates are increasingly scarce, with emerging skill shortages in the labor market in general."[26]

Close to 20 per cent of all Canadian teachers are aged 50 or more, and about 50,000 will reach retirement age in the coming 10 years. Schools already face problems in hiring good science, technology, and math teachers, and the Chemical Institute of Canada warns that "major shortages of chemistry teachers are projected by the turn of the century." In a 1988 study for the Ontario government, for example, Laverne Smith of York University forecast a 20-year teacher shortage in the province, the most important shortages being teachers in intermediate- and senior-level mathematics, science, technology, and French. The problem is not confined to the schools.

Canada's universities also have rapidly aging faculties. In 1988 almost 20 per cent of the full-time professors were 55 or over and another 38 per cent were in the 45-to-54 age group. "Faculty shortages will be a very serious problem for Canadian universities over the course of the next decade," the Association of Universities and Colleges of Canada predicts. "Such shortages could threaten the quality of university education in Canada and our ability to compete effectively in the 21st century with other countries with knowledge-intensive industries."[27]

Our future economy also needs a totally new approach to skills training. The Swedish approach offers one model; the German apprenticeship system, which moves 16-year-olds from school to work, is another. What is clear is that Canada's muddled approach is failing the young people who want to pursue skilled trades but also want a good foundation in literacy, numeracy, and technology, and it is also failing industry, which needs skilled workers on the factory floor as much as it needs engineering, marketing, and financial skills in head office. As the Ontario Premier's Council concluded in a 1990 report on education and skills, Canada's apprenticeship system "serves as a classic study of our inability to adapt our training system to meet the changing needs of industry and the economy in general."[28]

The Canadian system waits until students have left school and drifted into the workplace, rather than providing them with an organized school-to-work transition. As a result, many apprentices are high school dropouts and the average age of apprentices is 26, which is late for apprenticeship training. In Germany, the average age is 17. Not surprisingly, nearly half of all the apprentices never complete their training. Despite the urgent need, there was virtually no increase in the number of engineering and applied science apprentices during the 1980s. The number of registered apprentices in engineering and applied sciences rose from 45,504 in 1985–86 to 46,973 in 1988–89, in a workforce of more than 13 million; and many of these apprentices would never complete their training. Yet now that the skilled workers who came to Canada from Europe in the 1950s and 1960s are approaching retirement, there is an urgent need to find new ways to train skilled workers through the schools and community colleges and through a new apprenticeship system.

Some school boards, in partnership with local business and labour, are already moving in this direction. But a much more comprehensive effort is needed to enable young Canadians to develop needed skills, to broaden the apprenticeship system to the service sector, and to bring the high school dropout rate down to about 10 per cent by the year 2000.

At the same time that the apprenticeship system was failing, enrolments in community college career programs in engineering and applied sciences also declined significantly, from 60,468 in 1985–86 to 48,578 in 1989–90; in computer science and mathematics enrolments fell from 15,731 to 11,982, and in electrical and electronic technologies they fell from 18,092 to 12,544. Either students were not getting the message about the new workplace or they believed that community college programs were not worthwhile. These are ominous signs if we want to develop modern manufacturing jobs based on advanced skills.

Canada also faces serious future shortages of scientists and engineers, who will be essential if Canada is to build the ideas-driven innovative economy of the twenty-first century. Enrolments by full-time undergraduate students in science and engineering are falling behind future needs. In 1985–86 there were 41,352 students enrolled in engineering courses in our universities, but by 1989–90 the number had declined to 35,849 despite warnings of impending shortages. In mathematics and physical sciences enrolments fell from 29,264 in 1985–86 to 24,831 in 1989–90; not even computer science, one of the hot areas for the future, was spared, for enrolments fell from 10,970 to 8031. Students also shunned fields such as chemistry, physics, and geology, all of which had declining enrolments, though the number of students in mathematics increased by just 50 in this five-year period, to 8889. Biology was the only area that showed any significant increase in student interest. While total full-time university undergraduate enrolments rose 10 per cent in the second half of the 1980s, enrolment in science, engineering, and mathematics declined 5 per cent.[29]

Just as critical is the fact that although there was an increase, during the 1980s, in the number of students at the graduate level in science and engineering — the source of future researchers for industry and government and the source of future professors — the

Association of Universities and Colleges warns that the number of graduating PhDs in natural sciences and engineering "will decline in the latter part of the 1990s unless universities are able to increase the retention of bachelor's students through to PhD graduation."[30] This will seriously impede Canada's efforts to build a science-based economy as industry, universities, and government research organizations compete for needed talent from a total pool that is too small.

The Canadian Council of Professional Engineers warns that Canada could be short of as many as 33,000 engineers by the year 2000. But as council president John McDougall told a parliamentary committee, "the shortfall we have projected of 33,000 obviously can never really happen. What it really means is that our economy will grow more slowly than has been predicted."[31] Without the engineers it needs, Canadian industry will not be able to make the technology investments and new product development that will enable it to be competitive, and the Canadian economy will suffer through fewer jobs and slower productivity growth. It is a problem that threatens the growth of many industries, from telecommunications and computer software to aerospace, biotechnology, and chemicals. The Chemical Institute of Canada, for example, has stated that future industry needs will far outstrip student enrolments in chemistry, chemical engineering, and chemistry technology programs. "The advent of new technology requires employees in development, production, service and even marketing to be more highly educated than ever before," says a report for the industry. "Take, for example, the materials field: as plastics supplement wood and paper, as fibre optics replace metal wire and cable, as ceramics as well as steel are used, the 'scientific' content of development and production is increased." And "as products and processes become more technologically complex, then marketing and customer support requires personnel with more sophisticated training." Yet the industry is pessimistic over its chances of finding the people it will need.[32]

And the software industry faces a similar problem. It relies mainly on universities for entry level employees. According to a federal study, "there are insufficient graduates to meet the demand. The number of graduates from software-related programs has not grown noticeably in recent years and is not expected to change significantly."[33] In fact, the federal study reported, "there was a 30 per cent drop in enrolment in university computer-science programs between 1983 and 1988." While enrolments have now levelled off, they have done so at 1988 and not 1983 levels. The same study also found that "a negative image" of software workers among high school students was also contributing to the inadequate number of students entering the software field. So in addition to a current shortage — made worse by U.S. companies such as Microsoft hiring away Canadian graduates to work in the United States — there could be an even worse shortage in the future. And a similar problem exists for in-house software workers, who are drawn mainly from community colleges; not enough students are enrolling in the necessary courses.

Robert Kavanagh of the Natural Sciences and Engineering Research Council (NSERC) has stated, in a major research study, that in fields such as industrial engineering, computer science, and mathematics, Canadian enrolment in graduate programs is "strikingly low" compared with U.S. enrolments. He warns that "if, as seems likely, the next decade is one of growth in the Canadian economy, the modest growth in engineering numbers seems quite inadequate to meet the needs of industry."And while higher U.S. enrolments may reflect higher U.S. industrial research and development, "the lower growth rate in Canada will result in Canada slipping even further behind the U.S.A. in this respect."[34]

Looking at other fields, Kavanagh makes clear that, at the graduate level, "Canada may experience a serious under-supply of computer scientists" as well as shortages of top researchers in forestry, geology, mathematics, and physical sciences. These shortages will make it that much more difficult for Canada to improve its international competitiveness through increases in industrial research and innovation.

"We have predicted that increasingly in the 1990s we will find the country as a whole in the position of being short of trained manpower, and I think this is the key issue," Arthur May, former president of NSERC, told a parliamentary committee in 1990. "You can produce researchers only by doing research and funding research in the universities. This is the only way they are produced. So the extent to which university research funding is tight, young people are not attracted to science and engineering graduate school and the country will be increasingly short of the people it needs to develop the research capacity in the private sector, to maintain the research capacity we have in the universities and in government labs. The demographic evidence and the enrolment evidence all indicate this is a growing problem."[35]

This is what led the National Advisory Board on Science and Technology to conclude that "the overall picture in science, engineering and technology is bleak, given the future Canada faces. If we are to catch up and remain competitive, consistent policies and programs are needed to encourage many more people and many more of the best and the brightest, especially among women, to pursue careers in science, engineering and technology."[36] In 1988 the federal government launched a five-year $80 million Canada Scholarship Program that will fund up to 10,000 top science and engineering students, half of them women. But although this will help, it is not enough.

The Royal Society of Canada has warned that Canada faces serious barriers to realizing its potential in the twenty-first century unless a major new effort is launched to raise the level of physical and social science, engineering, and humanities education and research. "A society which fails to provide adequate support for the next generation of scholars, or for the broad base of skilled and committed researchers who sustain and extend the general pursuit of knowledge and understanding is unlikely to produce many superstars in the future," it said in a 1991 report.[37] "There can be little doubt that the next few decades will see heavy demands placed on the research capabilities of government, industry and the Canadian university system, and since the leading researchers of the first few decades of the 21st century will emerge from among the graduate students of the 1990s, the importance of them receiving an education of the highest quality can scarcely be overestimated."

Both the Royal Society and the National Advisory Board on Science and Technology have urged that there be a major increase in funding for the granting councils that provide the financial support for graduate students in science, engineering, medicine, social sciences, and the humanities. While NSERC funding, for example, grew 65 per cent in after-inflation dollars between 1978–79 and 1984–85, it grew only 8 per cent between 1984–85 and 1990–91. As a result, only half of those applying for research support could get funding, and in many instances it was well below the levels requested. The situation was even worse for medical researchers (only 35 per cent of those applying were able to get support) and for social science and humanities researchers (only 12 per cent of the applicants could win support). The National Advisory Board on Science and Technology called on the federal government in 1988 to double the budgets of the granting councils immediately and to tie future increases to 1.5 times the rate of economic growth. This was what was needed, the panel of business and academic experts told the government, if Canadian universities — and the economy — were to be put at the leading edge of scientific and technological research. These calls for new priorities continue to be ignored.

The federal government's own discussion paper on education and training acknowledges that "Canada's learning performance is simply not good enough to prepare us for the future."[38] The paper urges Canadians to develop "a new learning culture" that will commit the country to lifelong learning in a world in which Canadians will face a continual need to upgrade, broaden, and diversify their workplace skills and knowledge. This will create new challenges and opportunities for our schools, colleges, and universities. But it will cost money. As the federal government's study points out, compared with many other countries, Canada underinvests in higher education and apprenticeship-type training. Yet this same federal government has imposed a five-year freeze on federal payments for post-secondary education and has severely limited the capacity of its granting councils — the Natural Sciences and Engineering Research Council, the Medical Research Council, and the Social Sciences and Humanities Research Council — to fund more graduate students in areas of study that are essential to Canada's future.

However, if we want to attract more Canadians into science and mathematics, we have to start with our elementary and secondary schools and with the investment we are prepared to make in teacher training and teaching materials. A Science Council of Canada survey in the early 1980s [39] found that more than half the teachers at all levels — elementary and secondary — who were teaching science had not taken a university course in science or mathematics for at least 10 years, if at all; and although about three-quarters of the science teachers said they were prepared to participate in workshops outside school hours to improve their knowledge and teaching skills, they had little support from school boards.

The results of international science and mathematics tests organized by the International Association for the Evaluation of Educational Attainment are not reassuring, suggesting that Canadian teaching methods and teaching skills may be inequate. The performance of 10- and 14-year-olds in science can be considered "satisfactory," but results at the senior level are "highly unsatisfactory," says Robert Crocker of Memorial University, who was one of the organizers of Canada's participation in the international tests. Students at the senior level achieved less than 50 per cent correct answers "on a test made up of items on the specific subject matter of courses they were just completing at the time of testing." If these had been final exams, more than half would have failed.[40]

In an analysis of disappointing international mathematics test results, David Robitaille of the University of British Columbia concluded that "a great deal of mathematics is being taught in Canadian schools by teachers who are ill-equipped for the task." Moreover, "the situation is likely to become much worse as the current teacher shortage worsens."[41] But simply imposing more tests and pursuing a "back to basics" crusade will not resolve the more fundamental problems of teacher education and new curriculum and teaching methods that will inspire students to learn.

Our colleges and universities, as well as our schools, face serious challenges in preparing Canada and Canadians for the twenty-first century. In the first place, they must confront critical funding problems. According to the Association of Colleges and Universities of Canada, on a per student basis, public spending on post-secondary education as a percentage of GDP is only about one-third that of Japan; and in the United States, public support of state universities per full-time student is also much higher than it is in Canada.[42] In his study on university education in Canada, Stuart Smith found that while universities had done a good job in responding to financial restraint, the undergraduate students, the libraries, and the physical infrastructure were bearing the brunt of the cutbacks. Smith's report showed that Ontario universities received $7726 in grants per full-time student while state universities in the United States received $9193 in state government grants per full-time student. At the same time, while Ontario universities received the equivalent of $1370 in federal research contracts, U.S. state universities received the equivalent of $2872 in federal contracts per full-time student. Ontario tuition fees also generated less revenue: $2060 per full-time student compared with $3638 in a typical state university. Overall, Ontario universities had total revenues per full-time student of $13,230, compared with $17,600 for a state university — so a U.S. state university had one-third more money per full-time student to invest in education and research.[43] The situation in other provinces is not much different.

Universities also face a critical shortage of new equipment and technologies both for advanced research and for the education of scientists and engineers. A 1990 study by the DPA Group of Vancouver concluded that "there is a significant lack of the type of equipment necessary to do competitive world-class research, and that this lack in Canada is now worse than it was in 1981."[44] Libraries also have deteriorated. According to a special report from the Royal Society of Canada, "the budgets of university libraries have been constrained to such an extent that even the largest collections no longer have any hope of keeping up with the production of essential new materials." The problem is compounded by Ottawa's decision to raise the cost of its statistical and other publications that were once available at little or no cost.[45]

In a blunt speech in the mid-1980s, Chief Justice Brian Dickson of the Supreme Court of Canada attacked the lack of funding for Canadian universities, describing the situation as "bordering on the tragic." He warned that "second-class funding of universities will inevitably lead to second-class teachers, second-class students and — ultimately — a second-class nation."[46] While higher student fees can provide some extra funding, more taxpayer and business support is also essential.

As we approach the next century, education at all levels must be our most important concern. To create the new goods and services that are necessary to replace old industries and to sustain our society, it is essential that we equip young Canadians with the knowledge, skills, and lifelong learning opportunities that can make innovation happen. As David Vice, then president of Northern Telecom Ltd., told a Canadian Senate hearing more than five years ago, "the capacity of a society to generate new ideas, to adapt to change, to innovate, to make the most effective use of its natural resources, and to improve its productivity and international competitiveness are all critically dependent on an educated population. Therefore, education should be viewed as a capital investment rather than a cost. It must be seen and financed as the engine of future growth and prosperity."[47] Vice told the senators that knowledge must be seen as the raw material of the information economy. "In such an economy, the schools and universities are as much the primary producers as the farm, the mine, or the fishery — and the productivity and quality of the school is perhaps more crucial at a time when the world competes on brainpower and technical knowledge."

Many Canadians understand this. But, as a country, we continue to fail our students without realizing that we are also failing ourselves and our prospects for the future.

7

Our Science and Technology Building Blocks

NO MODERN COUNTRY has a greater or more urgent need for a national technology program geared to the twenty-first century than Canada. Caught up in the waves of a global revolution in science and technology, Canada is in danger of floundering in the after-current while others ride the crest to future prosperity. Accelerating advances in computers and communications, semiconductors and software, biotechnology and new materials, based on constant investment in knowledge and ideas, are driving the new economy, not only in the rich nations of the industrial world, but increasingly in South Korea, Taiwan, and Singapore — as they will in the future in Mexico, Brazil, and Chile. The need for science, technology, and innovation applies as much to old industries, such as pulp and paper, steel, and food processing, as it does to computers, telecommunications, and other industries of the future. Yet among the nations of the world, Canada is adjusting badly to the innovation economy after more than a century of relying on natural resources to provide the wealth to support a modern economy.

Now, Canada is having to make up for lost time. The country's science and technology base is weak, which means that the foundations for future economic growth and prosperity also are weak. Canada has one of the lowest levels of R & D spending among industrial countries — 1.4 per cent of gross domestic product (GDP), compared with roughly double that level among its competitors —

TABLE 25	
Spending Per Capita on Research and Development*	
Britain	$323.00
CANADA	260.60
Denmark	223.60
Finland	270.60
France	342.00
Germany	431.40
Italy	173.20
Japan	439.60
Netherlands	297.20
Norway	304.10
Sweden	428.20
Switzerland	506.40
United States	582.20
*1989 current PPS dollars	

SOURCE: OECD/STIID Database (Paris: OECD, 1992).

and it also has one of the lowest levels of business spending on R & D. Another indicator of innovation is the pace of investment in new machinery and equipment; for the past 30 years, Canada has invested a smaller share of its GDP in new machinery and equipment than any other major industrial nation. Government-funded R & D, as a share of GDP, is also one of the lowest among industrial nations. As well, Canada is at or near the bottom of the list in the number of high-tech industries with a positive trade balance, the number of patents per capita, and the number of scientists and engineers per 1000 workers.

Although we have some able scientists and engineers, including two Nobel winners, and some highly enterprising and innovative companies, our overall performance in science, technology, and innovation is dismal. There are many explanations for this, ranging from a too-easy ability to create wealth by exploiting natural resources to a high level of foreign ownership, but the underlying problem is that science, technology, and innovation are not part of our political, business, or educational culture. For Canada to prosper in the twenty-first century, then, it has to undergo nothing less than a cultural revolution, raising science, technology, innovation, and the concept of an ideas-driven economy to the highest levels of policymaking. Canada has to invent new institutions for innovation; but in the process, if successful, it could achieve economic results that are beneficial to every part of the country.

Technology matters because Canada's ability to compete and export while maintaining a high standard of living, with secure, high-skill and high-pay jobs, depends on its ability to improve its productivity. This in turn depends on its ability to develop and use new technologies — whether in producing auto parts or processing fish, or designing a new business jet or cellular telephone. So technology is one of the critical factors in sustaining and raising real incomes of Canadians. Countries that are unable to innovate successfully and develop new technologies face declining wages and a declining standard of living; they become poorer.

"The need to change is imperative," a Canadian Manufacturers' Association strategy paper warned five years ago. Pointing to Canada's deficiencies in science and technology and its lack of capacity for innovation, the strategy paper warned that "Canada will become a Third World country by the end of this century if we continue to rely primarily on resources and fail to strengthen our ability to compete in technology."[1] Much the same warning was sounded by William Curlook, then the executive vice-president of Inco Ltd., who told a 1988 conference that without bold science and technology policies "we'll get plant shutdowns, economic downturn, economic deterioration, associated economic brain drain, until we get to become a Third World industrial power."[2]

In a detailed study of Canada's high-tech trade, two Economic Council of Canada economists, Sunder Magun and Someshwar Rao, found a growing trade deficit that was largely the result of a lack of investment in the R & D that is crucial to an economy based on innovation and ideas. Canada's poor performance, they argued, suggests "serious competitive problems for Canadian high-tech industries in the medium- to longer-term, unless Canada broadens and deepens its industrial base of high growth and emerging industries in a major way very soon." Most Canadian high-tech sectors lost significant market share in the 1971–86 period, and Canada failed to make any penetration of the Asian market. So the prospect for our high-tech trade "looks bleak and the technology gap between Canada and its major foreign competitors could further widen," the two economists warn, unless Canada changes its ways fast. "These problems will have a significant adverse impact on our future growth in productivity and living standards and our international competitiveness. Therefore, Canada needs to undertake a major review of its science and technology policies."[3] The Canadian Advanced Technology Association estimates Canada's high-tech trade deficit at $12 billion.

In a subsequent draft paper, Someshwar Rao, Farah Tcharkari, and Tony Lampriere of the Economic Council found that competitiveness had slipped so badly in about half of Canada's manufacturing industries that by 1985 "these industries were not price competitive even at 73 U.S. cents (per Canadian dollar) in that year."[4] In fact, it was the substantial deterioration of the past 25 years in Canadian cost competitiveness in relation to the United States that led to the sharp devaluation of the Canadian dollar between 1975 and 1985, a devaluation that was reversed by monetary policy, with harsh consequences for Canadian manufacturing, just at the time when barriers came down under the Canada–U.S. free trade agreement. Almost all manufacturing sectors in Canada have been facing difficult adjustment problems, which these economists predict will weaken the industrial base over time "unless Canada broadens and deepens the industrial base of high-growth and emerging industries in a major way and substantially improves its relative productivity performance." What is at stake, they warn, is "the sustainability of Canada's current high standing in the world economy over the medium to longer-term, measured in terms of per capita real income."

Moreover, they stress that the competitive pressures from the other G-7 countries (the United States, Japan, Germany, France, Italy, and Britain) and the Asian newly industrializing countries (South Korea, Taiwan, Hong Kong, and Singapore) can only intensify in the future. Therefore, the sustainability of Canada's high standard of living will critically depend on productivity performance in its manufacturing companies: "The fierce competitive challenge to

Canada from its trading partners could threaten its relative standing in the world economy, unless Canada moves up the value-added scale in a major way and substantially increases its market share of world technology- and skill-intensive manufactured exports."[5]

Similarly, a draft confidential discussion paper from the federal Department of Industry, Science and Technology in 1990 stressed that Canada's economic future depends on innovation and productivity; but it made clear that "the private sector on its own cannot fully realize the potential of the Canadian economy."[6] Summing up the dismal situation, the paper said that only 3 per cent of manufacturing firms had any research capability and that most had no staff capable of identifying or acquiring best-practice technologies; indeed, about 70 per cent did not employ a single engineer. Less than half of all Canadian manufacturing companies had taken up one or more of some 22 leading manufacturing technologies, and Canada placed twentieth out of 26 countries in the adoption of flexible manufacturing systems. Canadian management was a big part of the problem: "Traditionally, Canadian business culture is characterized as relatively risk-averse and parochial in outlook, not aggressive and well-informed in trade matters, limited in its understanding of science and technology and often too dependent on government." Looking to the harsh new demands of the global economy, the federal officials said that an "integrated, comprehensive strategy" on innovation was needed and that "decisive national leadership" was essential. But instead of this, Canadians got the so-called Prosperity Initiative, a federal consultative process — with the result that nearly two years later the federal government was still floundering in its efforts to provide the required leadership.

The discussion paper stressed that the federal government needed "as a matter of priority a series of mutually reinforcing policies and programs designed to bootstrap Canadian industry into the acquisition and adaptation of best practice technologies," as well as new initiatives to lever greater private-sector participation into R & D, perhaps through a civilian version of the U.S. Defense Advanced Research Projects Agency. As the paper observed, Canada's lack of "globally-oriented, technologically sophisticated management" was at the heart of the problem because this meant that business leadership was not demanding innovation.

An OECD study, *Technology in a Changing World,* had even more humiliating news for Canada. Looking at the R & D intensity of different countries, as measured by business spending on R & D as a proportion of GDP as well as by the growth in intensity, it divided countries into four categories: technological leaders, other high-tech countries, middle-tech countries, and low-tech countries. Canada found itself lumped with India and Mexico as a middle-tech country. The technological leaders were Germany, Japan, Sweden, Switzerland, the United States, and South Korea. The other high-tech countries were Belgium, Finland, France, the Netherlands, Norway, Taiwan, and Britain. The middle-tech countries, in addition to Canada, India, and Mexico, were Austria, Denmark, Ireland, and Italy. The low-tech countries were Argentina, Australia, Greece, Iceland, New Zealand, Portugal, Spain, Turkey, and Yugoslavia. While Canada's R & D intensity is increasing, "the gap with the 'new' technological leaders is widening, despite significant public R & D support over the most recent period," the OECD report said. Moreover, in terms of the relative competitive position of Canada

TABLE 26			
Research and Development as a Share of GDP			
	1971	*1981*	*1990*
	(%)	*(%)*	*(%)*
CANADA	1.36	1.23	1.37
Britain	2.10	2.41	2.25*
France	1.88	1.97	2.42
Germany	2.20	2.42	2.81
Italy	0.85	0.87	1.36
Japan	1.71	2.13	2.80*
Netherlands	2.06	2.32	2.17*
Sweden	1.49	2.30	2.76*
Switzerland	2.27	2.29	2.86*
United States	2.47	2.45	2.88
*1989			

SOURCE: OECD/STIID Database (Paris: OECD, 1992).

vis-à-vis the United States, the widening technology gap "could have negative implications in terms of future growth and international competitiveness."[7]

In one of the Economic Council of Canada's last reports before it was abolished in 1992 by the Mulroney government, it analysed Canada's poor science and technology performance and weak capacity for innovation. "One might expect Canada's resource-based manufacturing sector to be relatively research-intensive, given its importance to the Canadian economy," the Economic Council said. "That does not appear to be the case, however. For example, the R & D propensity of the resource-based manufacturing industries is only about 40 per cent of the average of the overall manufacturing sector. This situation contrasts sharply with that in smaller countries such as Sweden, which invest heavily in research in their key sectors (food-processing and pulp and paper). In Canada, there is no such commitment."[8]

A series of sector studies conducted for the federal government by the Science Council of Canada shows how critical technology, innovation, and research and development are to virtually every industry in the country. These same surveys show that for almost every one of the 15 industry sectors studied (telecommunications is an exception), Canadian industry is starting from behind and is ill-prepared for competition in a global economy that demands continual innovation. "Much of the Canadian economy has chosen to compete on the basis of cost, rather than innovation and quality," the Science Council noted.[9] But as developing countries move into a growing number of industry sectors, Canada will find it increasingly difficult to pursue a low-cost strategy; no matter how much Canadian wages are held down, Mexico, Brazil, South Korea, Taiwan, India, and China will always have a wage advantage. Moreover, a low-cost, low valued-added strategy will not generate the standard of living that Canadians aspire to; instead, it points to a future of diminished expectations.

The Science Council identified three innovation strategies pursued by Canadian companies: adopt and adapt, which means acquiring foreign technology and adapting it to Canadian needs; innovation, which means incrementally improving a winning technology to gain a greater share of the market or to maintain a competitive edge; and breakthrough, in which a company seeks to leap ahead of the competition. Most Canadian companies, the council said, pursued an adopt and adapt strategy, the main emphasis being on adoption; but since this strategy is easily copied, it provides only a short-lived advantage. Moreover, it requires a timely access to the technology of others, which cannot be assured, does not provide for integration into a clear vision of the market, and exposes companies to a fundamental threat to products from advanced technological change: "For a high-wage country, adopt/adapt strategies as the dominant technology strategies are becoming a high-risk approach."

Canadian companies should be pursuing innovation strategies. But because of problems with the availability of capital, a weak technology base, poor managerial skills, and high risk, a national technology policy is needed to create a climate of innovation. Canadian business tends to compete on the basis of low-cost production of commodity products, but the future economy will be driven by customer needs and global competition, and this will require a broader R & D profile, greater R & D investment, and greater emphasis on

TABLE 27

Business Spending on Research and Development as Share of GDP

	1985 (%)	1990 (%)
Britain	1.44	1.48*
CANADA	0.76	0.73
France	1.32	1.49
Germany	1.98	2.07
Italy	0.64	0.77
Japan	1.85	2.08*
Netherlands	1.18	1.28*
Sweden	1.96	1.83*
Switzerland	2.24	2.14*
United States	2.13	1.93

*1989

SOURCE: OECD Main Science and Technology Indicators 1991:2 (Paris: OECD, 1991).

marketing and management. The Science Council's 15 sector studies concluded that many of Canada's most important industries will face a bleak future unless they can shift to high-value activities based on R & D, continual innovation, and global marketing.

Canada's non-ferrous metals industry — which produces copper, aluminum, nickel, gold, lead, zinc, titanium, and all the other metallic minerals aside from iron — is one of the largest in the world, and Canada is the world's largest exporter of minerals. Yet while it has built up great technological skills in mineral exploration and development, along with extraction and smelting and refining, the industry is in trouble because it is not a leader in the downstream activities of advanced alloys and products and new materials. Future developments in ceramics and high-strength composites, for example, could have a devastating impact on Canadian metals companies. With growing competition from low-cost developing countries, Canadian metals producers have been losing their share of the market and, because of their lack of advanced products, have found themselves forced to compete on the basis of costs. Since Canada depends heavily on its mining and metals companies to provide jobs and to generate foreign exchange to pay for imports, a decline in the industry has serious implications.

The level of R & D in Canada's non-ferrous metals industry is "very low" compared with that in other countries. "At less than 1 per cent of sales, it is lower than virtually all Canada's competitors," noted the Science Council of Canada.[10] In fact, R & D spending by the industry declined during the 1980s, from just $86 million in 1981 to $72 million (in 1981 dollars) in 1988. In the same period, spending by Japanese metals companies rose from US$457 million in 1981 to US$813 million in 1988, or about 2 per cent of sales (compared with 0.8 per cent of sales by Canadian companies). One federal study of R & D as a per cent of mining GDP found that Canada's was the lowest of the eight countries studied: 0.5 per cent of mining GDP was spent on R & D, compared with more than 2 per cent for most of the other countries, which included Finland, Germany, Sweden, the United States, France, and Britain.

Because of the abundant worldwide resources and the lower-cost offshore resources, as well as weak growth in demand, Canada's non-ferrous metals industry will face a lacklustre future unless it

TABLE 28
Business Share of Research and Development Performed

	1971 (%)	1981 (%)	1990 (%)
Britain	—	61.8	65.9
CANADA	35.2	48.7	53.6
France	56.2	58.9	61.6
Germany	63.7	70.2	73.5
Italy	55.9	56.4	57.1
Japan	64.7	66.0	74.3*
Sweden	66.5	63.7	65.9*
Switzerland	79.0	74.2	74.8
United States	65.9	70.3	69.1

*1989

Source: OECD/STIID Database (Paris: OECD, 1992).

moves to new and advanced materials — especially when there is increasing demand for high-value products and growing substitution. Japan, in contrast, has recognized the need for high-value finished products. "In fact, the downstream end of the non-ferrous metals sector is increasingly dominated by Japanese metals companies. Japan has few mineral resources, but has a huge domestic market for metals products," according to the Science Council. And despite its lack of mineral resources, "Japan is as significant a producer as Canada." But it has a deliberate strategy to develop high-value products in order to reduce its vulnerability to swings in commodity prices. This is why Japanese companies have substantially increased their R & D.

The Science Council of Canada quoted a manager from Mitsubishi Metals as saying that although conventional business operations accounted for 50 per cent of total revenues, they received only 10 per cent of the R & D budget. "The other 90 per cent goes to new areas, mainly new materials and new product development." Japan is by no means alone in taking this approach. Outokumpu Oy of Finland is aggressively moving into downstream activities.

Driving this activity is the fact that the demand for metals is changing, with growing competition from plastics, composites, fibres, and other new materials, and there are increasingly stringent demands from manufacturers for higher quality or more specialized metals. Yet Canadian companies tend to be specialized commodity producers — Inco and nickel, Alcan and aluminum — and they tend to focus on upstream activities. In fact, Canada runs a trade deficit in semi-fabricated metals. "Japan's success in the non-ferrous metals sector suggests, however, that the real challenge North American companies face is to develop a business and technology strategy that emphasizes advanced materials and new products, not the production of commodities."

Canada's mining companies do deserve credit for their achievements in exploration, development, and extraction technologies. These activities are heavily high-tech today, using robots, sensors, and computerized systems. Inco now needs one-third of the labour it needed 20 years ago to operate its mines and process control system. But "there is a serious question whether the sector can be sustained at any significant scale over the next decade in Canada by maintaining a primarily upstream strategy. The strong likelihood is that pressures will drive increasing investment in mining operations and competencies overseas." But "the downstream path will require some significant capital investments, mergers and acquisitions, imaginative R & D, strong leadership and a concerted effort by all levels of government to provide a supportive policy environment. A strong sense of urgency should permeate the national debate and discussion as to how to support and sustain those firms taking this path, if the sector is to survive profitably over the next 10 years."[11]

The Canadian steel industry faces an equally difficult future, the Science Council said. With heavy losses in the 1991-92 recession, it has to compete against a rejuvenated U.S. steel industry (partly through investments by Japanese steel producers) as well as formidable competition from Japan, Europe, South Korea and, in the future, developing countries such as Brazil and perhaps China. Canadian steel producers have concentrated on commodity steel instead of developing high-value specialty products, and this makes them especially vulnerable to a rising Canadian dollar and rising wages. "Canadian steel firms have followed a strategy of technology purchase, supported by limited R & D for minor adaptations and improvements," the Science Council said.[12]

The industry is being hit by the downsizing of automobiles and the switch to other materials, such as plastics and aluminum. The role of new materials could affect many traditional steel applications in the future. This is why more than 50 per cent of R & D spending by Japanese steel companies, which are the most technologically advanced in the world, is going into new materials. Nippon Steel spends more on R & D than the entire U.S. steel industry, and it plans to reduce steel to less than half its business by 1995. Kawasaki Steel will reduce steel to 60 per cent of its business by the year 2000, and by that same year Kobe Steel plans to be a "comprehensive materials producer." While Japanese steel companies spend 1.5 per cent of sales on R & D, Canadian steel companies spend 0.25 per cent. The South Koreans invest 0.87 per cent of sales, the Germans 0.67 per cent, the British 0.57 per cent, and the American industry 0.42 per cent of sales. Canadian companies have had a short-term outlook on R & D: "It has been regarded as expendable when company fortunes decline, rather than as an investment in the future of the company."

Because of poor finances and lack of technological expertise, the Canadian steel industry is in a weak position as it looks towards the next century. "The Canadian integrated steel companies know they can no longer afford to cater only to traditional, declining markets, if they are to survive without being subject to foreign takeover," the Science Council warned. Unlike the Japanese companies, which use steel profits to finance R & D in new materials, Canadian companies lack the profits to follow that strategy. "If the Canadian steel industry is to raise its level of performance of R & D it will almost certainly require large partners or substantial support from government funding. The industry, which lacks the financial resources to make any significant attempt to develop leapfrog technologies on its own, must enhance its chances for government support and other private sector funding by trying to establish a strong R & D proposal bringing together many suppliers, customers, universities, and perhaps even governments, in a major consortia."[13] In fact, "unless they merge or joint venture, possibly with other Canadian materials companies and/or selected end users of steel such as auto parts manufacturers and construction companies" Canadian companies will face few opportunities for twenty-first-century technology. Both Stelco and Dofasco are depending on Japanese technology and Japanese capital to build new plants to supply the auto industry.

The Canadian forest-products industry, by far the largest source of Canada's trade surplus ($21 billion in 1990), also faces a daunting future, according to the Science Council. The industry's success in Canada — from lumber to pulp and paper — has depended on access to high-quality forests, cheap electricity, and investment in imported technology." But new competitors are expanding, especially in Oceania and Latin America, taking advantage of low-cost, high-quality, and plantation-grown fibres, as well as a much shorter growing period for replacement trees (7–10 years compared with 50–70 years in Canada). At the same time, recycling requirements have "potentially serious implications, accelerating the loss of Canadian market share in North American and European newsprint" and "further threatening the survival of many small papermaking towns."[14] Moreover, the fast-growing segments of the market require greater technological expertise and R & D, the areas of greatest Canadian weakness. In addition, the industry must invest heavily to meet environmental standards.

The forest-products industry has invested little in R & D, spending less than 0.5 per cent of sales, compared with about 1 per cent by major U.S., European, and Japanese companies. For the most part, Canada's forest industry "has focused primarily on producing commodities rather than higher value-added products, whose development tends to be more research intensive." Moreover, since many Canadian forest companies are foreign-owned, their major R & D efforts are based outside Canada.

Yet Canadian-owned companies, too, have failed to pursue technological innovation. "It is extraordinary," said the Science Council report," that in a sector on which so much of Canada's creation of wealth depends, only two forest-product firms conduct in-house R & D on solid-wood products," despite the great potential in the light industrial and commercial construction markets in North America. One exception is MacMillan Bloedel, which spent $150 million over 20 years to develop Parallam, a composite wood product that is three times as strong as natural wood and competes with construction steel and concrete beams. Forintek, a government-industry research institute, is also a source of innovation, although it depends heavily on government rather than industry funding.

In the pulp and paper industry, Canadian companies spend 0.3 per cent of sales on R & D, compared with 1.25 per cent in the United States and 1.35 per cent in Sweden. Moreover, the Science Council said, "cutbacks in R & D by several Canadian firms during the recession of the past two years are of concern, particularly because it takes time to build good research teams and because of the need for innovation." As a result of the lack of investment in people, Canada's forest industry is further handicapped: "European forest-products firms have better-trained people throughout their organizations. There are more graduates in line management, and senior hourly and operating personnel have more formal training, such as a two-year diploma in pulp and paper. The result is that Canada's technical competence lags behind that of Sweden, Finland, Norway and Germany."[15]

R & D trends in the Canadian forest-products industry are "profoundly disturbing." For example, the industry reduced in-house R & D staff from 600 people in 1980 to only 500 in 1990. While Canadian forest scientists have show that they are capable of highly creative work, commercialization is poor, "due in part to the lack of a vibrant machinery-manufacturing sector in Canada." Canadian forest companies import technology from foreign companies, especially Scandinavian companies, and it is the equipment suppliers who do much of the R & D. Yet Canadian companies, the Science Council stressed, "will require greater technological capabilities and more proprietary R & D" as the world market demands wood and paper products that are of higher quality and more customized. Thus, Canada can no longer remain competitive by buying technology from other countries. This gives no competitive advantage. Yet "such an advantage will be needed to develop new markets, especially in the Pacific Rim and Europe, and to make inroads into new North American markets for higher value-added wood products."[16]

The Canadian auto parts industry is another that faces a vulnerable future, according to the Science Council. Its fortunes are closely linked to the U.S. Big Three automakers, and as the Big Three lose market share to Japanese companies, the Canadian parts producers face declining prospects. The Japanese transplant manufacturers in Canada and the United States have not helped, because they allocate only 12 per cent of component purchasing to independent domestic parts producers, compared with the 45 per cent allocated by the Big Three U.S. automakers. In addition, developing countries such as Mexico, Brazil, and Taiwan are a growing source of competition.

As a result of these competitive forces — especially the lean production structure developed by the Japanese auto industry — the auto parts industry is restructuring into three tiers. Only tier-1 companies will supply the auto assemblers, and they will supply complete assemblies such as door assemblies and air-conditioning systems; tier-2 parts companies supply subassemblies to tier-1 companies, such as seat rails and window-winder mechanisms; and tier-3 companies supply parts of subassemblies produced by tier-2 companies, such as metal stampings and moulded plastic parts. One implication of this new system is that there will be far fewer parts companies; another is that the companies that survive will have to have the technology and financial strength to conduct R & D for the automakers; General Motors, for example, says that its suppliers must spend 1 per cent of sales on R & D.

Yet few Canadian auto parts companies conduct R & D or design the parts they produce; R & D spending as a percentage of sales remains low in Canada compared with that in the United States and other auto-producing countries. As a result of the Canada–U.S. auto pact, "control over the Canadian parts industry became centralized in the United States, just as had occurred with vehicle assembly. Research, design, and development activities, and key production decisions in Canadian branch plants of multinational parts firms were taken over by the parent firm. Essentially, the Canadian branch plants became solely production-line facilities," the Science Council concluded.[17] But since 1970, Canadian ownership in the parts industry has grown from just 4 per cent to nearly 20 per cent, led by companies such as Magna International, A.G. Simpson, and the Woodbridge Group. Nonetheless, Canada tends to focus on low-end, labour-intensive parts and in 1990 ran a $6.4 billion parts deficit with the United States (and a surplus of $8.2 billion in assembling vehicles).

Canadian auto parts companies have largely been unsuccessful in gaining sales to Japanese auto plants in North America or in exporting outside North America. This is not surprising, the Science Council said, because Canadian parts companies lack the necessary "innovative engineering capability." Their high level of foreign ownership is one reason. In 1986, for example, Canadian-owned auto parts companies accounted for 6 per cent of all auto industry shipments, including assembled autos, but for 46 per cent of auto industry R & D. "The lack of R & D in the Canadian parts sector adversely affects prospects for competitiveness" since the big auto companies are demanding technological and innovation capabilities. Most Canadian auto parts companies import foreign machinery that is as close to state-of-the-art as possible and rely on lower Canadian labour costs (resulting in part from Canada's public health-care system) to compete — a strategy that the restructuring of the industry calls into question. If production costs rise, multinationals can pull out of Canada and go to the southern U.S. states or to Mexico. "In general, very few Canadian parts firms — perhaps only about 2 per cent — have a technology strategy of innovation, using either proprietary technology or manufacturing processes as a basis for differentiation." However, the most successful Canadian companies have relied on innovation for their rapid growth.

In the new competitive environment, the Science Council said, "Canadian firms not only have to reach world-class technological capability, but they also have to demonstrate that they can sustain it over the long term." Unfortunately, there are few Canadian parts companies that qualify as tier-1 suppliers; this means that unless Canada develops more large tier-1 companies, the tier-2 and tier-3 parts companies in Canada will have to establish links with tier-1 companies in the United States, and perhaps even Japan, if they are to survive. In this case, they might find it more attractive to move to the United States so that they would be closer to their customers. To develop tier-1 companies in Canada, supporting strong tier-2 and tier-3 companies, is an enormous challenge, said the Science Council: "It is legitimate to wonder where the money will come from in Canada to pay for the involvement of suppliers in R & D, for increased capital spending, so that suppliers can accommodate increased business caused by fewer parts companies selling to the auto companies, for robots, for training, for communications, and for Computer-Assisted-Design/Computer-Assisted-Manufacturing equipment. It is unlikely that internally generated funds will be sufficient, and the cost of capital for many companies is too high to justify their required short-term returns on investment."[18]

The non-electrical machinery industry — which supplies a wide variety of machinery, ranging from forestry and metalworking equipment to moulding machines, machine tools for the tool and die industry, and agricultural machinery — is one of Canada's weakest industries, despite the presence of a small number of creative and entrepreneurial firms, reported the Science Council.[19] Canada runs a major trade deficit in machinery, and most Canadian companies are small and unable to undertake "significant R & D." Moreover, "Canada's strong development of resource industries has not led to the development of a significant related machinery industry." Massey-Ferguson (now Varity), once the leading Canadian farm machinery manufacturer, operated on a global scale, but it collapsed because of "indifferent management and missed opportunities," including a lack of R & D and a consequent failure to develop new products. At the same time, "high levels of foreign ownership in key customer segments, such as petrochemicals, automotive, and manufacturing, means purchasing decisions are made by foreign head offices, effectively downsizing an already small domestic market."

Canada's weak position in machine tools "has contributed to the limited scale of domestic machinery manufacturing," said the Science Council. "Machine tools, particularly advanced flexible manufacturing systems, are a critical part of most machinery manufacturing processes," and the lack of a machinery industry means that imports supply 71 per cent of the non-electrical machinery sold in Canada. Canada does have some "threshold firms" — Husky Injection Moulding, Hymac, Timberjack (Finnish-owned), Harricana, Groupe Denis, and CAE Machinery Ltd. — which invest an average of 3.4 per cent of sales in R & D; but foreign-owned subsidiaries account for 53 per cent of machinery sales in Canada, and they spend 1.6 per cent of sales on R & D, compared with an average of 3.6 per cent spent by their parents.

In non-electrical machinery, Canadian companies spend 1 per cent of sales on R & D; this compares with 2.6 per cent that is spent in Germany, 1.7 per cent in Japan, 1.5 per cent in the United States, and 3.3 per cent in Sweden. Adjusted for inflation, Canadian R & D spending actually declined 25 per cent in the 1980s.

One reason for the industry's weakness, the Science Council said, is that "the lack of strong links, in particular, between resource companies and resource-based machinery companies has almost certainly had an adverse impact on both groups of sectors. The synergy between a vibrant domestic machinery manufacturer and, say, the pulp and paper sector is still missing, to the detriment of both." Moreover, Canadian firms are generally too small to undertake global marketing programs. "They lack the scale, visibility and R & D support of more high technology firms in sectors such as telecommunications."

The best growth prospects for Canadian machinery firms, the Science Council study says, are in specialized machinery, most of which must be exported to be viable for development in Canada. But Canadian companies lack the money and skilled people (especially experienced engineers, managers, and skilled machinists) for R & D, as well as lacking the resources to market globally. Since Canada is so dependent on machinery imports — with all the balance of payments implications — this may be one area in which the government should act directly "to obviate a major structural weakness in the economy," the Science Council said, though this in effect would mean starting a sector "from scratch."

There is also a problem with Canada's petrochemical industry, which is heavily locked into commodity chemicals that compete on price alone, rather than moving into specialty chemicals that are based on high levels of R & D and compete on the basis of the functions they perform and their reliability. The problem is that Canada has "limited unique product or process technology with which to exploit opportunities in specialty chemicals," the Science Council said.[20] As in steel and non-ferrous metals, Japanese chemical companies are targeting higher value-added products, and they may use Mexico as a platform to produce high-performance plastics for the auto, aerospace, and other industries in Canada and the United States. "The great danger for Canadian and U.S. firms in any major expansion of Japanese technological innovation is clear. That is, the whole of the North American petrochemical industry — and the United States is as vulnerable here as Canada — could be overtaken by Japan's new technology in much the same way as was the North American iron and steel industry."

As a result of a highly targeted industrial strategy by its provincial government, Alberta now accounts for more than one-half of Canada's petrochemical capacity. The next largest centre is Ontario, and a smaller part of the industry is in Quebec. But the Canadian petrochemical industry does not have a "total systems capability" of its own; it exists as a "rationalized segment of a North American industry." The only Canadian petrochemical multinational, Polysar, was broken up during a hostile takeover by NOVA Corporation, and a large part of its business was sold off to Bayer, the giant German chemical company. R & D spending by Canadian chemical companies is low (about 1 per cent of sales) compared with a range of 2–7 per cent among the large U.S. chemical companies. And Canadian companies pay $50 million a year in royalties and related fees to foreign companies for technology (which is about 41 per cent of their R & D spending). Canadian companies focus on the commodity market by accessing the latest technology and process improvements from foreign parents. "But Canada is left without the technology base on which to build broader innovation and remains dependent on external technology," said the Science Council.

Dominated by Northern Telecom and its related Bell-Northern Research, the Canadian telecommunications industry is the only high-technology sector in which Canada has been able to achieve clear international success. In 1987, Canadian telecommunications companies spent 16.9 per cent of revenues on R & D, well above the international benchmark of 11 per cent, with Northern Telecom and Bell-Northern together accounting for about 80 per cent of the spending.[21] But because of accelerating advances in digital communications, fibre optics transmission, cellular communications systems, and software systems, companies will be forced to invest heavily to remain competitive in an era of intensifying competition. Much of the future growth in markets will take place outside Canada, but "as yet, many Canadian suppliers have limited exposure abroad," the Science Council warned. The same is true for service providers; for example, while companies such as British Telecom and AT & T are moving abroad, Canadian phone companies have almost no international presence. "If British Telecom is correct in forecasting fewer service providers, the Canadian service providers, unless they establish international networks soon, may well be placing themselves in a tenuous position."

Much of Canada's future potential rides on Northern Telecom's success; but fears, whether well-founded or not, that the company may shift its home base to the United States — relocating management decision making, R & D, global marketing, and manufacturing south of the border — raise uncertainty over Canada's future technology capacity. According to the Science Council, Northern has employed a strategy of "innovation" rather than "breakthrough," investing in a technology only when it believes the technology is mature enough to be developed rapidly into new products and services that can quickly be marketed — a strategy that has worked well in digital switches and fibre optics. Nevertheless, "Northern is still vulnerable to the effects of fundamental breakthroughs in core technologies by competitors able to invest far more than Northern itself in basic research." For the smaller Canadian telecommunications hardware and software suppliers, the challenge is even more awesome.

"In the years ahead, Canadian companies will face the challenge of new technologies being developed elsewhere; they will have to learn to deal with the subsequent effects on the telecommunications industry," the Science Council warned. "These new technologies may come from different countries or different industries. The fact that Japanese companies are investing heavily in photonic computer technology, for example, should mean the development of much faster switching than is available using current electronic technology. Unfortunately, Canadian firms by themselves do not have sufficient funds to invest in the basic research needed to develop such 'breakthrough' technologies, photonic or otherwise. Moreover, as R & D in telecommunications becomes more sophisticated, enormous investments will be required to achieve a major technological advance or 'breakthrough.' Thus substantial market entry barriers will be erected and only large firms will be able to meet the demand for resources."[22] This will put strains even on a Northern Telecom which, while big by world standards, ranks number five among the world's suppliers of telecommunications equipment (the leaders are AT & T of the United States, Siemens of Germany, Alcatel of France, and NEC of Japan; Sweden's L. M. Ericsson ranks just behind Northern Telecom).

Canada's greatest challenge, however, is in the telecommunications services sector. "If Canada's equipment industry is to achieve its growth targets, it will need a dynamic service sector from which to launch new products into the international marketplace," the Science Council said, arguing for deregulation and expanded opportunities for new services. This also means that, because of Canada's small market size, it must become a much greater exporter of telecommunications services. At present, the services of Canadian phone companies (aside from Bell Canada's role in providing some cellular phone services in Mexico) are largely confined to Canada because of Bell Canada's failure to win in competing bids for phone companies in Mexico and Venezuela.

As this survey of some of our most important sectors of industry shows, Canada faces a formidable task in bringing its technological capabilities to a level that will yield new competitive advantages in the global economy. Since the service sector represents more than 70 per cent of jobs in the economy, it is tempting to dismiss the role of manufacturing. This would be a costly mistake, because it is hard to visualize how Canada could sustain its standard of living without a competitive manufacturing industry. While manufacturing's share of employment has declined in Canada over the past 30 years — and will likely decline over the next 30 — this is mainly because of productivity gains from new manufacturing technologies and a more highly skilled workforce. As a result, manufacturing value-added in the economy is greater than its share of employment. In addition, many functions previously performed within manufacturing companies are now contracted out to the services sector.

Today, manufacturing generates much of the demand for business and other services, such as transportation, power utilities, communications, financial services, computer software and services, engineering, management consulting, advertising, and marketing. Without a domestic manufacturing industry, Canada's service sector would be much smaller and less competitive, lacking the opportunity to develop skills at home that it can sell abroad. Manufacturing is also important because of its continued capacity for productivity gains, which until now have exceeded productivity gains in the service sector. Finally, manufacturing matters because a declining manufacturing sector would increase Canadian manufactured imports and Canada's chronic balance of payments deficit. In fact, a more efficient and technologically advanced manufacturing sector offers Canadians the best hope of breaking out of a growing foreign debt by generating bigger trade surpluses.

Canada's technology policy for the twenty-first century must therefore be ambitious in its goals, and it must set ambitious targets for the country. Perhaps the single most important target is to raise the annual investment in R & D from 1.4 per cent of GDP today to 2.5 per cent by the year 2005, with an interim target of 1.9 per cent (still well below that of most other industrial countries) by the year 2000, as the House of Commons Committee on Industry, Science and Technology suggested in 1991. The federal government has dismissed these targets as being "of questionable relevance," and there are indeed limitations to such targets. But the government's resistance can probably be attributed to its own mediocre performance in developing Canadian science and technology. Whatever the limitations, this approach is, as the Economic Council has argued, "a good proxy for innovation," and setting a national R & D target would given Canada something to aim for as well as providing a reference point for measuring progress. At the same time, the federal government should be required to present a science and technology budget, on a revolving five-year cycle, at the same time as it brings down the spending estimates each year — just as the United States does with its budget.

To build an ideas-driven economy, Canada also needs to create new institutions that will help to create and encourage the consensus and debate for innovation policies. The National Advisory Board on Science and Technology (NABST) was established by the prime minister in 1987, modelled on a Japanese institution chaired by the prime minister of Japan, and on the Premier's Council in Ontario. But despite ambitious plans for Prime Minister Brian Mulroney to chair its meetings, he has averaged fewer than two meetings a year with his advisers.[23] Moreover, in spite of the production of detailed reports on almost every aspect of science and technology policy, the advisory board has had only modest impact. More recently, the federal cabinet turned down a proposal from the House of Commons Committee on Industry, Science and Technology to have the NABST reports referred to the committee for public discussion. At the same time, the federal government in its 1992 budget abolished Canada's two main research institutes that study policy issues affecting science, technology, and innovation, the Science Council of Canada and the Economic Council of Canada.

A future government should create a new institution, based on the experience of the Science and Economic councils, to make sure that the Canadian public has access to independent research and ideas affecting the country's future and to provide an annual report on competitiveness and technology policy — and this institution should be at arm's length from government and therefore beyond the reach of vindictive civil servants and politicians. As two U.S. experts, David Mowery and Nathan Rosenberg, point out, investment in research is not enough. Institutional structure matters too. It "heavily influences the ability of nations to realize the economic payoffs from research. Not only does the structure of institutions matter, but their historical development affects innovative performance."[24]

While Canada can rightly claim that it has one of the most generous R & D tax-incentive systems in the industrial world (though its value was reduced in 1987 tax "reforms"), there are several deficiencies in it. One of the most serious is the narrow definition of R & D that qualifies for the incentives. Although companies face enormous paperwork, together with delays in winning approval for qualifying spending, the regulations exclude many of the necessary expenditures that companies must make to bring a product from initial R & D to market. Some experts have suggested that the incentive should be extended through almost all of the innovation cycle, since the R & D stage represents a relatively small part of the cycle. The Economic Council estimated that applied research represents just 6 per cent of the costs of innovation. The biggest shares (35 per cent and 49 per cent) come from prototype or pilot plant costs and from tooling and manufacturing equipment and new facilities.[25]

At the same time, relying largely on tax incentives for R & D means that investment will be attracted only to areas that already have the best chances of payoff, and there will be underinvestment in high-risk areas of innovative, leading-edge projects which the market does not see as being quickly profitable, says U.S. expert Kenneth Flamm.[26] While tax incentives move market forces, the need is to move beyond market forces and beyond projects where profit is almost assured. A more recent review of U.S. technology policy came to much the same conclusion. Calling for greater funding for precommercial R & D and technology adoption, the study, headed by former U.S. secretary of defence, Harold Brown, said, "A reliance on broad tax measures to stimulate investment in R & D, although helpful, is insufficient in the absence of other measures to meet the needs of improving U.S. performance in technology."[27] A mechanism that brings greater selectivity to channel R & D resources to socially and economically beneficial projects (where the investment yields benefits to a larger group of users) is also essential. For Canada, this is an even greater concern. A 1989 study by the Canadian Manufacturers' Association found that in the United States government grants and other forms of non-tax support amounted to 35 per cent of industrial R & D, while in Canada it was only 12 per cent.[28]

If Canada is to develop an innovative economy, government will have to play a much more ambitious role as facilitator or catalyst by creating new institutions to increase R & D and to stimulate innovation. One of Canada's most urgent needs is to accelerate precompetitive R & D that links the technologies of the future with many of Canada's resource and other mature industries. There are potential linkages between biotechnology and the forest, food, mining, and chemical industries; between microelectronics and the auto parts, telecommunications, machinery, and appliance industries; and between new materials and the auto and auto parts industries. A small start has been made in the semiconductor or microelectronics sector. But a more comprehensive approach is needed. A Canadian Technology Corporation, funded by government at $1 billion over a five-year period, could underwrite half the costs of precompetitive R & D projects and promote a more rapid rate of technology development in Canada. Operating at arm's length from government and with an independent board of directors, so that it could not be used as a political pork barrel, it would participate in industry-driven projects, based on clear economic and scientific analysis.

Its role would be to lever private-sector money into pursuing major R & D projects which are of clear benefit to the Canadian economy but which industry, on its own, would not undertake because of the high risk. This would force companies to work together at the precompetitive stage of R & D without sacrificing competition after commercialization. As two U.S. experts, David Mowery and Nathan Rosenberg, argue, "the Japanese example suggests that cooperation among firms in pre-commercial research can support the diffusion of knowledge among participant firms and facilitate their utilization of such knowledge in competitive development of new product and processes. Precompetitive research cooperation is not only compatible with but also in all likelihood intensifies interfirm competition in commercial product markets." [29]

If Canada is serious about building a new economy based on ideas and knowledge, then other institutions will also be needed. One of these is a risk-sharing agency to help individual companies commercialize risky new products. An embryo of such a program already exists in Ottawa under the out-of-date name of the Defence Industry Productivity Program. It provides risk capital, mainly to companies in the aerospace industry, which is repayable along with royalties on successful projects. This program could be renamed, say, the Canadian Industry Program, and extended to assist all manufacturing sectors as well as the software industry.

An effective technology policy must also accelerate the use of best-available technology by Canadian companies, especially small and medium-sized companies. Canada has one of the best programs in the world to do this, the Industrial Research Adjustment Program (IRAP), which is so good that other countries have copied it. Yet it has been underfunded and mismanaged by the federal government. The program provides funding and advice to companies to help them acquire the latest technologies, which they can use to make their companies more efficient or to produce new products. Measured in constant dollars, IRAP's funding fell from $82 million in 1984–85 to $64 million in 1991–92. A parliamentary committee on science and technology in 1991 called on the federal government to raise IRAP's annual funding to at least $100 million so that Canadian small and medium-sized businesses had a better chance of gaining access to it. But although the government admits that IRAP is one of its "most successful and popular programs," it has kept the lid on funding — thus slowing down the adjustment of Canadian industry to free trade and global competition. Likewise, despite repeated pleas from technology companies, the government has refused to reinstate the $25 million Unsolicited Proposals Program, which allowed companies to seek funding for innovative R & D projects that could lead to cost savings for the federal government and to the development of new products.

To be sure, there are other requirements for a national technology program, including greater funding for the granting councils that support graduate students in science, engineering, and other important fields of study; continued support for basic research; and much more creative use of government procurement to help launch competitive products and services. For example, by developing leading-edge requirements for information networks and databases, Canada could provide strong support for software development and systems and new telecommunications hardware. While some business leaders argue that Canada should concentrate on applied research and treat basic research as a luxury, U.S. experts Mowery and Rosenberg contend that the distinction is "highly artificial." Basic research is the "ticket of admission to an information network," they maintain. It is necessary so that one can better understand where to conduct applied research and so that one can evaluate the outcome of applied research, and monitor and evaluate research being conducted elsewhere — as well as advancing the state of knowledge.

While the most fundamental need for a national technology policy is to ensure Canada's capacity for innovation, there are two additional reasons for such a policy. One is that if Canada fails to develop an attractive technology environment, not only will international companies be reluctant to undertake R & D activities here, but Canadian companies will locate their R & D activities in the United States. The Economic Council feared that a growing number of Canadian companies might already be doing so. "The implications are particularly serious if Canadian firms find the United States a more attractive environment to do research and development — for example, if it is easier to recruit highly skilled personnel there or if there are efficiencies in locating R & D activity in communities with high concentrations of high-tech firms and research facilities."[30]

Although the evidence does not reveal "a clear shift of 'home base' activities from Canada to the United States," the Economic Council said that it does raise "a warning flag."

Peter Morici, a U.S. trade economist and Canada-watcher, says that instead of worrying about U.S. trade actions against Canadian science and technology policies, "a much greater threat to the development of Canadian R & D–intensive activities could be posed by a shift in U.S. industrial policies from passive support for high-technology to more aggressive American responses to Japanese and European Community competition."[31] Morici argues that more favourable U.S. incentives and other support for high-tech industries would make the United States a more attractive location than Canada for international corporations, so much so that Canadian high-tech companies, too, would find it preferable to locate R & D activities there. As a result, Canada would be left with "more routine and less sophisticated fabrication and assembly operations."

A second urgent reason to develop an effective technology policy is that increasingly Canada should be seeking to participate in science and technology megaprojects that originate in other countries. Without an effective policy to identify and support national technology interests, as well as world-competitive technology-based companies, Canada will be ill-equipped to join in international projects such as the U.S. space station. In that project, Canada has competitive companies and technologies and is committing one-third of its space budget to provide an advanced version of the Canadarm that is used in the U.S. space shuttle; this facilitates advances in Canadian capabilities in artificial intelligence, vision systems, and robotics. Similarly, Canadian businesses are engaging in joint ventures and strategic alliances with foreign partners.

The Science Council has pointed out that international collaboration in science and technology will accelerate.[32] It identified four factors as driving transnational science, technology, and innovation activity: scientific and technical advances, as shown by worldwide computerized communications and transportation and by the increased scale of projects, requiring substantial participation from both the public and private sector; economic factors, including a worldwide movement towards corporate networking, as shown by the increasing number of strategic alliances, interindustry R & D consortia, and regional economic integration; geopolitical factors, including a global shift to market liberalism and an urgent need for coordination on economic development, investment, and trade; and a multitude of environmental issues that could drive international science and technology collaboration through the 1990s.

The emergence of an international science and technology system is especially important for a middle-sized country such as Canada, although it also raises legitimate concerns about the loss of east-west ties within the country if R & D activities are increasingly linked to U.S. activities and if Canadian high-tech firms operate primarily as suppliers to U.S. industry. This could result in a Canadian economy in which few industries have much linkage with one another. An effective technology policy, though, could offset these pressures and could help Canada participate in international projects in a more beneficial way.

In view of Canada's relatively small economic size, it has to look to major technology projects in other countries to augment its own capabilities, especially the kind of project that it cannot afford to undertake on its own but which could provide a critical opportunity to strengthen Canadian industry. An example is the U.S. High Performance Computing and Communications Project, a multibillion-dollar program to provide the United States with the fastest and most powerful electronic data system in the world. It will have far-reaching implications, not just for the computer, telecommunications, and software industries, but for a wide selection of users, ranging from business, government, and university research institutes to schools and hospitals. Given Canada's telecommunications and software interests, it would make sense for it to buy into the project, with some role for Canadian companies and university researchers. But for this kind of international effort, Canada needs an institutional capacity to identify opportunities, to work with industry to establish core technology interests, to draw up a business strategy, and to negotiate with a foreign government and its industry groups. We do not have that today.

While there is considerable room for debate over the details of a national technology policy, there can be little disagreement over the fact that Canada is going through a painful period of economic change. Stagnation in living standards, poor industry productivity and a decline in competitiveness, high unemployment, and weak capabilities in the new technologies are all signs of an economy in trouble. Most Canadians recognize that the nation's problems cannot be solved simply by lowering inflation and interest rates. Science, technology, and innovation are the keys to a brighter future. Without an ambitious technology policy, Canada's hopes for a prosperous future are in peril.

8

Money Is the Bottom Line

THE CANADIAN ECONOMY faces a decade of far-reaching restructuring. The Canada–U.S. free trade agreement and its expansion to include Mexico, the emergence of new global competition in Asia and Europe, the rebuilding of U.S. industry, and the impact of transforming new technologies are all combining to force major changes in Canada's traditional resource and manufacturing industries. The large number of permanent plant closures since 1989 is just one painful indicator of these changes, and there are more to come. The Canadian economy will have no choice but to diversify into new and higher-value goods and services.

All of this will take investment. Without investment, Canada will be unable to sustain its standard of living. Investments will be needed for new machinery and equipment, especially energy-saving and material-saving technologies; for research and development and all the subsequent stages that take new products from laboratories to store shelves; and for the pursuit of foreign markets and the training of employees. The cost and availability of capital and the profitability of Canadian companies will determine whether we can make the needed investments and thus the transition to a new economy. If these ingredients are lacking, Canada will become a poorer country, unable to support the health care, social, environmental, and cultural aspirations we have as a country.

Building up strong Canadian companies is one of our greatest challenges as we prepare for the next century and the new economy.

It is through companies that we use the skills and knowledge of people, together with the potential of science and technology, to create the products and services of the future and to sell them around the world. Companies are the vehicles for economic growth, embodying management and organizational know-how, research and development capacities, production skills, and distribution networks. Without companies that are able to grow, all our efforts to improve education, to promote skills training, and to invest in science and technology will be of little use. Companies are essential to exploit the new knowledge coming from our universities and research laboratories and to provide opportunity for the next generation of educated Canadians.

Unfortunately, we are not doing a good job of growing our own businesses in Canada. Many of our promising companies — especially the medium-sized ones that should become big companies — cannot find the equity capital they need to finance their growth. The real cost of capital is too high for companies of all sizes, forcing them to drop investments in innovation and in new high-value activities because they cannot afford to adopt long-term strategies. Many of Canada's potential high-tech winners are being forced to sell out to foreign corporations because they cannot find the capital in Canada to grow into world-scale Canadian-based companies. Changes in tax laws can help. But new institutions are also needed to provide new sources of equity and risk-sharing financing for the next generation of made-in-Canada products. Even our underlying system of business organization and corporate governance needs to be questioned, causing new forms of business organization to emerge.

One of Canada's best chances for the future is to foster strong medium-sized companies — those with up to 500 employees and sales of $50 million plus a year — and help them grow into big companies. These companies can be technology-intensive, can compete in specialized niches, and can operate in world markets through strategic alliances and other kinds of partnership. Medium-sized companies provide better jobs than most small businesses and have the capacity to be at the leading edge of new technologies.

Because of new manufacturing technologies and information systems, these companies can develop and sell new products and services without having to reach the size of a big business; and because they are not too large and bureaucratic, they have the flexibility to seize new opportunities faster than big companies do. Medium-sized companies have been raising their research and development budgets faster than large corporations. "From a public policy point of view, therefore, there are many reasons for Canada to pay additional attention to the state of health of medium-sized companies," says investment banker Gordon Sharwood.[1] Yet these are the companies that today are facing the most serious difficulties.

Although medium-sized companies represent only one-sixth of total investment or employment in Canada, their contribution to the nation's economic vitality "outweighs their statistical clout," says Sharwood. They are present in all parts of the country and in all sectors of the economy, especially in manufacturing. But their growth is lagging behind that of medium-sized companies in the United States. Moreover, a far smaller proportion of Canada's small and medium-sized businesses ever grow into big businesses. Between 1978 and 1986 only about 0.4 per cent of small businesses in Canada grew into medium-sized businesses, compared with 15 per cent in the United States; and almost none of the medium-sized Canadian businesses graduated to large corporations. While about 5 per cent of new businesses in the United States grow to become big businesses with more than 500 employees, less than 1 per cent in Canada ever become big businesses. This means, Sharwood says, that most medium-sized companies are "stalled" in the process of graduating to large-sized companies. Moreover, too many "are being taken over by foreign companies after they grow to a certain size."

So despite their potential, Canada's medium-sized companies are not "harbingers of the leap to world-class economy which Canada must achieve to be fully competitive." Small business cannot fill this role, and neither will the subsidiaries of foreign multinationals. Few foreign-owned subsidiaries in Canada will obtain real world product mandates from their parent companies: "The challenge, then, falls to the mid-size sector to graduate organizations with the necessary financial resources and entrepreneurial skills to bolster the Canadian economy and ensure that production rationalizations following in the wake of free trade are not all in favor of U.S.-based companies and plants. It is these Canadian mid-sized companies on which we must rely to succeed in the liberalized world trading environment by establishing foreign facilities, entering into joint ventures and strategic alliances, and growing through mergers and acquisitions." But these companies are highly vulnerable and many are ill-prepared for the new competitive environment. "They remain poised at the threshold, but unable to marshall the financial resources to graduate into the upper echelon of the Canadian corporate environment."[2]

The venture capital industry, a critical source of funding for small and medium-sized companies, is not strong enough to support the growth of technology-based Canadian companies into the international league, according to a Science Council of Canada study.[3] This was one reason why the number "reaching the threshold level necessary to be competitive internationally is not impressive," Mary Macdonald, author of the study, says. While the United States has seen companies such as Apple Computer, Digital Equipment, Genetech, Lotus, Sun Microsystems, Compaq, and Federal Express graduate from small enterprises to world-scale companies, there are almost no similar success stories in Canada. Macdonald blames this on lack of funding, weak management in high-tech companies, and a venture capital industry that is not well attuned to new technologies: "Canadian technology companies are definitely playing in the minor leagues when it comes to the support they get from the venture capital industry." While about 70 per cent of U.S. venture capital goes into new technology companies, less than 25 per cent of Canadian venture capital does; and if it were not for government venture capital funds, which provided 22 per cent of venture capital financing for technology companies in 1985–89, the Canadian position would be even worse.

In other countries, large corporations play an important role in nurturing small and medium-sized companies by providing financing, management and technology advice, and distribution, as well as developing the companies as suppliers. "Unfortunately, few large Canadian companies are actively partnering with Canada's young technology companies," Macdonald says. "The most suitable corporate partner for a small technology company is often a global industrial corporation with a related technological focus. Major chemical, pharmaceutical, communications, electronics, information technology, and industrial equipment companies are the primary candidates for corporate partnering relationships. These firms have the resources, the R & D capability, the manufacturing know-how, the global distribution channels, and the marketing intelligence to add value to their young partner." However, Macdonald could find only six major companies in Canada that actively try to build up small and medium-sized Canadian companies.

In fact, small and medium technology companies face a worsening situation because private-sector venture funds are leaving the Canadian technology market at the same time that capital requirements are actually growing. This will mean more foreign takeovers in the future because "many of the more promising Canadian firms, when unable to find venture capital in Canada or elsewhere, will sell out to larger, better-funded corporations, usually foreign owned," predicts Macdonald. "This pattern is already particularly evident in the Canadian software industry, where a number of firms in the $2 million to $5 million revenue range have recently been acquired by large U.S. software companies. The effect of these acquisitions will be to substantially reduce the base of technology companies from which highly successful Canadian 'threshold' firms might grow."

When Canadian technology companies are acquired by foreign owners, their potential may be curbed and the high-value activities and jobs may be transferred out of the country. This problem was illustrated in a Canada Consulting Group report. A Canadian company recently acquired by a U.S. company had come up with a new product, had sold it to a few major overseas customers, and had built up the development team to take it to a wider market. "Not long after the development work began, the new foreign parent found that its own development staff were about to have considerable spare capacity. Rather than lay them off, it transferred the development of the product in question from its Canadian operation to its foreign headquarters, and disbanded the Canadian development team."[4]

Canada's biotechnology industry also fears that Canada is at "a singular disdavantage" in developing industries of the future. One problem is that Canada's major resource and manufacturing companies have failed to invest in leading-edge technologies. Consequently, they are neither a market nor a partner for technology-based companies; nor are they a source of future executives who have the experience to head up high-tech companies. The other disadvantage is a lack of funding, which means that the companies are unable to expand their equity base and pay the significant costs of bringing new products to market. The result is that "for their long-term survival, many Canadian companies have been forced to sell a portion of their proprietary technology, or an equity share, to foreign investors and have thus lost control of their technologies or their companies," the biotechnology report says.[5]

Many studies have documented the serious financial barriers to building an innovative economy in Canada, but little has been done to change things. The problem is not that Canadians lack ideas or the capability to develop innovative enterprises. Companies such as Husky Injection Molding, Imax, Alias Research, Ballard Technologies, Gandalf Technologies, Cognos, Videotron, CAE Industries, Glenayre Electronics, and Quadra Logic Technologies show that Canadians can develop truly innovative enterprises that are highly regarded all over the world. What we do not know is how many opportunities have been lost because Canada does not provide the equity capital for companies to grow.

A 1988 study by the Canadian Chamber of Commerce found that "while Canada has a sophisticated debt system, it has an inadequate system of equity financing for the new environment which companies face today."[6] This is not just a problem for small companies; larger companies in the industries of the future, which are developing "soft assets" such as software systems in knowledge-based areas, also have problems. "In part this is due to Canada's traditional investor culture, which has been nurtured on capital-intensive resource-based projects." The Chamber of Commerce report says that Canada's investment community does not understand how to invest in the new economy of soft-asset, knowledge-based companies, which have different requisites for success: "Yet it is these very companies that are propelling today's economy. As a result, a new agenda for financing business has to be developed, one which takes into consideration the new need for equity financing." The report points out that Canada is moving away from its traditional resource economy to "a more complex economy" where research and development, information systems and software, and employee training are the ingredients of success, and that this requires great amounts of capital, just as the bricks and mortar and heavy machinery investments did in the past.

Another problem is the high cost of capital. A study by the Canada Consulting Group points out that this means that Canadian companies are less able or willing to invest in innovation than their foreign competitors, and this discourages the long-term and high-risk investments that are essential for future jobs and economic growth.[7] The cost of capital is the minimum before-tax real rate of return that an investment project must generate in order to be justified economically and to pay its after-tax financing costs. It is determined by the cost of a company's funds — the payments it must make to its debt and equity holders — offset by the economic depreciation of the investment and tax policies, including the tax treatment of that depreciation, the taxation of corporate profits, and whatever tax incentives are available.

Canada has a much higher cost of capital than Japan and Germany, the National Advisory Board on Science and Technology found, although the cost is comparable to that of the United States and Britain.[8] In its research for the National Advisory Board, the Canada Consulting Group found that the after-inflation or real after-tax cost of capital in Canada averaged 4.8 per cent in 1977–88, compared with 4.9 per cent in the United States, 2.5 per cent in Germany, and 2.0 per cent in Japan. The lower the cost of capital, the longer is the period of time a company has to generate a return on its investment; when the cost of capital is high, companies have to adopt a short-term perspective. "Competitors with lower capital costs can justify investments that Canadians must decline, and can afford to wait longer for their returns," Canada Consulting said. "They invest more intensely and more patiently, while Canadian companies cannot justify many of the investments needed to keep them globally competitive."

This high cost of capital also hurts resource-based and mature manufacturing companies that need to upgrade and innovate. "Resource-exploitation industries face diminishing returns in the future. . . . Real prices for the unrefined product have been falling over the past 15 years and there is no reason to expect that this trend will be reversed," states the National Advisory Board. "However, such industries have the opportunity to transform themselves through science-based innovation. The transformation, for example, could involve the evolution of a mining or mineral processing company into a materials company specializing in advanced alloys and compounds needed by the industries of the future."

The problem that Canada's resource and mature manufacturing companies face is that competition from low-wage developing countries has pushed the returns available to less than their cost of capital, and therefore they cannot finance investments to become more competitive. This means that they are no longer able to drive economic growth in Canada or to provide rising real wages. In fact, according to Canada Consulting, in real terms, the assets of Canada's 300 largest companies have hardly expanded at all since the early 1980s; and of 22 large resource and mature manufacturing companies studied by Canada Consulting (in industries such as forest products, mining, and metals), only two managed to earn their cost of capital in 1982–88; the remainder shrank in value. "This problem at the individual company level translates into a disaster for the economy as a whole, since it will lead to a steady erosion of our competitiveness and a lowering of our standard of living," says the Canada Consulting report.

"Where will the new growth in high value-added industries come to take up the slack from our downsizing resource and mature manufacturing sectors?" the report then asks. Even though technology-based companies have a better record in earning their cost of capital (9 of 16 technology companies studied by Canada Consulting did so in 1982–88), they still face serious problems arising from the high cost of capital. This forces them either to spread their efforts too thinly over product development and marketing or to concentrate on too few product areas and markets — and both courses make them vulnerable to competitors or takeovers.

This high cost of capital is one of the reasons why Canadian and U.S. companies often pursue short-term strategies while German and Japanese companies are able to pursue longer-term objectives. If the cost of capital is 6 per cent, a company is likely to seek a payback within three years; if the cost is 1.5 per cent, it can wait 12 years. Even with tax incentives, R & D can be expensive in Canada. Canada Consulting calculated that in 1988 a Canadian company would have to earn a 19.4 per cent rate of return to justify an R & D project with a 10-year payoff. This was far above the 8.7 return required to justify the same project in Japan and the 14.8 per cent return required to justify the project in Germany. Australia, a country similar to Canada, boosted its R & D tax deduction to 100 per cent of costs and was able to lower the return that an Australian company would need from the same R & D project to just 11.5 per cent.

When differences in the cost of capital persist for extended periods, they have a profound effect on the behaviour of companies, warn three U.S. experts: "The type of people who rise to the top in a corporation and the culture of the firm evolve in response to what works best in its prevailing environment. Place a firm in an environment where the cost of capital is very low, and it will do its best when it takes a long view, largely disregarding current profitability. In time, this long view becomes part of the company's way of doing business. Place a firm in an environment where the cost of capital is high, and the firm's interests will be best served by a short-term focus, and this too becomes part of a company's culture."[9] This helps explain some of the differences between corporate behaviour in North America and Japan.

This is why "a relatively high cost of capital is a significant threat to Canadian industrial competitiveness and hence to our economic future," the National Advisory Board concluded. "It poses more difficult problems than relatively high material or labor costs, which at least stimulate business to use these resources more efficiently, usually through innovation and investment. High capital costs make investment more expensive. This reduces the range of products that can be financed, with a severe impact on investments in research and development or other aspects of industrial innovation." The failure to make long-term investments eventually catches up with a company and a country. Companies find themselves unable to compete because they are using dated technology or because their products and services have been overtaken, and a country finds itself with higher unemployment and less economic growth.

So what can be done? How can we reduce the cost of capital and also ensure that the supply of capital is there so that Canadian companies can grow to world scale? Canada will not be able to field its own team of players in the world economy if Canadian companies are unable to make the necessary long-term investments in science and technology.

Lower interest rates from low and stable inflation and declining government deficits will help reduce the cost of capital, but that is not enough to narrow the gap. Moreover, while interest rates began a sharp decline in Canada starting in 1991, real or inflation-adjusted rates remained high. With a prime rate of 7.75 per cent and an inflation rate of less than 2 per cent, the cost of money was no bargain. There must also be appropriate tax policy because Canada needs a decade of strong investment to revitalize old industries and create new ones. Yet in his "tax reforms," former finance minister, Michael Wilson, eliminated incentives that could help lower the cost of capital (for example, accelerated depreciation for key investments in new production technologies, and the use of an investment tax credit which, if fully or partially refundable, could benefit companies that have low or nonexistent earnings but need to restructure).

The Canada Consulting Group estimates that the Wilson tax changes in 1987 raised the cost of capital to Canadian companies by about one-third. In 1980, an investment made in machinery and equipment with a 20-year life benefited from a 50:50 two-year writeoff and a 7 per cent investment tax credit, resulting in a 5.2 per cent cost of capital. By 1990, the elimination of the investment tax credit and the introduction of a 25 per cent declining balance depreciation schedule had raised the cost of capital to 6.9 per cent. Wilson even reduced the value of Canada's R & D investment tax credit. Since Canada ought to be increasing R & D spending, not only should the value of the R & D credit be increased, but the definition of R & D should be expanded to become an innovation tax credit covering a larger portion of the costs from basic research to commercialization. Moreover, says Karen Wensley of Ernst & Young in a study for the Canadian Advanced Technology Association, R & D and other tax incentives for small businesses — Canadian-controlled private corporations — do not work well for high-technology companies. These companies "grow very quickly, have enormous needs for capital which generally cannot be obtained from banks, must make significant investments in R & D and marketing in order to take advantage of narrow windows of opportunity, and often enter into strategic alliances with larger companies." As a result, high-tech companies "can very quickly lose their eligibility for the tax incentives they need to stay competitive."[10]

Wilson's aim was to create a neutral tax system, one that did not discriminate between investments in shopping centres and investments in new manufacturing technology. But in a period of intensive international competition, a neutral tax system does not make sense. Canada is starting from behind in the world innovation race, and industry faces a costly challenge to catch up and get ahead. If we are to reduce the cost of capital and encourage investment, we should use the tax system to increase investment where it is needed. Canadian workers benefit when industry has the capital to invest in new technology, since this makes the company and the workers more competitive. So it makes sense to have low tax rates for capital that is used for investment in the economy (for example, a fully or partially refundable tax credit for investment in new machinery and equipment and in R & D). On the other hand, capital should be more highly taxed when it flows out of companies and into the hands of shareholders; in other words, the principal tax burden should be on individuals who benefit from the growth of companies rather than on the companies themselves. This could be done through income tax and some form of inheritance or estate tax.

In addition, a reduction in the capital gains tax targeted to investments in companies that compete in international trade could lower the cost of capital by reducing the returns an investor would have to get from making an equity investment in clearly defined businesses (in particular, manufacturing and certain knowledge industries, such as software) if the shares were held for at least five years. A register of qualifying companies could be developed by an independent panel, based on criteria set by the government. Retailing, real estate, distribution, and financial and personal service firms would not qualify for the reduction, as the National Advisory Board has suggested.

Quebec has used another tax device — the Quebec Stock Savings Plan (QSSP) — to attract equity capital into Quebec-based businesses. Pierre Lortie, a Quebec businessman, has proposed that Ottawa should consider an equivalent Canada Stock Savings Plan.[11] Under the plan, Quebec taxpayers get a tax deduction for investments in new issues of stock by Quebec-based companies, with the incentive biased towards smaller companies. Since its inception in 1979, the QSSP has helped raise more than $8 billion for Quebec-based companies, according to the Quebec Ministry of Finance. At one point it encouraged overpriced issues from weak companies, but Lortie says that overall it has been a success, acting as "a powerful engine for economic growth." This, he says, is because "the corporations most likely to benefit are those that have the greatest need for the plan because, for them, the most difficult hurdle is getting easier access to risk capital." Cascades Inc., a successful Quebec paper and packaging company, went public with a $5 million stock offering under the QSSP in 1982 when its annual revenues were $29 million. In 1991 its revenues were $806 million, and $1000 invested in the company in 1982 had an annual compound growth rate of 33.1 per cent to February 1992. The QSSP was "the element that helped us make the decision to go public," according to company executive Michael Provencher. "It was very, very helpful to our company."[12] Quebec also helped launch the Quebec labour movement's Solidarity Fund to invest in promising companies. Today it has assets of more than $500 million and ties with venture capital funds in the United States. Ontario and Saskatchewan have since facilitated similar labour-run venture funds, such as the Canadian Federation of Labour's Working Ventures Canadian Fund.

In the final analysis, Canada has no choice but to look at all the possibilities for attracting capital into the productive businesses that will form the dynamic core of a new competitive economy. A study that the former Economic Council of Canada chairman, David Slater, made for Investment Canada found that even "relatively small increases in productivity growth require substantial future investment efforts."[13] Productivity growth in Canada has lagged behind that of all the major industrial nations aside from the United States for the past 45 years, and Canada's investment in machinery and equipment, as a share of GDP, has been the lowest of any of the G-7 countries for the past 30 years.

Canada's overall rate of investment has been at about average for the industrial countries in the postwar period, though below that of Japan, Germany, and France. But as Slater points out, Canada has needed a high level of investment just to equip all the baby boom generation of workers joining the labour force, as well as to meet the needs of capital-intensive resource industries and to accommodate Canada's cold climate and long distances. "From this perspective, the fact that Canada was at the OECD average might suggest that not enough investment took place." More important, Slater fears that Canada may not be able to meet the investment levels needed to achieve better productivity through the 1990s. This would have serious implications for our ability to support our social system, to meet the needs of an aging population, to adjust the economic structure to meet the new environmental imperative, and to finance the infrastructure necessary to maintain the quality of our cities.

With three projections of Canada's future investment needs — from a low of 20.6 per cent of GDP to a middle range of 23.0 per cent and a high range of 26.9 per cent — Slater says that even the highest projection would yield productivity increases that are "consistent only with the sluggish levels of the last decade." Since 1980, investment has run just below 23 per cent of GDP, compared with just over 23 per cent from 1955 to 1980. So Canada faces a critical challenge in the 1990s to set the stage for a more productive economy that will be able to generate the jobs and wealth we will need as we move to the new world of the next century.

One of the most important potential sources of capital for technology-intensive firms is the $200 billion or more held in Canada's trusteed pension funds. In fact, pension funds are our biggest pool of capital today, and no group has a greater stake in Canada's future prosperity than the millions of individual Canadians whose savings are held by these funds. Canadians also hold a great deal of their savings in registered retirement savings plans (RRSPs) and insurance policies (according to Slater, 60 per cent of the savings of Canadians are in pension plans, insurance, or RRSPs). So, as Slater points out, the role of pension fund managers, insurance companies, and the banks and trust companies handling RRSP savings is crucial to the kinds of investment that are made in Canada. Much of this money is currently invested in bonds, mortgages, and other forms of debt, and in real estate; the challenge is how to get more into the equity base of Canadian industry, including emerging and threshold companies, so that these savings can be put to work for Canada's future.

The National Advisory Board on Science and Technology has called for a tax incentive to persuade pension funds to put 1 per cent of their money into technology-based firms. Those that failed to do so would have to pay a penalty of 10 per cent of the amount not invested — for a maximum yield of about $200 million a year. This could encourage the expansion of specialized venture capital funds that invest pools of capital from pension funds and insurance companies in small and medium-sized businesses with sales of up to $50–$75 million. While pension fund managers argue that this could risk the retirement income of Canadians, the National Advisory Board responds that "the retirement income, indeed the economic future of Canadians is at risk now unless Canada improves its international competitive position through industrial innovation. Pension funds must be asked to participate in the financing of our economic future."

The 1991 budget proposed tax incentives to get pension funds to shift more of their resources into the equity of Canadian companies by eliminating "the existing bias in favour of debt investments by pension funds." Canadian pension funds had 35 per cent of their assets in equities, compared with a figure of 46 per cent for U.S. pension funds. However, the plan ran into strong opposition from pension funds and was quickly withdrawn, but the Department of Finance made no attempt to defend or explain it, leaving the impression that this was what it had wanted all along. Yet with $200 billion in trusteed pension funds, about $100 billion in RRSPs, and more than $55 billion in the Canada and Quebec pension plans, we need to find better ways of using these resources.

Quebec has done just that. Its Caisse de dépôt et placement du Québec, with $41.1 billion in assets, is the biggest pension fund and biggest stock market investor in Canada. Established by the provincial government in 1966 to manage the funds for the Quebec Pension Plan, public-sector pension plans, and other insurance assets, it has played a key role in building up Quebec-based companies and encouraging Quebec entrepreneurs. By being there as a source of patient equity capital and as a partner in strategic acquisitions and restructurings, the Caisse has sent a powerful message to Quebec business. It can own up to 25 per cent of a company. In an extension of this role, it announced in 1991 that it would allocate $100 million to buy shares of smaller, publicly traded Canadian companies. Yet in that recession year of 1991, it was still able to earn a 17.2 per cent return on its investments. Over the past 10 years, the Caisse has earned an average annual return of 14.4 per cent, which puts it among the top performers in the Canadian investment industry.

In the United States, many state governments are looking to their public pension funds as tools for economic growth by pushing them to invest in their local economies. "Economically targeted investments will be more and more in the forefront as states and municipalities continue to feel the impact of fiscal strain," predicts Francisco Borges, state treasurer in Connecticut, who wants to see 3 per cent of the state pension fund in Connecticut-based enterprises.[14] A 1989 survey of the largest U.S. state and local pension funds, conducted by the Institute for Fiduciary Education, found that 41 of 99 retirement funds had economically targeted investment programs.

Influenced by the role played by the Caisse, Ontario has drafted plans for an investment fund to help finance the growth of small and medium-sized companies by making equity investments. But instead of using public-sector pension funds, it is hoping to attract funds from public- and private-sector pension plans on a voluntary basis, aiming for somewhere between $1 and $2 billion over 5 to 7 years. This suggests that it will be much less effective than the Caisse in building up industry, because there will be no assurance that it can attract funds for strategic investments and because the participants are likely to limit its effectiveness.

In another approach, the National Advisory Board on Science and Technology has proposed the establishment of an Industrial Innovation Merchant Bank to provide equity and debt for technology-intensive companies. Government would provide some of the capital, and the banks and trust companies would provide the remainder. The proposed bank would also "take the lead in facilitating deals, such as creating cross-equity holdings to create a critical mass" in an industrial sector, much like the Japanese *keiretsu*. The National Advisory Board said that "consultants to the committee have identified a number of individuals in the financial and industrial communities who support this concept in principle." Such a bank would provide an alternative for Canadian companies that are forced to sell to foreign multinationals because they cannot raise capital in Canada.

If finding new sources of equity for Canadian companies is one key to a more prosperous future, another is helping companies finance the high-risk development of new products — from basic research to international marketing. One model is the Swedish Industrifonden, or Industrial Fund. This fund, which was set up by the government but is managed at arm's length from the government, shares up to 50 per cent of the costs of high-risk innovation projects to develop new products or processes. It aids some of Sweden's biggest companies as well as many small and medium-sized ones, and it does so without a big bureaucracy. The fund operates with a small staff, using outside consultants to make financial and technology assessments. All the investment decisions are made by the fund's board, which has minority representation from the government. The other members — the majority — all come from the private sector. Industrifonden recovers the money from successful projects through the repayment of funds and through royalty rights. Taxpayer money is not recklessly spent, because companies still have to put up half the funding themselves. According to Canada Consulting, the fund has earned a 7 per cent rate of return since its establishment about a decade ago.

The Ontario Premier's Council recommended a similar fund in its 1988 report, *Competing in the New Global Economy.* This fund would play a critical role in facilitating innovation; for many medium-sized companies, the risks of new technology are especially high, forcing management to bet the company whenever a new technology or product is pursued. Under the council's proposal (which was endorsed by top executives from Northern Telecom, General Motors, Dofasco, Abitibi-Price, Weston Foods, and Union Carbide, who were on the council) loans would be provided for up to 50 per cent of total project costs, including new product development, design, and placement of prototypes. The loans would be repayable on a sliding scale, with no payback if the project failed and with an above-market rate if the project succeeded.[15]

The National Advisory Board on Science and Technology has proposed a similar national risk-sharing fund, capitalized ultimately at $1 billion by the federal government, to finance half the industrial innovation costs of high-risk industrial projects. According to the board, Sweden's Industrifonden and the U.S.–Israel Fund both show profitable results even though they plan for failure rates of 15–20 per cent. So far, the federal government has ignored the National Advisory Board's proposal.

In another possible approach, Mary Macdonald, in a report for the Canadian Advanced Technology Association, has proposed that government allocate $150 million to several technology-focused venture capital funds, in partnership with pension funds and other private-sector investors. "To remedy the shortcomings in the financial infrastructure, a critical mass of technology-focused venture funds managed by experienced and knowledgeable technology investors must therefore be created," she says.[16] But qualified technology investors are unlikely to enter the market unless they can raise sufficient capital to establish a viable fund. Yet without such funds, capital sources such as pension funds and insurance companies are unlikely to make more capital available to technology companies. So government should help, she says.

If Canada is to have the economic structure that can create through ideas and innovation the wealth needed to build a better future, even more sweeping changes may be required in our corporate structures and system of corporate governance. A fundamental problem in Canada and the other English-speaking countries is that business is preoccupied with short-term goals and with the constant threat of hostile mergers and acquisitions. This is not just because of the high cost of capital; it is also because of the way companies are owned and measured. In countries such as Germany and Japan the structure of business is significantly different, and corporations are able to focus on long-term rather than short-term goals.

A crucial difference is the stability of ownership in Germany and Japan, says American management expert Peter Drucker. This allows businesses to pursue long-term strategies instead of having to cater to the casino-style capitalism of Canada, the United States, and Britain, where the daily fluctuation in stock prices is often the measure of performance. German and Japanese shareholders expect companies to sacrifice short-term profits and dividends to achieve long-term goals, but Canadian, American, and British executives would be in trouble if they cut the next quarter's dividend to finance R & D. The lack of long-term patient shareholders is a major structural problem for many Canadian companies, undermining their ability to focus on long-term objectives.

One major reason for the difference centres on the banks' involvement in business. "In Germany, the country's three major banks have long controlled about 60 per cent of the share capital of the larger companies, partly through direct holdings, partly through the holdings of their customers that, under German law, the banks manage and vote on," says Drucker. "In Japan, the majority of large companies are members of a small number (10 at most) of industrial groups, the now familiar *keiretsu*. In a *keiretsu*, 20 per cent to 30 per cent of the share capital of each member company is held by the other members and by the group's bank and trading company, and practically all credit to the member companies is provided by the group's bank."[17]

German banks and the Japanese *keiretsu* reject the idea that the job of a corporation is "to maximize shareholder value" as the term is normally understood in Canada (where it means a higher share price within 6 to 12 months). "Such short-term capital gains are the wrong objective for both the enterprise and its dominant shareholders," says Drucker. Instead, the objective should be to "maximize the wealth-producing capacity of the enterprise." If this is the objective, then the long-term importance of research and development, employee training, search for new markets, innovation, workplace organization, production systems, and labour-management relations become the focus of management. The key shareholders in both Germany and Japan, Drucker contends, "support management regardless of short-term results as long as the company performs according to a business plan that is designed to maximize the enterprise's wealth-producing capacity — and that is agreed upon between management and whatever organ represents the owners." Consequently, management has the continuity and stability it needs. The results, "to judge by German and Japanese business performance, are clearly superior to running the enterprise as a 'trustee' for stakeholders or to maximize short-term gains for shareholders."

Because the major banks are long-term shareholders in leading German corporations, they can play a strategic role in building the strength of a corporation. The Deutsche Bank, for example, holds 28 per cent of Daimler-Benz and was instrumental in expanding the company from automobiles to aerospace. "The German 'universal' banks, pre-eminent players in all financial markets, contrast sharply with the more specialized banks of the Anglo-American system. For 'universal' banks equity investments and loans are alternative means of providing corporate finance," U.S. economist John Zysman says.[18] As shareholders, German banks have an interest in the long-term health of the companies in which they have holdings; and when corporate crises occur, they play an "almost parapublic role," mediating with government and labour and other corporate entities. In effect, many German bailouts and corporate restructurings are engineered and led by the banks rather than by government.

There clearly are benefits. As well as enabling industry to take a long-term approach, the banks provide a strong defence against unfriendly takeovers and make it virtually impossible for foreign corporations to take over important German companies. German bankers are highly critical of the hostile takeovers, mergers, and acquisitions that characterize North American business. Hilmar Kopper, head of the Deutsche Bank, calls these activities "financial acrobatics."

In Canada and the United States, corporate takeovers are used to bring about corporate restructuring. But one consequence, as British experts Stephen Woolcock and Michael Hodges point out, is that "by facilitating takeovers, the Anglo-Saxon model also militates against corporate-led consensus, because an environment in which change of ownership is commonplace is not conducive to the maintenance of explicit, let alone implicit, social contracts: new management is not bound by previous management's commitments. Thus the structure of capital markets and forms of industrial finance influence the nature of corporate governance."[19]

Similarily, Japan's system of corporate ownership emphasizes long-term strategic management and implicit but productive contracts between employees, suppliers, customers, creditors, and shareholders. These corporate families, or *keiretsu*, are typically organized around a major bank, trading company, and large industrial corporation. There are at least 10 major *keiretsu*, bringing together more than 1000 companies that account for 25 per cent of total sales and the same proportion of paid-up capital of all Japanese companies. About half of all companies listed on the Tokyo Stock

Exchange are members of a *keiretsu*. Membership means much more than sharing a common name — such as Mitsubishi, Sumitomo, or Mitsui. What binds a *keiretsu* together is the reciprocal ownership of common stock: all the members own shares in one another.

Take the Mitsubishi *keiretsu*, for example. Mitsubishi Heavy Industries owns 3.5 per cent of Mitsubishi Bank, and Mitsubishi Bank owns 4.6 per cent of Mitsubishi Heavy Industries. Altogether, more than 20 per cent of the outstanding shares of companies in the Mitsubishi *keiretsu* are held by other companies in the group; and there are agreements not to sell shares held reciprocally — so all the companies in the *keiretsu* have a core of stable shareholders.[20]

The cross-stock holdings of Toyota, which belongs to the Mitsui group, provide another example. The top 10 shareholders of Toyota, which account for about 38 per cent of Toyota stock, include five commercial banks, one long-term credit bank, two life insurance companies, one component supplier, and one distributor. At the same time, Toyota holds 20 to 40 per cent of the shares in each of the main subsidiaries in its production *keiretsu*.[21]

Typically, a *keiretsu* consists of an inner core of about 20 companies, with a tiered structure of capital holdings and interrelated lending from the inner core to a middle core of 50 or so companies, with a similar structure cascading out to a larger group of companies numbering into the hundreds. Mazda, which is in the Sumitomo *keiretsu*, is a typical case, says Kenneth Courtis, strategist and senior economist for Deutsche Bank in Tokyo. "Stakeholders in this group hold roughly 60 per cent of Mazda's overall shares. Mazda, in turn, holds between 20 and 40 per cent of the equity of its 15 major suppliers. These suppliers in turn hold significant equity positions of their suppliers and so on down the chain."[22] Although the Tokyo stock market has one of the largest capitalizations in the world, only 30 to 35 per cent of the shares are ever traded. The other 65 or 70 per cent are held through this type of corporate cross-holding.

There are other reciprocal arrangements as well. Mitsubishi Bank is a major lender to Mitsubishi Electric but is also a purchaser of its electronic equipment. Mitsubishi Steel sells steel to Mitsubishi Heavy Industries and buys equipment and construction services from it too. Thus, long-term relationships are developed.[23] In the period 1975–87, the companies belonging to the six largest *keiretsu* purchased 54 per cent of their computer requirements from companies belonging to their own *keiretsu*.[24] At least as important is the fact that a *keiretsu* provides an awesome system of information exchange. Once a month, the 26 top presidents in the Mitsui group meet to exchange information; no substitutes can be sent, and allegedly no minutes are kept. These secret gatherings are a powerful way for companies in different industries but in the same corporate family to trade ideas, information, and analysis, and to share technology, management, capital, information, personnel, and risk. They also help turn around the performance of a weak company in the *keiretsu*. As well, they organize low-cost and high-risk capital to support new promising companies that can be brought into the group. In this respect, they operate as venture capitalists.

Each *keiretsu* is centred around a core bank, which is the main though not the only provider of capital. The core bank monitors the economic performance of the member companies, is strategically involved in financing the borrower's innovation, and acts as the lender of last resort. "These stable customized relationships bring benefits to lender and borrower alike," says Masaru Yoshitomi of the Japanese government's Economic Planning Agency. "The banks can minimize the costs of reviewing and monitoring corporate performance, and the borrowers can obtain credit at lower interest rates thanks to lower risk premiums." He cites the relationship between NEC, a large Japanese electronics company, and its main bank, Sumitomo Bank, as an example of the benefits. In the late 1970s, NEC aggressively out-invested Hitachi and Fujitsu in constructing semiconductor plants, largely because Sumitomo had intimate knowledge of NEC and backed the new technology. "Stockholdings of financial institutions, coupled with the main-bank system, appear to have contributed to Japan's longer-term strategy of business investment. Cross-stock holdings have sharpened the separation of power between management and ownership, shielding the management of member firms from the the short-sighted interests of individual stock holders," says Yoshitomi. "The main-bank system has promoted a long-term strategy of business investment and R & D expenditure."[25]

The *keiretsu* system also encourages Japanese companies to invest in new business activities, which facilitates industrial adjustment and restructuring (rather than closing plants and laying off workers, as a typical Canadian company would do). "Both labor and capital in the declining sector of a Japanese firm are transferred to new activities by establishing subsidiary firms which are mainly financed by the parent company," the Organisation for Economic Co-operation and Development points out.[26] The workers from the declining activity move into the new subsidiary. In 1986, for example, about half the sales of Japanese synthetic fibre or textile firms were in new products such as films, light fibres, and medical products. Japanese companies are constantly pushing R & D into new areas, and this accelerates adjustment. In 1984, 25 per cent of the R & D budgets of Japanese food companies was in pharmaceuticals, 41 per cent of those of textile companies was in chemicals, 24 per cent of those of metal products companies was in electrical machinery, 19 per cent of those of pulp and paper companies was in chemicals, and 19 per cent of those of non-ferrous metal companies was in telecommunications. Canada Consulting cites the example of Nippon Mining, a member of the Mitsui *keiretsu,* to show how a mature company in a *keiretsu* can use the support of the *keiretsu* bank and work closely with other members of the group — in this case the electronics company, Toshiba — to diversify away from its traditional business in copper mining and refining into new, high-value business activities. In 1986–90 Nippon spent US$154 million or 3.1 per cent of sales on targeted R & D, most of it for technologies that could lead to new areas of business. Nippon decided that its best opportunities lay in copper foil, which is used in the semiconductor industry; and having made this decision, it acquired Gould Corporation in the United States, the world leader in the technology.

"In principle, by tying themselves to one another in industrial groups bound by an intricate network of reciprocal ownership and reciprocal trading agreements, yet eschewing outright ownership and control, Japanese companies have been able to enjoy the best of both worlds," says Carl Kester. "They have been able to harness the high-powered incentives of the market that derives from independent ownership of assets while relying on selective intervention by large banks, trading companies, or other key equity owners to adapt contracts to new circumstances as needed. When given the choice between owning another company outright or embracing it with bilaterally self-enforcing constraints, most Japanese companies have opted for the latter wherever possible."[27] Membership in a *keiretsu* protects a company against the threat of a takeover and allows it to pursue long-term strategies and investments to expand markets and develop new technologies; managers of Japanese companies do not have to focus on short-term results because they have the security against a takeover through the cross-holdings of shares among the *keiretsu* companies.

How can Canadian companies respond to the competitive advantages of the German and Japanese systems? The Canadian financial system, says Deutsche Bank's Courtis, operates like a utility with almost no direct role in the management of the real sector of the economy. "In a sense, as a country, we find ourselves in a situation where we do not allow ourselves to lever the growth potential of what is one of this economy's great structural strengths, that is its financial system," he says. "It is, perhaps in part, a question of economic doctrine. But now we confront enormously competitive economies that operate differently and the numbers indicate that not only are they outperforming Canada, but the gap seems to be widening. Under these circumstances, can we continue to remain attached to an economic doctrine despite the accelerating shift against us that is now occurring in the international balance of power? I believe not."

Canada has some large business conglomerates, but they do not operate in the same strategic fashion as a Japanese *keiretsu*. BCE Inc., for example, controls Bell Canada and Northern Telecom and even owns a financial institution, Montreal Trust. But BCE's confusing and contradictory investment policies in the past decade, getting in and out of oil and gas pipelines and oil and gas exploration, and getting in but not out of a disastrous real estate investment that cost it several hundred million dollars in losses, suggest the lack of a coherent business strategy. Aside from the Bell Canada–Northern Telecom links (and even there, BCE is presiding over the possible Americanization of Northern Telecom), there is nothing to suggest that BCE is using its huge economic potential to build up a network of business enterprises, strategic alliances, and partnerships along the lines of the *keiretsu* model.

Canadian Pacific, with its holdings in transportation, forest products, telecommunications, real estate, and waste management, is another large Canadian business enterprise. It has the potential to form a *keiretsu*-type structure, linking up with machinery and electronics companies, for example. But it has shown no such inclination. The same can be said of the huge Hees-Edper empire, whose assets include Noranda Forest, Noranda Mines, John Labatt, Royal Trustco, London Life, Canadian Hunter, Bramalea, and Trizec. Subsidiaries that might have formed the basis of stronger industrial enterprises (for example, Lumonics, Federal Pioneer, and Canada Wire and Cable) have been sold off to foreign industrial groups. The interlocking Hees-Edper empire is a cascading network of companies whose financial continuity depends on a constant stream of dividends upwards to the senior Hees-Edper companies. But there is no evidence of a corporate vision to generate added value from this huge agglomeration of companies.

One way we could change our corporate system would be to encourage the banks, major trust companies, and leading pension funds to become long-term equity holders in Canadian companies so that they can participate in Canadian-style *keiretsu*. Banks are permitted to own up to 10 per cent of a company, but they rarely do so — except as a last-resort tactic when loans are at risk and a debt restructuring takes place. In Quebec, however, there is support for links between financial institutions and industrial enterprises. Pierre Fortier, a former junior finance minister in Quebec and head of the Société financière des caisses Desjardins Inc., a $5 billion financial holding company, says that it is vital for Quebec to have its own powerful groups to confront foreign competitors: "We had to envisage and encourage the emergence of industrial, commercial and financial conglomerates which, by joining forces, could give Quebec the means to act either at home or abroad."

It is possible, Fortier told a Senate committee, to have commercial links between financial institutions and industrial companies while regulating insider trading and possible conflict of interest. The real problem, he said, is that "large industrial groups are coming into the province and buying our commercial and industrial companies. We were not very happy in Quebec when the Dutch group purchased Le Groupe Connue, nor were we very happy when Stone Container purchased Consolidated-Bathurst. That is why our philosophy is to ensure that our financial institutions can develop commercial links so that we would remain the masters of our economy. ... I do believe as a Canadian that we should have a series of financial institutions helping Canadians to remain owners of our economy. We in Quebec think it can be done and we believe it could be done at the Canadian level as well."[28]

We should also look at the possibility of establishing our own version of a *keiretsu* — or joining a Japanese one. Masaya Miyoshi, president of the powerful Japanese business association, the Keidanren, has proposed that each Japanese *keiretsu* invite non-Japanese companies to join its corporate family.[29] The Canadian Institute for Advanced Research is pursuing ways of establishing a Canadian-style *keiretsu*, which it would call a Nunaligiit, or innovative business enterprise. Similarly, the Canada Consulting Group has concluded that "new institutional arrangements between the providers and users of capital may be the best long-term solution to our cost of capital problem." One option, it says, would be to create a Bank for Industrial Innovation, which would operate like a main bank in a Japanese *keiretsu* and become the nucleus of a home-grown *keiretsu* in Canada. This would require the cooperation of Canadian financial institutions. But as the world moves towards more technology-intensive industries, we cannot afford to miss opportunities to form links between Canadian resource and high-tech enterprises.

Pension funds are another potential partner in a Canadian-style *keiretsu* (or as long-term shareholders of important Canadian companies). The trusteed pension funds are already major owners of shares in Canadian companies, and they hold approximately 30 per cent of the shares listed on the Toronto Stock Exchange. But pension funds do not behave as owners in the way that German or Japanese banks do. Their interest is simply in the stock market performance of a company. Yet there is a strong argument for them to behave like owners: pension fund holdings are so large that they cannot easily sell the shares they own. Peter Drucker contends that they should behave as real owners and promote long-term economic growth: "A country perishes if those who have the power do not exercise responsibility — and the pension funds have power."[30]

Two New York corporate lawyers, Martin Lipton and Steven Rosenblum, have proposed a new "quinquennial system" of corporate governance that would also refocus corporate attention to long-term objectives. The system they propose "is designed to make shareholders and managers think and act like long-term owners."[31] Under their system, every fifth annual meeting of a corporation would become, in effect, a referendum on corporate strategy and control. Between these five-year reviews, they would severely limit the ability of shareholders to change control of the company. Directors would be elected for five-year terms and would be elected on the record of the company over the previous five years and on its strategic plan for the next five years. In the year of the quinquennial meeting, the company would distribute to all its shareholders a detailed report comparing its performance over the past five years with the strategic plan as well as detailing the company's plan for the next five years, including return on investment and management compensation. In addition, an outside firm, such as an investment bank or accounting firm, would provide an independent evaluation of the company's performance in the past five years and the feasibility of its plans for the next five years. In other words, the company would focus on maximizing its wealth-creation capacity instead of the short-term focus of maximizing shareholder value.

Drucker argues that institutional investors, such as pension fund managers, have done enormous harm to industry by focusing on short-term results — a policy that forces corporations to do the same: "The short-term focus has been a major contributing factor to the bad performance and decline of a U.S. company or industry: it explains in large measure why General Motors failed to respond in time to Japanese competition. Everyone who has worked with American managements can testify that the need to satisfy the pension-fund manager's quest for higher earnings next quarter, together with the panicky fear of the raider, constantly pushes top managements toward decisions they know to be costly, if not suicidal mistakes."[32] And the damage is greatest, Drucker warns, where North America can least afford it, "in the fast-growing, middle-sized high-tech or high-engineering firm that needs to put every available penny into tomorrow — research, product development, market development, people development, service."

As Canada moves towards the next century, it is vital that we create new institutions and policies that will enable us to grow a strong team of Canadian companies. We need them in order to compete successfully internationally, to generate new jobs and opportunities for better educated and better trained Canadians, to use new science and technology that Canadian scientists and engineers are clearly capable of producing, and to join in strategic alliances, joint ventures, and partnerships with companies around the world. If we are successful, we shall attract high-quality foreign investors who want to tag on to a more dynamic and innovative Canada because it is a good place to be. This will require new attitudes on the part of policymakers, bankers, pension fund managers, corporate management financial analysts, and Canadians in general. It will also require recognition of the fact that, since corporations are the vehicles for economic growth and opportunity, the vision of our business executives will have to shift from short-term thinking to the longer view: an emphasis on maximizing the wealth-creation capacity of our businesses and on the R & D, skills training, labour-management relations, employee empowerment, and other factors that make for long-term success.

9

A Workplace for the Year 2000

NYONE WHO WANTS TO SEE the future of work should start with Shell Canada's chemical plant in Sarnia, Ontario, a high-technology installation that requires careful monitoring and close attention to quality control. For more than a decade now, its unionized employees have been running the operation through a system of work teams that was jointly designed in a partnership between the company and the Energy and Chemical Workers Union. There are only two types of worker: process operators and maintenance technicians; the six process teams work 12-hour shifts and the maintenance technicians work weekdays only. Not only do these employees largely run the plant, but all the members of the teams are trained in a variety of skills and can handle routine maintenance and quality control by themselves.[1]

There are other features that make the Sarnia workplace remarkable. The employees have much of the responsibility for training one another as well as for final hiring from a short list prepared by management. They plan their work assignments and training programs, authorize overtime, and schedule vacations. Moreover, the more skills each worker develops, the higher his pay, with all workers being allowed to strive for top pay rates. Supervisors have been replaced by coordinators, who serve on the process teams as representatives of management. An entire layer of management was eliminated, as were management dining facilities and reserved parking spaces. The plant facility itself was designed to accommodate the new workplace structure, and both management and employees are continually striving to redesign the system to make it work better. Workplace consultant Jacquie Mansell says that "the most important innovation in the technical system is in the communications and information network. The computer system provides direct information at various levels in the organization in forms and frequencies that would never occur in traditional plants." For instance, it provides the information, including financial information, and the decision-making capacity to permit individual employees to make key decisions on what course of action to follow.[2]

Shell Canada and its union are not alone in persuing new workplace arrangements, but this example underlines the fact that if Canada is to pursue a high-skills, high-pay economy, producing high-value goods and services for world markets, new partnerships between companies and their employees are essential. Moreover, while productive partnerships do not require unions, they will have a much better chance of success if employees are able to exercise their collective voice through healthy labour unions. Recognizing the important role of unions as a key institution is essential for our future economic success; and even where employees do not seek to become unionized, new forms of employee representation will be necessary if Canada is to have the highly productive, highly skilled, and innovative workforce that it is going to need.

A number of developments are putting strains on the old-style workplace with its authoritarian structure of command and its sharp distinctions between management and employees. Demographics will play a pivotal role. An aging workforce will mean that companies will have to find new methods of retraining and upgrading skills to keep their workforce flexible and up to date, as well as finding new ways of motivating employees, since the number of aging baby boomers will far exceed the number of new positions for advancement. At the same time, as the number of young new workers declines, companies will end up hiring people they might have turned down in the past. And companies will have to pay even greater attention to the needs of working mothers (for example, the provision of child care) as they attempt to offset the slowdown in the number of new workers. Meanwhile, equity programs and others will force companies to adjust the workplace to the needs of the physically handicapped and to the needs of native populations and unskilled immigrants from developing countries with very different cultures.

Global competition is another major factor forcing change in the workplace. In the new economy, companies around the world can buy the same technology. A Japanese auto parts company and a Canadian auto parts company can have the same computer and the same machining systems. But if the Japanese company has a well-designed workplace with close labour-management responsibility for its operation, and if it has invested more in employee training, then it will get more and better output from its manufacturing systems than the Canadian company will. The competitive advantage comes from the skills of workers and the structure of the workplace. As trade barriers tumble and education and experience levels rise around the world, what happens in the individual workplace will become more important than ever before. This challenge has been put well by the United Steelworkers union in Canada: "If we compete in the same markets as new industrializing countries, using the same technologies, the odds are stacked against us. There is no long-term place for Canada based on low-skilled and semi-skilled jobs. Our future can lie only in skill-intensive industries and skill-intensive methods of production."[3]

Perhaps the greatest source of change is coming from the fast-evolving information technologies, which are upsetting the very nature of work and the structure of the workplace. The Economic Council of Canada has estimated that more than one-half of all Canadians "are now employed in occupations that are primarily concerned with the creation and use of data and knowledge." Jobs of this kind accounted for two-thirds of the net employment growth in Canada between 1971 and 1986.[4] In 1989, Statistics Canada found that 43 per cent of all employed Canadians — about 5.4 million people at the time — said that their jobs had been somewhat or greatly affected by the introduction of computers or automated technology sometime in the past five years. Two-thirds said that the level of skills required to do the job had increased, and 61 per cent said the job had become more interesting. Almost one-third of employed Canadians used computers in their work and more than half of them used a computer 10 hours or more a week.[5]

Increasingly, jobs consist of managing and manipulating data on a computer screen, whether the screen is an office terminal, an airline check-in desk, a salesperson's laptop, a control station in a steel mill or paper plant, or a machining centre in a factory. For banks, airlines, truckers, manufacturers, retailers, hotel chains, and stockbrokers, information technologies are now the key source of competitive advantage — so much so that an airline's reservations system is its most important asset, as is a bank's electronic network. The ways in which these systems are used and upgraded are the key determinants of how well a company can compete.

The new information technologies are also revolutionizing the resource industries and manufacturing. Continuous process control (in which information technologies are used to monitor and correct all the various stages in converting oil or natural gas to gasoline or chemicals, wood fibres to paper, and metal ores to steel, aluminum, or nickel) means that many of the jobs in these industries are for information workers, who sit in front of control screens monitoring the process flow and adjusting systems to gain the most efficient output. On the factory floor, computer-aided design is employed to engineer and upgrade parts and components, computer-aided manufacturing directs robots and other forms of automation, flexible manufacturing systems use unmanned machining centres to produce finely measured metal parts, and computer-integrated manufacturing is poised to link together the various systems of automation. Consequently, factory workers will increasingly have to be knowledge workers.

In a massive project surveying nearly 1000 companies in Canada on their use of information technologies, the Economic Council found that Canada was falling behind other nations. "Canada's persistent lag in the introduction and use of computer-based technologies is an urgent national problem of major proportions," the council said, warning that the slow diffusion of technology would impede Canada's competitiveness. In Japan, the council said, not only is the use of process technology far more advanced, but "workers are highly trained and, in fact, are often involved in the design and implementation of the systems."

The Economic Council stressed that technological change is more than new machinery and equipment: "As Japan and Sweden (among others) have demonstrated, success also requires an innovative organizational climate that can foster an involved, well-trained and committed workforce. In Canada, while almost everyone agrees that people are the key, too few organizations live by that principle." Job redesign and worker participation have not caught hold. Although there are some highly innovative workplaces, on balance "it appears that many firms in this country are operating according to traditional principles of work design and decision-making." Yet as the Economic Council concluded, "success depends as much on innovation in organization and the development of human resources as it does on technical expertise."[6]

These technologies, then, are radically transforming the workplace as we know it, putting new demands on both management and employees. But they have the potential to yield great gains in productivity and better-paying jobs, provided old-style management practices are replaced by new-style management. At issue is management's willingness to surrender its authoritarian controls and move to a more democratic workplace, where executives become coaches, workers become team members with management, and new partnerships are built.

Companies that want to pursue flexible design, development, and production systems must rely on their own employees "to anticipate possible problems, eliminate bottlenecks, avoid production shutdowns, and ensure quality," the U.S. Office of Technology Assessment (OTA) said in a study of the modern workplace.[7] These programs depend on continual improvement to cut costs and raise quality while reducing waste and scrap. Workers participate in group problem-solving as well as in other matters that require social and communications skills. At the same time, "new forms of work organization push responsibility and authority downward in the corporate hierarchy, from line managers and staff engineers toward the shop floor. Information systems bring business data previously restricted to managers — incoming orders, unique customer requirements, production schedules, cost and sales projections — directly to the factory floor," the OTA report says. "Shopfloor groups often must know how to interpret such information and apply it to their work. This change, more than any other, promises to fundamentally alter traditional workplace hierarchies and to create a new set of training requirements."[8]

The problem is that many companies, because they want to retain old systems of hierarchy and control, are using new technologies mainly to automate old-style jobs, says Shoshana Zuboff in a major book on the new workplace, *In the Age of the Smart Machine*. "Managers emphasize machine intelligence and managerial control over the knowledge base at the expense of developing knowledge in the operating work force," she says.[9] While this kind of manager uses technology to exert control over the employees, experience shows that such an approach is "fatally flawed in its ability to exploit the informating capacity of the new technology." It leads to antagonism in the workplace and the loss of knowledge that workers might possess and that could lead to high-value outcomes. As long as the traditional system of management control and hierarchy is preserved, the company fails to gain the full benefits of new technology that are available to its competitors, and its business suffers accordingly.

There is no doubt that the development of a well-informed and interactive workplace that can realize the full potential of new technologies — what Zuboff calls an "informating strategy" — does threaten old-style management, whose power comes from tight control over the knowledge base of a company. But as long as managers are unwilling to share information, employees cannot be expected to show any enthusiasm for the new technologies. "New roles cannot emerge without the structures to support them," says Zuboff. Managers and employees alike will need new methods of evaluation, new career paths, and new ways of determining rewards. The defining difference in this new workplace is that there is access to information and knowledge, and a focus on continual learning.

The increasingly intellectual content of work blurs the traditional lines between management and employees, in large part because employees gain access to information that previously was the preserve of management and the source of its authority. "Under these circumstances, work organization requires a new division of learning to support a new division of labor," says Zuboff. She points out that today's vocabulary does not express the realities of the new workplace. "We remain, in the final years of the 20th century, prisoners of a vocabulary in which managers require employees; supervisors have subordinates; jobs are defined to be specific, detailed, narrow, and task-related; and organizations have levels that in turn make possible chains of command and spans of control. The guiding metaphors are military; relationships are thought of as contractual and often as adversarial." New concepts are therefore needed to reflect the new reality of information technologies and the sources of competitive advantage where value-added is the key objective. The new vocabulary, says Zuboff, is "one of colleagues and co-learners, of exploration, experimentation, and innovation. Jobs are comprehensive, tasks are abstractions that depend upon insights and synthesis, and power is a roving force that comes to rest as dictated by function and need."[10]

This new workplace puts difficult new demands on both managers and employees. Managers who want to see their organizations prosper can no longer behave like little Napoleons. They will have to behave more like coaches, facilitators, or coordinators, developing a learning environment, motivating people, and, in the forthcoming period of skills shortages, having to spend more time finding ways of keeping good employees. In the old workplace, managers could treat employees as one of several inputs, along with raw materials, parts, and energy; in effect, employees were objects whose output could easily be regulated and measured, and who could be laid off if the economy slowed down. For their part, employees could do their jobs without any commitment to the company and managers did not have to pay attention to their feelings so long as they did their jobs. But in a learning environment, says Zuboff, "how people feel about themselves, each other, and the organization's purposes is clearly linked to their capacity to sustain the high levels of internal commitment and motivation that are demanded by the abstraction of work and the new division of learning." New kinds of management skills and styles are thus essential.

Nowhere has this been more bluntly stated than in the comments by General Electric chairman John Welch in his company's 1991 annual report, in which he described the type of leader found in his company and the type it wanted throughout the organization, starting at the shop floor. It was the fourth type of leader that Welch focused on. "That leader delivers on commitments, makes all the numbers, but doesn't share the values we must have. This is the individual who typically forces performance out of people rather than inspires it: the autocrat, the big shot, the tyrant." This kind of manager may have been acceptable in the past, Welch said, "but in an environment where we must have every good idea from every man and woman in the organization, we cannot afford management styles that suppress and intimidate."[11]

These changes in workplace organization will be difficult for labour as well as management. For many employees, the traditional workplace provided a high level of personal security and autonomy. A labour contract defined the worker's job, pay levels, and advancement through seniority, as well as the protection of rights through grievance and arbitration procedures. So long as one carried out one's job properly, there was no problem. "A worker need not buy into the purposes or values of the organization in order to perform competently and enjoy the rewards that he or she has earned," explained Zuboff. "There is no need to be liked by those around you, either superiors or peers, when one's primary obligation is to fulfill the demands of a narrow job description." This relationship gave workers a great sense of personal autonomy.

The new workplace is very different, and many workers fear that they will be brainwashed into some notion of company loyalty that impinges on their personal independence. Their tasks are more abstract, the demands of their jobs more uncertain, the need to work and collaborate with others much more important, and the benchmarks of performance far less clear. In the old workplace an employee just had to worry about doing the job properly; in the new workplace one may have less control over one's work because of being a member of a team, something totally new. So while the old rules and hierarchies will disappear, "informed organizations will have to pay careful attention to developing a constitutional infrastructure that legitimates public debate and mutual influence," Zuboff warns. "The clarity of individual rights within the enterprise is likely to become extremely important to the extent that the learning community requires the participation of the 'total person' in its endeavors. Because such a system will exert considerable pressure on an individual's psychological boundaries, it will require mechanisms that can arbitrate competing interpretations of rights and obligations."[12]

The new workplace will create other tensions as well. Older workers with less education could have a hard time fitting into new structures that favour young, more flexible, and better-educated people.

The new workplace may also create tensions among the workers — between those who race ahead with the new technologies and those who resist being put on what they fear is a management treadmill that demands greater and greater performance to keep their jobs and their seniority. And since the real value of new information technologies will come from the willingness of employees to experiment and innovate with systems, the managers will be under enormous pressure to win the commitment of employees and to find forms of reward that do not add to antagonisms and divisions in the workplace.

If the new workplace is to benefit both employees and employers, effective democracy within companies is essential so that employees can balance the power of employers. Laws help and so do unions, so strengthening labour laws to remove barriers to unionization would help some employees. But as labour law expert Paul Weiler points out, even with stronger laws on labour standards, health and safety, pay equity, and protection against unfair dismissal, many employees still have a "representation gap" which they do not want to deal with by joining unions. Non-union workers often feel powerless to pursue their legal right; and unions, though effective at protecting workers, have failed to provide the participation in the governance of the workplace that many employees desire.

Many of the larger non-union companies recognize the need to retain employees (especially when they have invested in their training and skills upgrading) as well as to gain their commitment and cooperation to help compete in the new global economy, says Weiler, and they have therefore introduced different forms of employee involvement, such as quality of working life programs, work teams, quality circles, and other forms of participation. But ultimately this is "participation without real power," he says. Management can ignore employee recommendations that it doesn't like. "Thus a Quality of Working Life committee of employees has no independent power base from which to challenge management's action — to insist, for example, that there will be drug testing only when there is a reasonable suspicion that a particular employee is using drugs, and to tie management down to such a position in a written contract."[13] Moreover, in these days of mergers and acquisitions, there is no guarantee that a new owner would accept continuation of worker participation programs — or even that a new chief executive officer would feel bound to continue such an arrangement.

U.S. research that examined more than 1000 manufacturing companies using labour-management committees found that those in unionized companies were more effective, because although unions can say no as a group, "they can also collectively say 'yes.'" In non-union companies, employees had much less to trade. The researchers found that "among those plants which have adopted new technology within the past five years and when there is both a union and a collaborative problem-solving committee structure, blue-collar workers have a significantly better chance of having their jobs redesigned to include the new skill-enhancing responsibility of programming." By contrast, non-union workplaces with joint labour-management problem-solving committees "are significantly less efficient and less likely to provide employment security than is a traditional union-based system of workplace governance." The lesson? "For collaborative problem solving to succeed, it must be possible for employees to achieve outcomes that also empower them. In management-initiated schemes, the narrow focus and limited scope for which these programs were designed are quite possibly frustrating these aspirations, undermining the trust and commitment so necessary for success."[14]

Weiler argues that if employee involvement is to be effective, there has to be "a cohesive worker organization capable of effective representation of employee interests." Unions have played this role and continue to do so, but for a shrinking proportion of the private-sector workforce. In 1989 some 3.8 million Canadians, or 34.1 per cent of the workforce, belonged to unions, including 737,889 manufacturing workers or 36.3 per cent of the manufacturing workforce, and 1.3 million service industry workers, or 34.6 per cent of the service sector workforce. But the fastest growth in union membership is coming from the public sector, including health care, social services, public administration, and education. Fast-growing parts of the economy, such as business services with a unionization rate of just 3 per cent, have very low levels.[15] Although unions have been effective in protecting the interests of workers, they have not succeeded in strengthening employee participation — partly because the unions themselves have been divided over whether union members should engage in ongoing workplace discussions with management, and partly because the very nature of collective bargaining confines real discussion to contract negotiations once every two or three years.

The United Steelworkers union, in a forward-looking policy paper on the new workplace, recognizes this limitation and wants to do something about it. "The duty to bargain ends when a collective agreement is ratified. For the next two to three years the employer focuses on the right to manage while the union focuses on the right to grieve in an attempt to make sure that agreed-to limits on management rights are in fact respected," the Canadian steelworkers said in this policy paper. "Typically, during this period of the administration and enforcement of the collective agreement the union is shut out of all decision-making concerning the operation of the company. . . . In this situation, the only role for the union is a reactive, adversarial one — to challenge management decisions by litigating the procedural or substantive validity of those decisions." In other words, the current system "is not well suited to deal effectively with long-term issues such as training, skill development, occupational health and safety, or adjustment to change. The more important such longer term issues become, the less appropriate the current labor relations system is," said the steelworkers, calling for innovative mechanisms to allow companies and unions to engage in "creative ongoing discussions on the longer term issues."[16]

But the movement to employee involvement could also bring collective agreements and the role of national unions into question, Weiler argues. "Once employees begin to deal directly with managers about a variety of immediate concerns in the production process and the workplace, it is virtually impossible to insulate the terms of the union contract and the prerogatives of union leadership from their purview," he contends. One reason for the various forms of employee involvement — aside from a desire to give employees a greater sense of participation and to counter employee alienation — has been to help adjust the business to the demands of new technologies and global competition. But lengthy, tightly written collective agreements, by narrowly defining the roles of employees and management, may impede necessary adjustments. Weiler suggests that this could be why the General Motors contract with the United Auto Workers for the Saturn plant in the United States is only 20 pages long and mainly sets out the mutual goals of the auto company and its union, leaving the resolution of problems to a joint committee structure throughout the organization. In fact, Weiler argues, a major shift in the power and structure of the unions could be underway, with national unions giving up power to local unions that work much more closely with local management. National unions would become loose federations of company-specific locals, with the national head office providing a range of services and resources to the locals.

Although unions need to play a larger role in the governance of the workplace, it is unlikely that they will represent more than a large minority of private-sector workers. So what is also needed, says Weiler, is labour legislation that provides "some meaningful voice in the governance of the workplace" and that "would be good for its workers and for its broader political economy." The law could mandate some form of participatory procedure for employees within all companies above a certain size, one that would not necessarily mean union representation. Such a procedure would offset the significant power that management exercises over the lives of employees and would pave the way for more productive participation by employees in their companies, with benefits for the companies as well.

Weiler's model is the German Works Council, or *Betriebsrat;* he calls his version the Employee Participation Committee. The works councils have played a significant role in Germany's human resources policy and in the country's economic success. Under Weiler's proposal, every company with 25 or more employees would be required to establish an Employee Participation Committee; companies with just 25 employees would elect a single member to the committee; bigger companies would elect a larger number. All employees would be eligible for election (including professional, supervisory, and middle management) except for senior management and those in charge of human resources or industrial relations departments. In companies that had operations at different locations, a company-wide committee would coordinate this exercise of employee influence. "The aim of this entire structure would be to develop an in-house, bottom-up system of employee representation that acknowledges that the work force as a whole has a common stake in the human resource policies and other programs of the employer, whatever the specific responsibilities and status enjoyed by any one occupational category."

The employee participation committees would deal with a wide range of issues. Employers would be required to provide them with ongoing and detailed information, not just on personnel policy but on the broader financial, investment, and profit position of the company. Employers would have to consult on changes in their criteria for salaries and wages, benefits, hiring, training, adjustment policies, layoffs, health and safety, employment equity, technology changes, plant closings and relocations, and organizational changes. Discussion would take place on a regular basis.

The employee participation committees would be weaker in some respects than unions; for example, in lacking the resources of a national office. But they would have access to more information than unions normally get and would have ongoing access to senior management, which would be required to sit down and talk with the committee. As Weiler acknowledges, these committees would need financial resources to train their representatives and to hire outside expertise to help in their discussions with management (for example, pension experts, labour lawyers, economists, and scientists). He suggests that companies be required to pay part of the cost, though employees would have to help with the financing.

"When elected, informed, trained and well-advised representatives of the employees meet regularly with their opposite numbers in the senior management team to address a continuing series of employment issues, one can expect the employees eventually to develop considerable persuasive influence on the ultimate policies and practices of the firm," Weiler argues. His scheme would go far beyond the type of employee-involvement programs of non-union firms, since employees would be operating through a collective voice and would have greater leverage to influence corporate decision making. Of course, there could still be areas of sharp disagreement, and here employees would have to calculate whether they wanted to take the next step of joining a union, and management would have to consider whether it was worth making a compromise in order to avoid unionization.

Unions need not be threatened by the emergence of employee participation committees, since some committees would almost certainly lead to unionization; in the meantime, national unions could be a service and resource centre for the employee participation committees, selling advice on pensions, health and safety, and other issues and offering some kind of associate membership status. In the case of already unionized plants, unions could, if a majority of employees agreed, become the employee voice on employee participation committees. The system, Weiler argues, would guarantee all employees, wherever they worked, "a structure for elected and informed representation of their interests in the firm." And it would extend democracy into the workplace, where it is badly needed.[17]

The implications of such a move would be far-reaching, raising the status of employees to that of stakeholders who have interests that are as important as those of shareholders. In the new economy, where the real capital of companies is knowledge — much of it embedded in the skills and experience of employees — it is time for the status of employees and their role in shaping the business enterprise to be increased. This has gone furthest in Japan where, according to Koji Matsumoto, a former high-ranking official of the Ministry of International Trade and Industry, "employees replaced shareholders as the main structural elements in larger Japanese companies" — so much so that "as a social reality, the big corporation in Japan is a body of its employees." With its job security, its sharing of gains in productivity, and its well-structured forms of labour-management consultation, Japan has created a unique corporate system.

"For its part, the company cannot replace employees easily, like it can other production factors, such as land and raw materials," says Matsumoto. "The company, therefore, had to concern itself with maintaining and developing employee abilities and morale." At the same time, employees know "that if the company were to prosper they would benefit economically from higher salaries, promotions, improved health and welfare benefits as well as socially from the company's higher prestige." In other words, employees feel a close link between their well-being and the well-being of their employer. This linkage is missing in countries such as Canada, as Matsumoto points out: "The only relationship employees have with a corporation is providing part of their occupational functions in return for a salary, and, in a sense, rather than receiving economic compensation from their company, one can say they receive it from their functions."[18]

In their minds, Japanese executives represent the employees, from whose ranks they have risen, rather than the shareholders. While Canadian executives are concerned primarily with maintaining and increasing shareholder value in the form of dividends and capital gains, which means a top-down system of management, Japanese executives include employees in the internal corporate structure where decisions are made. More than 90 per cent of large Japanese companies have a labour-management consultation system, according to the Japan Productivity Centre, and employees are involved not only in decisions that directly affect them in the workplace but in broader questions affecting such matters as the modification of production lines, the establishment of new plants, and foreign investment.

Few companies go as far as the giant Kao Corporation, a leading Japanese soap and detergent maker, where every employee has equal access to all corporate information. Each employee may access any information in the company's computer data base, attend meetings of the company's board of directors, and participate in monthly conferences on research and development. The goal is to encourage creativity and new product or process innovation, says Sheridan Tatsuno, an expert on Japanese technology development.[19] The Japanese system helps explain why Japanese companies have become world leaders in building the "knowledge-creating" company that thrives on continual innovation and the rapid embodiment of new knowledge into new products, says Japanese management expert Ikujiro Nonaka. "The centrepiece of the Japanese approach is the recognition that creating new knowledge is not simply a matter of 'processing' objective information," Nonaka says. "Rather, it depends on tapping the tacit and often highly subjective insights, intuitions, and hunches of individual employees and making those insights available for testing and use by the company as a whole. The key to this process is personal commitment, the employees' sense of identity with the enterprise and its mission." Japanese companies are able to do this, he says, because they put "knowledge creation exactly where it belongs: at the very centre of a company's human resources strategy."[20]

In Canada, although there is widespread recognition that the workplace has to change to reflect the impact of new technologies and the aspirations of a better-educated workforce, there are still enormous barriers to real change. One indication is business's continuing hostility to an expanded role for unions and to changes in the labour laws that would make it easier for unions to gain representation and achieve first contracts — this despite the fact that, as economists Richard Freeman and James Medoff found in a major research project, on balance, unionization appears to improve rather than harm the social and economic systems. As these economists also point out, "the extent to which a union is a liability or an asset depends crucially on how management responds to it." If management uses collective bargaining "to learn about and improve the operation of the workplace and the production process, unionism can be a significant plus to enterprise efficiency." Unions can "increase the development and retention of skills, provide information about what occurs on the shop floor, improve morale, and pressure management to be more efficient in its operations."[21] But if management sticks to old-style hierarchies and views its employees simply as cogs in the organizational machine, the workplace will be one of confrontation.

Trust is an essential ingredient of the modern workplace, yet this appears to be one of the weaknesses of Canadian management. Peter Drucker, the U.S. management expert, highlighted this problem in a seminar for members of the Canadian Manufacturers' Association in the mid-1980s. "Your obsolete and old-fashioned labor relations climate is 20 years behind the rest of the developed world," he told the Canadian executives. "I would consider labor relations a priority. And I would ask myself, 'Have I really used the strengths of people?' because you Canadians are singularly poor in this regard. You're so conscious of the fallibilities and weakness of people that you are not looking for their strengths."[22]

A similar point has been made by Gail Cook Johnson, a human resources specialist. "There aren't many differences between American and Canadian organizations, but the key one is that Americans train and develop their people and make them feel as though they're using all their skills to a far greater extent than Canadians do," she says. "We do a very good job on rigorous one-to-one supervision. We have much safer workplaces. We have more rigorous control procedures in place. But we don't take risks with people. Why don't we? Because we tend to invest in the things that control people as opposed to the things that develop people."[23]

One striking indicator of the need for change in management attitudes is the low level of private-sector job training in Canada. The Advisory Council on Adjustment, headed by then BCE Inc. chairman Jean de Grandpré, reported in 1989 that "the private sector does not have a training mentality." Although some companies (for example, the large banks) are major investors in employee training, they are in the minority. "A general private sector training effort is urgently required and will benefit both employers and employees," the council said. "If everyone were involved in such an effort, employers who do training would not see their staff raided by employers who do not invest in the skills of their workforce. Employees' satisfaction would also be greatly improved as they would be able to achieve their utmost potential." This, said the council, is why business must completely rethink its approach to training. "Training is not a residual activity. It must become part of work." While governments have the responsibility through the education system to equip people with the basic literacy, numeracy, and scientific skills, "ensuring that workers can meet the challenges of tomorrow's occupations remains a private sector responsibility. . . . Only private sector training and retraining, on a continuing basis, will allow firms to meet their skills requirements, workers to maximize their abilities, and firms and workers to adjust and win."[24]

It is difficult to obtain reliable statistics on how much training Canadian employees actually get, but it seems clear that they are getting less than employees in countries with which Canada competes. The fact that Canadian business is slower to use new technologies than business is in other countries and that it is less willing to train its employees helps to explain why Canada has a competitiveness problem. Although there are some notable exceptions in our business community, overall Canada is not fielding a world-class private sector to compete in the global economy. It is not investing sufficiently either in the best available technologies or in the best available skills. Without this productivity potential, then, Canada is forced to keep zeroing in on wage and other costs to find a place in the global marketplace.

In 1988, the average Canadian worker received 6.7 hours of formal training, compared with 17 hours for an Australian worker, 170 hours for a Swedish worker, and 200 hours for a Japanese worker, according to the National Advisory Board on Science and Technology.[25] The same study cited a Statistics Canada 1987 survey that found that Canadian companies had spent about $1.4 billion on training, about one-half the level of U.S. companies and less than one-quarter the investment of German companies. In fact, less than one-quarter of Canadian companies spent anything at all on training their employees; small business is particularly negligent. A survey of 136 companies in Ontario by the Premier's Council also found a serious deficit in skills training: "Companies investing seriously in training were the exceptions in the survey rather than the rule."[26]

Moreover, according to the Economic Council of Canada, "when employer-sponsored training is provided, it is heavily concentrated among highly-skilled, well-educated male workers: the rest of the work force has far less access, particularly to comprehensive training opportunities."[27] The Conference Board of Canada came to much the same conclusion in a survey of 444 medium and large-scale companies: "Although the Canadian companies surveyed are investing in training for all categories of employees, professional and management staff receive the most training annually. It seems that the remaining employees are receiving significantly fewer training hours per year on average."[28]

To underline the critical importance of training, the Canadian Labour Market Productivity Centre estimates that two-thirds of those who will be in the workforce in 2005 are already part of it. "This means that the problem is becoming increasingly a question of upgrading the basic skills of those currently in the labor force," says Andrew Sharpe of the centre.[29]

Training is not only an issue on the factory floor. It is of critical importance in service industries as well — as the banks, for example, are increasingly recognizing. In its report on skills, the Ontario Premier's Council contrasted the difference between the training of

German and Canadian bank tellers. In Germany, the tellers go through the country's highly organized apprenticeship system; they are better educated than tellers in Canada, and there is low turnover. They are therefore able to inform customers about loan costs, interest rates, and various bank products. Now that Canadian banks are moving to offer a wide range of new services, as well as their long list of existing products, ranging from mortgages and car loans to RRSPs and mutual funds, it is surprising that Canadian bank tellers are not equally well trained. The banks explained their reluctance to upgrade tellers "by citing concerns about high turnover and the often low expectations they have of new workers' capabilities," the Premier's Council said.

The auto industry is one of Canada's most important manufacturing industries, supporting an enormous number of suppliers; but in a new era of continental free trade, Canada will have to work hard to maintain its share of the business.. Much of this effort will have to come through employee training. In 1985 some 62 per cent of the blue-collar jobs in Ontario auto parts companies were in unskilled work that required less than one month of training; by 1995 only 33 per cent of blue-collar jobs in the auto parts industry will be unskilled. On the other hand, the proportion of skilled jobs — in which a worker must spend two years to acquire proficiency — will more than double, from 13 per cent in 1985 to 32 per cent in 1995.[30] Will our companies be able to meet this challenge? While there is widespread concern about the great strength of the Japanese auto companies, there is less recognition of the fact that Japanese auto and auto parts companies invest much more in training and quality control than the big U.S. companies that dominate the Canadian auto industry.

According to research by the Office of Technology Assessment in the United States, experienced production workers in Japanese auto companies get three times as much training each year as their American (and presumably Canadian) counterparts. The differences are even more striking for newly hired workers. They get more than 300 hours of training in their first six months on the job in Japanese plants, compared with fewer than 50 hours in U.S.-owned plants in Canada and the United States; and the Japanese transplants in Canada and the United States provide about 275 hours of training

in the first six months of employment.[31] As we move to make training a higher priority, there will be a multitude of opportunities for
training providers, from community colleges to consulting firms. In
what may be a sign of things to come, there are now four training
companies listed on the London Stock Exchange, whereas there were
none in the mid-1980s.[32]

While much remains to be done to raise the availability of training in Canada, there are signs of progress — often in industries
where there are active unions. Steel, food, plastics, aerospace, electrical products, and forest products are among the sectors that have
taken steps in this direction. One example is the Sectoral Skills
Council in the electrical and electronics industry, which has established a sectoral training fund, paid for by industry, government,
and workers, to finance worker training and skills upgrading in the
industry. Reflecting the differences in attitude within the labour
movement, three unions (the Communications and Electrical
Workers of Canada, the United Steelworkers, and the International
Brotherhood of Electrical Workers) have agreed to have their mem-
bers help pay for the program, while two other unions (the
Canadian Auto Workers and the United Electrical, Radio and
Machine Workers) have refused. Another organization, Skills
Canada, was launched in 1989 to give skills a higher profile; in 1990
Canada became the thirtieth member of the International
Organization for the Promotion of Vocational Education, which
allows young Canadian workers to participate in the International
Youth Skills Olympics. The first national skills contest in Canada is
to be held in 1994.

Nevertheless, the Advisory Council on Adjustment, better known
as the de Grandpré Report, concluded that the private sector cannot
be counted on to increase its training effort "simply because it is
exhorted to do so." As the Economic Council of Canada found in a
1987 research report, "Canadian firms have not undergone major
human resource adjustments. The technology-driven retraining that
has been carried out appears to have been of a short duration and
unstructured nature, aimed predominantly at integrating the new
technologies with existing skills."[33] This is why the de Grandpré
Report concluded that government action was needed to ensure that
companies start living up to their training responsibilities. To

accomplish this, the Advisory Council on Adjustment proposed a corporate tax liability equivalent to 1 per cent of payroll to be offset entirely if the company provided training to its employees; this would roughly double the level of training that Canadian companies provide their employees (the 1987 human resources survey by Statistics Canada estimated that companies spent about 0.6 per cent of payroll on training in 1987). The purpose of the tax liability would be to stimulate training, not to raise revenue, but the council suggested that if companies did not meet the training target, the government should use the money to develop training programs in consultation with industry and labour so that Canada would enter the twenty-first century with a highly skilled workforce. Although the suggested training levy was not very high (for example, France had a 1.3 per cent requirement for some time, which it recently raised to 1.5 per cent), the federal government has not adopted the proposal. Yet as Anthony Comper, president of the Bank of Montreal, says, the scheme "should represent no additional burden for companies which are already doing their part."[34]

Companies also have a major role to play in restructuring apprenticeship systems so that Canada will have the skilled workers it will need in the future. "For many years," says Peter Larson of the Conference Board of Canada, "Canada has coasted off the apprenticeship system of Western Europe. For decades, thousands and thousands of skilled tool and die makers, electricians, millwrights and mechanics poured into Canada from England, France, Germany and other countries. As a result of that, our own apprenticeship programs in many fields have been weak and underdeveloped." But the days when Canada could rely on other countries for trained workers are over. "In every sector of industry there are dire predictions of impending labor shortage — precisely in the area of skilled and technical labor unless immediate steps are taken to remedy current trends."[35] Canada has serious problems in the school-to-work transition, as indicated by the 30 per cent high school dropout rate and the parallel lack of young trainees in skilled trades. Part of the problem is perception: young Canadians do not realize that skilled trades lead to challenging jobs and high incomes and to the opportunity to start one's own business, or that there is plenty of room for young women in Canada's skilled trades.

But a bigger problem is the lack of an effective apprenticeship system, like the one found in Germany, to help teenagers combine a high school education with apprenticeship training. Business should be taking the lead in developing a strong apprenticeship system; but to make it work, companies would have to ensure that apprentices are given high-quality training in the workplace as well as an assurance that there would be no layoffs during a downturn in the economy. Meanwhile, the quality of apprenticeship training being provided by companies in Canada may well be inadequate. According to the Toronto office of the Canadian-German Chamber of Commerce, "the growing demand for skilled labor in high technology companies is simply not being matched by the education level of the apprentices."[36] And a national apprenticeship survey by Statistics Canada found that "a surprisingly high proportion of Canada's apprentices do not complete their programs."[37] Among the reasons cited for dropping out was the inadequate teaching of skills to meet requirements for the various trades.

There are some signs of improvement by industry. Quebec's aerospace companies have teamed up with the province and the Montreal Catholic School Commission to establish an aerospace trade school that will provide an 18-month course for high school graduates and shorter courses to upgrade worker skills. Inco Ltd. has teamed up with Cambrian College in Sudbury and the Ontario government to establish a new mining and minerals processing certificate program that combines college courses and paid, on-the-job training. And in Nisku, Alberta, the oil and gas industry and the Alberta government have funded a new petroleum industry training service, which provides specialized courses for Canadian oil and gas workers, as well as for some students from other countries. Although they are not enough, these examples show what can be done.

In Germany, about two-thirds of the workforce have completed an apprenticeship program, financed by industry and government. Not surprisingly, the South Koreans turned to Germany for help when setting up their vocational training programs. When German students reach the ages of 16 to 18, they sign contracts with employers stating the training and education they are to receive. As well as getting on-the-job training and stipends from their employers, the apprentices must attend school part time and must write interim and final exams to gain certificates showing that they can meet the standards of the skilled trade they have been studying. A national Institute for Vocational Training manages the system, its board being drawn from business, labour, and government. The institute has developed standards for nearly 400 occupations, and nearly 70 per cent of young Germans enter the job market through this apprenticeship system.

In our search for better forms of corporate governance and workplace democracy, Germany's system offers a good model. Known as "codetermination" and imposed on all publicly traded companies by the 1976 Act of Codetermination, it requires each company to have a board of management and also a supervisory board that includes representatives of both the shareholders and the employees; the size of the supervisory board depends on company size and ranges from 12 to 20 members.[38] The board of management actually runs the company and includes the chairman and other senior executives, but none of its members may serve on the supervisory board. This reduces the capacity of a single individual — the chief executive officer — to impose his or her will on the company.

The supervisory board appoints the members of the management board for terms of up to five years, and when the contracts come up for renewal, it decides whether they should be renewed. It also deals with a number of employment issues, such as plant closings and foreign investment. The German law requires that half the members of the supervisory board represent employees, and unions representing employees choose several of the members. The other supervisory board members represent the shareholders, and there is strong participation by the German banks, which vote the shares they hold in trust. The chairman of the supervisory board is elected from among the shareholder directors, while the vice-chairman is elected from the employee directors. German companies also have elected workers' councils, as mentioned earlier, and these councils must agree on key questions that affect them.

Although codetermination is not a perfect system, says Harvard Business School professor Jay Lorsch, on the whole it has three benefits: "It allows top management to remain focussed on long-term strategies; it keeps employees committed to their companies; finally, if there is a failure in management, it provides a mechanism to correct it."

The very idea of employees having such legal rights in a corporation would send shivers down the backs of Canadian executives who have either been educated in the United States or been largely influenced by U.S. business practices; but German executives seem able to handle the system and also to see benefits. Asked whether Volkswagen can move competitively when it has union members on its supervisory board, Carl Hahn, then chairman of Volkswagen, replied, "Emphatically, yes. The velocity of our decision making is second to none. It has been my experience that when labor representatives, who are highly accomplished in their own jobs, come on the supervisory boards, they can come to agreement with board of management over complex and painful business decisions, as long as they know all of the facts." He points to decisions to expand in Spain and Czechoslovakia, where labour costs are much lower than in Germany. In fact, Hahn says, "labor participation may even speed up strategic decisions, if the employees understand the issues. The important thing is to maintain the spirit of understanding with open communication and continuous information."

To make codetermination work, Hahn says, executives must be on top of their business. "Codetermination works when persuasive information becomes the basis for agreement. Workers' representatives on our supervisory board are apprised of the facts of life — Korean and Japanese competition, the state of all our factories. They know we have problems, like everybody else." But Volkswagen is also a company where top executives are close to the production. "My colleagues and I are close to the shop floor, we walk around," says Hahn. "We can feel the vibrations from the stamping presses in our offices."[39]

Canada's economic prospects depend critically on the quality and commitment of its workforce and the skills and knowledge found in its business enterprises. Technological change, demographics, global competition, and the information revolution are all converging to make the quality of the workforce and the workplace more important than ever before. But to gain the new partnerships that we will need in the workplace of the twenty-first century, new forms of management-employee cooperation and commitment will be required. To achieve this, the institutional structure of the corporation will have to be reinvented, as will the role of unions. In the knowledge-based economy, partnerships are the only way to thrive, but they must be based on real democratic change and not simply on tokenism.

10

Getting It All Together

FOR MORE THAN A DECADE, much of the world has been living under a "conservative revolution," symbolized in the policies of Margaret Thatcher in Britain and Ronald Reagan in the United States, and emulated by Brian Mulroney in Canada. But this revolution has lost its currency, and countries are searching for new ways to achieve economic and social progress. The conservative revolution, says economist Andrew Britton, was born in the world slowdown of the 1970s, a period of stagflation, or low growth and high inflation, which made public opinion ready for a change in direction in economic policy. "The feeling, rightly or wrongly, was that society in the West had 'gone soft,'" says Britton, head of Britain's National Institute of Economic and Social Research. "Too much attention was being paid to income distribution, not enough to income generation. The market system was being thwarted by excessive regulation — well-meaning regulation, perhaps, but inimical to business efficiency all the same."[1]

At the same time, "workers began to wonder if trade unions served the private interests of all their members. Social solidarity became less important. Individual achievement was more admired." This weakening of the power of employees was matched by a tolerance for high unemployment and by growing criticism of social welfare. Central banks, including the Bank of Canada, took control of economic policy, and full employment was abandoned as a national economic or social goal. Fighting inflation became the sole policy objective, leading to the suspicion, according to Britton, that "the pressure of lower demand was a deliberate choice, made partly to reduce inflation, but also in the belief that markets worked better if there was overall some margin of slack." Privatization, deregulation, a squeeze on discretionary government spending, and tight monetary policy were all elements of the conservative revolution. "One distinguishing feature of the conservative economic policies is the wish to minimize the influence of government decisions on the economy," says Britton. In effect, government's role was to be confined largely to monetary policy, controlling the money supply, with interest rates and exchange rates left free to find their own levels.

These policies clearly succeeded in bringing down inflation. But the cost in unemployment was high. During the boom of the mid-to-late 1980s, for example, Canada's unemployment rate never dropped to the levels it had been before the 1981–82 recession; instead, Canada is experiencing a long-term ratcheting upward rate of unemployment. This represents a significant loss to the economy, as well as being a waste of human potential: if each worker in Canada produces an average of $54,000 in goods and services, and if each additional percentage point of unemployment represents about 140,000 jobs, then the economic loss resulting from the increase in unemployment from 7.5 per cent in 1989 to 10 per cent in 1991 represents nearly $20 billion in annual output; this figure does not include the additional social welfare and other costs of high unemployment that contribute to fiscal deficits. As Alan Blinder, a leading American economist, points out, economists underestimate the economic damage caused by high unemployment, and they overstate the economic damage caused by a rise from one stable rate of inflation to another stable rate.[2]

The weakness in the conservative revolution, beyond the cost of higher unemployment, was that it did little to encourage economic growth through training, investment in infrastructure, or science and technology policy, says Britton. The gains in productivity were modest and were achieved mainly by forcing the closure of less competitive plants and by concentrating on a narrower range of products. Conservative policies were better at achieving the more efficient use of existing resources and technologies than at stimulating economic growth by expanding the potential from training and from science, technology, and innovation. In fact, the conservative revolution was not intended to encourage economic growth in any direct or explicit way, Britton says: "Policies towards research and development were little changed. Little was done to encourage investment as such. Little was done to promote labor mobility or vocational training. It was recognized that all these are essential to growth, but it was for the market, not government, to determine how and when economic growth occurred." Thus, the main impact of the conservative revolution "has probably been to bring forward reorganizations and rationalizations of production which were long overdue, not to push forward the frontier of technological efficiency."

It is clear that an economic growth agenda for a new ideas-driven economy requires a new economic philosophy, one that recognizes the central importance of knowledge and innovation in economic growth, the need for new institutions, and the importance of government as a partner in facilitating economic and institutional transformation. While cost-cutting will always be a crucial factor in competitiveness, it will not be enough. Canada's future will depend on productivity gains from the ideas of science and technology and their commercialization through investments in education, training, research and development; it will depend on management skills and new institutions, new workplace relationships and structures, and greater consensus among government, business, and labour in setting Canada's future agenda.

None of this will be easy, because Canada's ability to change will be constrained by its past lack of investment in innovation (which means that there will be a big catching-up job to do) and by a weakness in management skills, as well as by a high government debt and high foreign debt. A new approach will also require a fundamental change of thinking by many of Canada's major business and governmental organizations.

It is not easy to change the thinking of a country in which established interests have the most powerful voices. Take, for example, the fact that the federal government was able to find several billion dollars to assist economically questionable oil and coal megaprojects while simultaneously cutting support for research and development in energy efficiency and new forms of energy, such as solar energy; or that the government subsidized the establishment of a defence industry plant from Europe in Quebec, to produce equipment that is no longer needed, while slashing the Industrial Research Assistance Program that helps bring new technologies into hundreds of small and medium-sized Canadian companies — its excuse being that the needed new funding was unaffordable at a time of big budget deficits. Established industries are well organized, with powerful unions, active trade associations, the backing of bankers, and the ear of politicians. The industries of the future have no such advantage. They are disorganized, made up of many small companies, their future is unknown, they lack the organized voice of an oil or forest industry, and the banks often do not understand them. Yet it is these innovative new industries that hold the key to Canada's economic future.

Making the right choices is doubly important because governments do not have much money. Although the budgetary deficit for all three levels of governments combined is expected to decline as a share of GDP as the economy slowly recovers (the combined budget

---

TABLE 29

Government Spending and Government Debt

		% of GDP		
	Spending		Debt	
Country	1979	1990	1979	1990
CANADA	39.0	46.4	12.0	40.3
United States	31.7	37.0	19.2	31.2
Japan	31.6	30.7	14.9	10.9
Germany	47.6	45.8	11.5	22.6
France	45.0	50.2	13.8	25.0
Italy	41.7	53.2	55.6	98.2
Britain	42.5	42.9	47.9	26.9
Australia	33.5	36.4	27.7	13.2
Netherlands	55.8	56.3	21.8	59.4
Sweden	61.6	61.5	−19.9	−3.7
Switzerland	33.9	31.8	—	—

SOURCE: *OECD Economic Studies, no. 17* (Paris: OECD, Autumn 1991).

deficit fell from 6.9 per cent of GDP in 1983 to 2.6 per cent in 1988, but the 1990–91 recession pushed it back up to 5.5 per cent in 1991), the net debt of government at all three levels is expected to continue to climb for years to come. The net debt of all governments in Canada was $328.4 billion in 1991, compared with $37.8 billion in 1981; it had risen to 48.3 per cent of GDP in 1991, compared with 10.6 per cent in 1981. As a result, net debt payments had risen to $36.6 billion in 1991, or 5.4 per cent of GDP, compared with $8.3 billion, or 2.3 per cent of GDP, in 1981.

The main reason why governments will be under strong pressure to eliminate their deficits through the 1990s is that these deficits are consuming too large a proportion of Canadian savings. If Canadian investment cannot be financed out of Canadian savings, Canada has to borrow money abroad. But as Canada's foreign debt grows, so does the debt burden, especially if the money is used to finance the servicing of debt and not productive investment. A growing foreign debt means that a growing share of what Canada produces each year has to be paid to foreign creditors instead of being used to Canada's own advantage. This rising debt also makes Canada more vulnerable to the demands of foreign creditors, which means, for example, that Canada's interest rates have to be maintained at a high level even if Canada has low inflation and needs low interest rates to encourage investment. Moreover, the 1990s will see an enormous demand for savings as the developing countries and the former Soviet bloc countries seek capital to build modern societies. When rich countries such as Canada and the United States dip into a tight pool of world savings, they force up interest rates, and the cost of borrowing becomes too expensive for the countries that most urgently need to improve their standard of living.

Canada's problem is compounded because its industry is not able to export enough to pay the interest on the already large and growing foreign debt. Canadian companies lack the range of competitive products and services that the rest of the world wants to buy — and this is one of the strongest reasons why Canada needs a new economic strategy. The problem has been made worse by an economic policy that has allowed the Canadian dollar to rise sharply relative to the U.S. dollar, making Canadian exports less competitive in the United States. The "Canadian catalogue" is not sought after in world markets because Canada has not invested in science, technology, and innovation to develop enough exciting new high-value products, and because its traditional industries have stuck to semi-processed products that developing countries can often produce more cheaply. So Canada is now having to borrow from Japanese, German, British, Swiss, and U.S. pools of capital to keep up the interest payments on its foreign debt.

The weakness of the "Canadian catalogue" is easy to see; while U.S. exports to Mexico more than doubled between 1987 and 1991, Canadian exports to Mexico, despite Mexico's strong economic growth, were lower in 1991 than they had been in 1987. Likewise, while the United States gained export sales after its dollar declined relative to the Japanese yen and the German mark, Canada's exports to Japan and the European Community declined in 1991 — despite the fact that the Canadian dollar also had been devalued relative to the yen and the mark. Instead of borrowing from the rest of the world to make productive investments, which would pay off in future years in new exports and output, Canada has been borrowing abroad to maintain its existing levels of consumption, and in the process it has been deferring the need to create a new, knowledge-based economy.

By accumulating this growing liability to the rest of the world, Canada is risking its future standard of living. And by making itself even more vulnerable to foreign creditors, it is making itself vulnerable to growing foreign ownership and control of the economy. At the end of 1991, Canada's net foreign debt was about $280 billion; and it was estimated, on conservative forecasts, that it would approach $340 billion by the mid-1990s. About $106 billion has been added to Canada's foreign debt over the past six years. At current interest rates, this means that Canada has to find about $5 billion more a year in exports to pay the additional interest (which it is hard-pressed to do, and which it finds even harder since anti-inflation policies have shrunk the size of Canada's industrial base); the alternative is to borrow more money to pay off this year's interest costs.

This is one more reason why Canada needs a healthy manufacturing industry; no other sector of the economy has the capacity to generate increased exports to help service and pay down Canada's foreign debt. In 1990, payments made to non-residents on Canada's net foreign debt totalled $24 billion, but because Canada gained a surplus of only $2 billion on its trade in goods and services, its foreign debt grew by $22 billion. In 1990, 3.5 per cent of what Canadians produced had to be sent abroad to pay foreign creditors.

Although governments in the Western world made some progress in bringing deficits under control during the 1980s, "a certain 'battle fatigue' is appearing after a decade of restraint," according to an OECD study.[3] Moreover, new pressures will emerge in the 1990s. There will be pressure to "catch up" from the restraint in the 1980s, when many programs were put under spending caps. Real wages of Canadian public-sector employees declined through the 1980s as well, so there will be "catch up" wage pressures, too. And public investment in infrastructure (roads, highways, transit systems, water systems, educational equipment) as a share of GDP has been falling since the 1970s. In the 1990s this decline will have to be reversed.

Social spending also will put pressure on public finances, with an aging population pushing up old-age security and health-care costs. Seniors of 65 and over represented 12 per cent of the population of Canada in 1991, compared with 8 per cent in 1971; this share is steadily growing and is expected to reach 25 per cent by 2036. At the same time, there has been a decline in the number of school-age children. In 1971 children under the age of 15 were 30 per cent of the population; in 1990 they were 21 per cent, and they will be 19 per cent in 2001. But this decline could be offset by increased enrolments in post-secondary institutions. Child care, too, will receive more attention in the 1990s, according to the OECD study, partly because there is more recognition of the importance of preschool care and partly because more subsidized day care will be needed if single parents are to be helped to re-enter the workforce.

Environmental concerns also will put more pressure on government budgets. While the polluter-pay principle should limit the need for government spending, aside from enforcement costs, governments will be under pressure to help ease the cost of adjustment to a sustainable economy, and they may also be forced to look after pollution clean-ups where the polluter has gone bankrupt or disappeared — for example, in the disposal of toxic wastes and the clean-up of tailings at old mine sites. Meanwhile, warns the OECD, there is unlikely to be a big peace dividend in most countries, despite the collapse of communism. In Canada, for example, defence spending accounts for only 1.7 per cent of GDP, so there are not significant savings to be made unless Canada abolishes its armed forces altogether.

These spending pressures will force governments to take various measures: to look to environment-related user charges and carbon taxes; to improve government efficiency significantly; and to turn to the private sector, where it can deliver some government services more cheaply. But even more creative approaches will be needed if there are to be sufficient savings so that new spending and investment priorities can be pursed, says the OECD study. For example, governments could raise the age of retirement by one or two years from the current age of 65. This would reduce pension outlays. Governments could also restructure social programs; for example, by increasing the skills of those on welfare and by providing other help to get them back into the workforce so that welfare costs would eventually be reduced. In Canada's case, there are significant savings to be gained from ending the duplication of federal and provincial activities, as well as the duplication of provincial and local activities, including school boards. Similarly the best available research on health-care costs suggests that dealing with the causes of ill health (such as stress-related illness arising from poverty and unemployment) and promoting a safer workplace and a healthier lifestyle is more important than putting more money directly into the health-care system.

The transition to a more competitive and innovative economy will be highly disruptive as many established industries, single-industry resource communities, and farmers all adjust to changes in the world, so social policy (including retraining of the unemployed) will have a central role to play. Any attack on social spending will be counterproductive; in fact, social programs will have to be redesigned to meet the needs of a new era. Social policy is important not simply because it is one benchmark of a civilized society. It is critically important because it can raise productivity by reducing the resistance to change and because it can raise production by helping to reintegrate unemployed or underemployed Canadians back into the workforce. By helping Canadians rejoin the workforce instead of providing long-term welfare payments, it will also be cost-effective.

The model should be what the OECD calls "an active society," rather than a social system that traps people in poverty. The premise of the "active society" is that most people want to participate, and for most this means having some kind of job. While there is an increasing emphasis on "active" policies in Canada, too little of the social spending is designed to bring people back into active participation in society: policies are "passive" and too often just pay people money to stay at home, out of sight. Canada spends 2.1 per cent of its GDP on labour market programs, but 76 per cent of this is for income support and only 24 per cent is for "active" policies to help the unemployed get back into the workforce through training, counselling, mobility assistance, and other programs.[4] More recently, Canada has begun to shift its policies — for example, by allocating an increased share of unemployment insurance funds to training, though this has been offset to some extent by cutbacks in other spending on training.

Sweden, a pioneer in "active" labour market policies, spends 2.4 per cent of its GDP on labour programs, but only 29 per cent of this goes to income maintenance; the other 71 per cent goes to active programs. Sweden's unemployment benefits run for 14 months, and during that period Sweden works hard to help the unemployed get back into the workforce. It does this through highly capable job counsellors, first-class training programs, temporary wage subsidies to employers who hire older or disadvantaged workers, and, as a last resort, temporary government jobs. In Canada, rather than being helped in this way, many of the high-school dropouts, single parents, and older workers are consigned to the margins of society, with a loss of self-esteem and few prospects for a better life; and society is confronted with a large and growing bill to provide a minimal standard of living to these same Canadians — as well as a rising health bill, since there is a direct connection between poor health and low income.

"Having a job — usually a salaried job — is more today than simply a means of earning a living. It brings with it dignity and status, social contacts, a sense of usefulness," says James Gass, the OECD economist who developed the idea of "the active society." "Employment, in short, helps integrate individuals into society — as the massive entry of women into the labour market eloquently demonstrates." Concern today over the cost of unemployment benefits and social welfare could provide "a new opportunity to reconnect economic and social progress," says Gass. Without a concerted effort to help unemployed Canadians become active members of society, a "dual" society could emerge, composed of "insiders" and "outsiders." This is not only wasteful but is incompatible with standards of social justice. The alternative, an "active society," is a society in which "government policies should help as many people as possible to participate fully in social and economic life."[5]

This approach is especially important in today's economy, as a report from the Economic Council of Canada, *Employment in the Service Economy*, warned in 1991. Canadian labour market programs "do not offer adequate opportunities for developing skills that would improve real long-term employability," this report contended. Moreover, it said, the rapid pace of economic change means that a growing proportion of workers will not have any expectations of a lifelong job, and consequently they will have little if any attachment to a particular employer. "Thus it will become more important in the 1990s for public policy to deal directly with those 'unattached' workers, many of whom experience substantial job insecurity. As well, the slowdown in the growth of the labour force will heighten the need to ensure that all Canadian workers can participate productively in the labour market." [6]

This is especially important in view of the 1990–91 recession, which has had a highly damaging effect on younger Canadians. According to the Economic Council of Canada, the unemployment rate for Canadians aged between 25 and 34 was running more than 5 percentage points higher in the 1990–91 recession than the levels for this same age group in the 1981–82 recession. "We have to worry," says Economic Council chairperson Judith Maxwell, "whether they've become permanently disadvantaged, that a continuing history of instability in employment impairs their work skills so that they have a lot of trouble ever getting into a stable pattern of employment."[7]

While education and training open up opportunities to participate in the job market, "failure, or relative failure, can be the first step in a downward spiral of unemployment, exclusion and poverty," says Gass. "The long-term unemployed, the handicapped, the single parent and the drop-out find it difficult to enter, or re-enter, the rapidly moving mainstream of opportunities — and the longer out of the labour market, the more difficult it becomes. The emergence of such persistently disadvantaged groups, sometimes referred to as an underclass, probably cannot be combatted by income maintenance alone, for it may foster the very dependence and alienation from which social policy should help them escape."[8]

This means that there must be an emphasis on preventive and remedial programs to keep vulnerable Canadians actively engaged in society. Although there is significant opportunity for many Canadians in the growing number of jobs requiring high levels of education and skills, Canada's weak economy over the past decade has generated a large number of what the Economic Council calls "nonstandard" jobs — part-time jobs, short-term (six months or less) work, self-employment, and temporary agency jobs. In the 1980s, jobs of this kind accounted for one-half of net new job creation, according to Harvey Lazar of the Economic Council; between 1975 and 1988, part-time employment accounted for just over 30 per cent of employment growth, and nearly half the growth in part-time employment was "involuntary" (which means that people took the jobs because they could not find full-time employment).[9]

Canada is plagued by structural unemployment too, Lazar says. This is the result of "a growing mismatch between the skills and locations of available jobs and the skills and locations of the people looking for work. "These trends raise serious social and economic questions. For example, they "suggest the possibility of a growing underclass, and the social tensions and political strife that inevitably would accompany such a development. At the economic level, they suggest an economy operating well below potential." Nor is there any evidence that the trends are likely to reverse themselves as technological change and international competition make themselves felt through the 1990s.

"If the aim of social policy is to assist individuals to earn an adequate income and, as far as possible, perform a useful role in society, only new combinations of work and welfare are likely to achieve that goal for people at risk," says Gass. These include programs of affirmative action for the handicapped and minorities, wage subsidies for companies to rehire older workers, special-education programs to overcome illiteracy, government measures to help unemployed and unskilled workers get on-the-job training and experience

TABLE 30
Percentage of Households in More Severe Poverty

Country	All Households(%)	Families with Children(%)	Single-parent Families(%)
CANADA	8.9	9.3	29.4
United States	13.6	17.5	44.9
Britain	7.0	8.6	7.7
Germany	3.2	3.1	12.5
Netherlands	5.7	3.9	5.1
France	6.1	5.3	10.7
Sweden	5.9	2.9	3.6

* Data for mid-1980s. More severe poverty is defined as household income of less than 40 per cent national adjusted median income, equivalent to the definition of poverty line used in the United States.

SOURCE: Joint Center for Political and Economic Studies, Washington, 1991.

through community programs with local businesses, child care to help single parents participate in training programs and return to the job market, retraining programs such as the training vouchers provided to older workers in Ontario, greater incentives for those on social welfare to earn extra money by permitting them to keep more of what they earn without sacrificing social benefits, and local employment initiatives. In an active society, social policy and labour market policy are closely linked. Rather than defining unemployment away so that the unemployed no long show up in official statistics, the goal of social policy should be to reintegrate as many people as possible by helping them become employable.

Social policy faces another challenge in facilitating the new economy: the high and rising incidence of child poverty in Canada, which has serious implications for the country's future. Statistics Canada estimates that nearly 20 per cent of Canada's children, or just over 1 million Canadians under the age of 16, lived in poverty in 1990.[10] There is growing evidence, says the Canadian Institute for Advanced Research, that the preschool years are critical in shaping a child's lifelong ability to learn and to develop social skills. There is a connection between "the attitudes toward learning and cooperation that are inculcated in the preschool years, and the actual way in which subsequent learning takes place — not just in school, but also in the workplace."[11] Young children who are raised in poverty and are socially marginalized are unlikely to have the early stimulation and encouragement that enhances their capacity to learn. "To a considerable degree, the intellectual competence, health and coping skills of any adult all have their roots in his or her early experience," the institute says.

There are many signs that society is not coping well with rapid social change; for example, the incidence of family break-up, the number of single-parent families, drug and alcohol addiction, and child abuse. Modern knowledge-based and innovative societies are dependent on a constant flow of new ideas, which in turn depend on skilled and motivated people. It is not enough, therefore, simply to allot additional money for education, the Canadian Institute for Advanced Research stresses. Human development goes beyond the classroom to the home life of young children. "Figures indicate that children are often the ones who must bear the greatest share of the burden that results from poverty. At the same time, the problems associated with large-scale immigration, with poverty, and with unemployment, are increasing and placing an increasing burden on our children and on the educational system that serves them."

In 1986 some 13 per cent of all Canadian children were in single-parent homes, compared with 9 per cent in 1976.[12] The growth in numbers is creating the need for additional forms of day care. More the 1.3 million preschoolers (less than 6 years of age) and 1.7 million schoolchildren aged 6 to 12 had mothers in the workforce in 1990, so alternative care arrangements were needed for up to 3 million children — but there were only 321,000 licensed day-care spaces.[13]

The unhappy truth is that "many children are growing up under conditions that are very harmful," and they pay a high price, says the Canadian Institute for Advanced Research: "Young children who have grown up in poverty are a full two years behind their more advantaged peers in pre-mathematics skills by the time they enter kindergarten. This early deficit has a cumulative effect." The school system is not set up to deal with these problems, and those who start off this far behind rarely catch up, which means that "they are effectively barred from full participation in science and other technical subjects. By adolescence, many of these students are very far removed from realistic opportunities to acquire these competencies."[14] For many, a poor start in life can mean a bad life: a high dropout rate from school, marginal employment, and poor health. This is why preschool programs will become more important in the 1990s and why child-care centres must become child-development centres, where a concerted effort is made to develop pre-mathematics and other skills. The workplace of the future will demand it; the children deserve it.

There is another reason why it is important to pay close attention to the early development of young children. In the new economy, lifelong learning and the ability of people to work together in teams will be essential. This is already well recognized in Japan. There, youngsters entering school are first taught the habits of social interaction and cooperation. As the Canadian Institute for Advanced Research says, these skills "will last a lifetime." Whereas the North American emphasis is on the individual student, the Japanese develop group skills, emphasizing the social environment, in the early years of school life. Not only do Japanese children seem to advance at a faster rate, but they stay together in this achievement: "The centrality of peer group techniques fosters the involvement of all the children and makes it possible for the slower ones to be assisted by their peers. No streaming is used, and all children must learn a lesson before the class can go on."[15] It is not surprising, then, that Japanese workers are able to cooperate in work teams, quality circles, and other forms of workplace social systems and that they appear to adapt easily to the concept of lifelong learning. Some countries are adapting much better than Canada. "The societies that appear to be adapting most successfully are those that have historically placed a very high value on learning, and regard it as a lifelong process," the institute says, adding that, "not coincidentally, they are also societies that invest heavily in mothers and children, that have a highly educated work force, and whose social institutions ensure that learning takes place across all social classes, and across the full life span." Canada has to become such a society.

In the light of these social and other demands, says Ian Stewart, a former deputy minister of finance, "it is difficult to see how 'good government' can absorb a smaller proportion of economic activity than it now does in Canada. Indeed, the growing numbers of elderly and of children living in poverty, the increasing demands for day care and affordable housing, environmental claims, the need for more education, training and retraining, and above all, government deficits make it seem unlikely that the taxing requirements of government will diminish."[16] This means higher tax levels than in the United States, where social values are different, but higher taxes do not necessarily drag down society, as the experience of Germany and Sweden shows. Canada's tax and transfer system means, for example, that in 1989 the top 10 per cent of income earners saw their share of total Canadian income reduced from 26 per cent to 22 per cent, while the bottom 10 per cent saw their share of income increased from 0.4 per cent to 2.9 per cent; the average person in the top 10 per cent of income earners still had nearly eight times as much income as the average person in the bottom 10 per cent.[17]

Despite the glaring inequalities that still exist, most Canadian families have higher incomes than their American counterparts, because the Canadian median family income is higher. "The U.S. has more poor families, and has middle-income families with lower average incomes than their Canadian counterpart," according to Michael Wolfson and B.B. Murphy of Statistics Canada. "But the wealthy in the U.S. are more numerous, and their high incomes bring the U.S. average family income above the corresponding Canadian average."[18] Not all Canadian business executives resent supporting social and infrastructure investments through their taxes. "I do not mind paying lots of personal income tax. In some ways I like it," Robert Blair, then chairman of NOVA Corporation of Alberta, said in 1989. "It's a sure measure you are producing. This country is a base in which I have made a good salary for a long time, plus excellent bonuses for the best performing years. When paying about half of that compensation in cash to Revenue Canada I have a feeling of fair return to the rest of the public whose presence and effort helped make my high rewards possible here, where I choose to live."[19]

Stewart points out, however, that if Canada is to create a society in which the social and political fabric is strong, the economic system must have widespread public support. In a paper for the Economic Council of Canada, he argues that consensus cannot simply be built around the notion of free markets. The challenges facing Canadians from demographic change, social and educational needs, the environment, the expanding role of science and technology, the impact of the information revolution, and the need to build a new economy all require a new consensus.

While today's mainstream economics minimizes the importance of public goods and the capacity of government to serve public purposes, the "role of collective goods and the skilful design of their provision, far from diminishing in importance, remain, and indeed may increase, as consensual foundations to the well-functioning of the market economy and economic performance generally," says Stewart.[20] Instead of dismissing the role of government, it is important "to discern what ought and what ought not to be considered appropriate for collective provision" and "to find the means of their provision most likely to sustain broad public understanding and support." But government should step aside, Stewart adds, "where private initiative, diversity and entrepreneurship may flourish." In the end, though, fairness is crucial if the public is to support a national strategy for economic growth. Too many economists, Stewart argues, believe that "running modern economies at less than full utilization and accepting socially undesirable distributions of income, wealth and amenity are necessary prices to pay and an essential discipline for the beneficence of market economies." It is this belief that helps explain why there is no commitment to full employment in Canada, despite the social and economic waste in high unemployment.

Unlike the Europeans and Japanese, Canadians (like the Americans and British) have never made a serious effort to build a consensus on national goals and the way in which the economic and social system should function. They have emphasized individualistic goals, rather than community or group goals. In Europe, though, one important feature "is the extent to which consensus, both within the firm and within society, is seen as an important policy objective," explain British experts Stephen Woolcock and Michael Hodges. " Here there is a clear division between the Anglo-Saxon model, which places little or no importance on such consensus, and the continental European approaches, exemplified in Germany, the Netherlands and Scandinavia, designed to create and maintain consensus." They note that "in Germany, consensus among management, owners and the workforce of each firm and with society as a whole is considered a prerequisite for sustained prosperity. Once established, agreements on acceptable conditions of work and the level of social welfare are often translated into statutes."[21] This is true in other countries, such as Sweden and the Netherlands.

By contrast, the English-speaking countries — notably Britain and the United States, with Canada following behind — are still locked in outdated attitudes and consider that efforts to establish a social consensus are damaging to prosperity. This explains the determination in both Britain and the United States to weaken trade unions, and it explains the open hostility of much of the Canadian business community to the trade union movement. In Britain, the United States, and Canada — the English-speaking world — "statutory provisions concerning employment conditions and social provision are in particular seen as increasing costs, reducing competitiveness and damaging prosperity. Wealth creation is seen as the exclusive responsibility of the entrepreneur and the benefits feed through or trickle down into the rest of the economy."[22]

This same hard-line approach has been characteristic of the fight against inflation, despite the high costs in unemployment and lost output, and represents a similar dividing line between the English-speaking world and other countries. But as the Economic Council warned in 1990, "excessive dependence on a monetary policy stance that strives to control inflation through credit restraint will periodically impose severe costs on some sectors or regions. We fear that those costs will accumulate over time, impairing Canada's capacity for adjustment." What Canada needs, the council said, is "another policy lever that can focus on growth and employment," because "Canada's approach is not likely to have any more success in meeting the challenges of unemployment in the years to come than it did in the 1980s."[23] This, argued the council, is why Canada must develop a social partnership or consensus that could include the adoption of guidelines or a voluntary incomes policy to contain inflation, as well as expanding other forms of consensus (in areas such as training, for example) to build a more productive and high-employment economy.

The Canadian Institute for Advanced Research argues that the reason every Canadian has a stake in the knowledge-based economy is that advances in Canada's science, technology, and innovation capacity are crucial to higher productivity and increased employment, as well as being the future source of revenues that will reduce deficits and finance future government activities. Today's level of technology "cannot provide all citizens in advanced countries with the standards of living accepted as normal by middle class citizens. Nor can it provide us with all of the public goods, such as free health care, government support of universities, arts and a host of other public goods, as well as social services at levels we think civilized."[24]

As an example of the precariousness of the Canadian situation, the institute says that Canadians should look at the effect of the increase in the interest bill on the national debt, which has risen from 10 per cent to 30 per cent of federal revenues. "This has caused the cutting of spending on many of the symbols which define Canada in many of its citizens' eyes, such as Via Rail and the CBC, to say nothing of cuts in education, research grants, and Statistics Canada funding." But if we are to "maintain and enhance the social services that we regard as important for Canadians, and the production of important public goods, we must generate the wealth that can support these worthy activities, all of which are financed by funds taken from the private sector where the wealth is originally created." So the challenge for Canada is "to create and sustain environments that are conducive to high rates of knowledge-driven, technological change, and to the economic growth that follows from it."

Paul Romer, who is one of the world's leading economists in new theories of economic growth (and a fellow of the Canadian Institute for Advanced Research), points out that even slight improvements in a country's growth rate can make a big difference over time. If per capita incomes in Canada grow an average of 1.6 per cent a year, it will take 43 years for them to double; but if per capita incomes grow 2.6 per cent a year, they will double in 27 years. (To find the doubling time for any growth rate, take the number 69 and divide it by the growth rate, he says.)[25]

But how is this growth obtained? Romer argues that societies grow by rearranging resources to create new recipes. No society grows indefinitely simply by cooking more and more of the same thing. Instead, recipes are improved and new ones are developed —

whether the recipe is to make a sheet of steel, a semiconductor, a plastic, or a medicine. This is the source of economic growth.

The potential for new recipes is enormous, Romer argues. The periodic tables contain about 100 different types of atom, so the number of different combinations of four different atoms is 94 million. The number of potential combinations from the 100 different atoms is infinitely greater, because combinations can be made up of more than four different atoms, different fractions of each atom can be used, and different temperatures and pressures can be applied. What really matters in a country is not a lack of resources or capital but having ideas and the ability to use them. A growth strategy, then, should focus on ways to stimulate ideas and to commercialize them — for example, through education, support for research and development, tax measures, patents, and the integration of applied research into the ongoing activity of business.

In looking to the future, Romer says, the challenge is to "invent an institution that supports a high level of applied, commercially relevant research in the private sector, and does so without imposing high efficiency costs or presenting large opportunities for political manipulation" (just as the invention of the patent system did in the nineteenth century and the agricultural extension system did in the early twentieth century). Moreover, Romer predicts, "the country that takes the lead in the 21st century will be the one that implements an innovation of this kind." In other words, says Janet Halliwell, chairperson of the Science Council of Canada, "for the first time in history, a nation's limits are being set by mental attributes and, further, how effectively they are used. We are living in a time when dreams have value, and our wealth can soar as high as the top of the Aurora Borealis or as low as the tundra. The scope and scale of our vision today determines the size of our pocket-book tomorrow."[26]

But is Canada ready to bring all of its resources together in partnership and launch an economic vision to raise productivity by developing a competitive, ideas-based economy? This must be an economy that can deliver the higher standards of living we need to grow our way out of our fiscal straitjacket; that can provide a higher disposable income for Canadians; that can finance the public or collective goods and services that help define the country in which we live — and that can leave some over so that Canadians can do their share and more to help raise the quality of life and the potential for economic progress in the developing world — and it must be able do all this in a way that is compatible with sustainable development. There is no reason why Canada cannot achieve this. Moreover, if we fail to act, our future will be bleak, because a stagnating standard of living and growing burden of foreign debt will make Canada a mean-spirited country and will drive away many of the nation's best and brightest, who will seek opportunities elsewhere.

Canada has the people. They can be found in our schools and universities, in the hundreds of high-tech companies that make up the Canadian Advanced Technology Association, and in the members of the business community who are working with local school boards to help young people stay in school and learn more about the world of work; they can be found in groups like Skills Canada, which is working to raise the prestige of skilled trades, and in companies and unions that are working together to develop programs for skills training and new workplace relationships. Sadly, the place we are least likely to find the people of the future is among our politicians and among the leaders of some of our largest corporations. There is a strong feeling throughout the country that we have to change our ways if Canada is to realize its potential in the next century, but this feeling is not well represented in our political life or in the financial towers of Toronto's Bay Street, the heart of our financial community.

If Canada does adopt a national strategy for the twenty-first century, what will it look like?

Education and training will be the most important priorities, because clearly the quality and skills of people are the single most important asset of a knowledge-based economy. Yet Canada's educational performance is inadequate — too many students are lagging behind in science and mathematics, too many drop out of school, too few pursue vocational courses, and too many students in college and university avoid science and engineering programs. In the workplace, training by business is glaringly inadequate — a situation that reflects a lack of commitment to employees by Canadian business.

Getting Canadian companies to use the best available technologies is crucially important, too. The combination of advanced production technologies and skilled workers is the key to higher productivity. The provincial governments can help by following the example of some U.S. states and implementing technology-extension services, modelled on the highly successful agriculture-extension services that helped farmers adopt new technologies at the start of the twentieth century. Businesses have to boost their capacities as well; one Ontario study found that 70 per cent of its manufacturing companies did not employ a single engineer. At the federal level, Canada has one of the best technology diffusion programs in the world, the Industrial Research Assistance Program (IRAP). But it has been severely underfunded and has been caught up in internal bureaucratic battles. It needs a major increase in funding and a stand-alone status as an independent agency operating at arm's length from government. Other forms of technical assistance to industry, including low-cost loans for new production technologies, should be considered as well.

Research and development is a serious problem for Canada. With spending at a mere 1.4 per cent of GDP, Canada has one of the lowest commitments to new science and technology of all the industrial countries, with spending that is well below that of its major competitors. Canada should set itself goals — 1.9 per cent of GDP by 1999 and 2.5 per cent by 2005 (by which time our major competitors could be spending 3.5 per cent of GDP) — but it also should target specific sectors of the economy. If Canada is to develop high-value products and services for the new global marketplace, including upgrading its resource industries, it must invest in university R & D through its granting councils, it must facilitate university-industry cooperation through expanded Centres of Excellence, it must increase precompetitive R & D through a Canada Technology Corporation, it must share the risk of commercializing new technologies through a Canada Industrial Investment Fund or Canadian Industry Program, and it must broaden the scope of the R & D tax incentives.

As well, new measures are needed to build up Canadian small and medium-sized businesses so that we can grow more Canadian-controlled companies that are able to operate on a world scale. Because of a lack of equity funding, a growing number of promising Canadian companies with significant potential are being forced to sell control to non-residents just so that they can stay in business. This means that Canada's potential future business giants become divisions of foreign multinationals instead of having the opportunity to realize their own potential. If Canada is to be a player in the new global economy, it must be able to field its own team. Alternatives to foreign takeovers are essential, and establishing a Canadian Industrial Innovation Bank, funded by the federal government but operating at arm's length, is one way to provide patient capital that can help businesses grow, with the equity investment being sold later when markets are more receptive. Other measures could include providing incentives for pension funds to adopt long-term thinking as shareholders and to invest capital in promising Canadian companies; encouraging Canada's business giants to play a greater role in nurturing Canadian suppliers; and creating a Canadian equivalent of the Japanese *keiretsu* system through the formation of Innovative Business Enterprises that would link different Canadian companies together in the pursuit of core technologies.

Building the infrastructure for the new economy is also of crucial importance. This means planning electronic highways as well as the Trans-Canada Highway. Just as, in the past, it was essential for Canada to develop its own transcontinental railways, highways, airlines, and broadcasting system because of the pull of the United States, it is now equally imperative that Canada have its own electronic spine, or telecommunications system. For a uniquely Canadian electronic highway to survive into the twenty-first century, the system must be flexible enough to facilitate the provision of competitive new services and to stimulate the development of new technologies; otherwise, it will be increasingly bypassed and Canadian software and hardware companies will lose the domestic market base from which to launch new international software and other services, as well as new hardware systems.

Meanwhile, Canada should look for international opportunities to upgrade its infrastructure capabilities — for example, by seeking to link up in R & D with the U.S. High Performance Computing and Communications Project, a multi-billion-dollar project to take the U.S. data network system into the information age of the next century. The quality of Canada's physical infrastructure — the electronic-guided highway, efficient airports, clean water, and quality transit

— are key considerations in business-location decisions in the new economy, along with the presence of good schools, colleges, and universities. Consequently Canada should make sure that it maintains and upgrades its infrastructure. Investment in infrastructure also provides the procurement opportunities that will help Canadian engineering, business service, and manufacturing companies develop new services, skills, and products with export potential.

Many of the changes needed in business cannot take place without a fundamental restructuring of the workplace. Companies cannot use new technologies unless they train employees and empower them to make many of the day-to-day decisions in the business; the new technologies have made the tyrannical boss in the corner office obsolete (even though many of them still exist). But if employees are to take on more responsibilities, as well as sharing in efforts to make businesses more competitive through quality programs and other measures, they must have a greater collective voice in the enterprise. One way of doing so is through unions, which play an important role in our economy. Improvements are needed to labour laws to strengthen the legal basis of unions and to remove impediments to new membership. Other methods of co-determination needed for the twenty-first century workplace include the adoption of a Canadian version of the German works council, which would give employees a greater voice in their jobs and would democratize the workplace — an important objective in itself.

Since building a new economy will bring disruptive changes to many Canadians, a creative social policy is essential to make sure that those who are not participating in the new economy are integrated into the new opportunities instead of being marginalized into welfare.

What is at stake is Canada's future. Canada has the potential to do much better than it is doing at present, but this will take an enormous commitment, a willingness by all groups in society to accept major changes and to make important compromises. The urgency of Canada's need to become much more productive and competitive should make this possible, because so much is at risk. To bring Canadians together, what is needed as much as anything is a vision of Canada's future. The Japanese know that they want to be a science superpower so that they can become the world's leading knowledge-based economy. The Europeans have their vision of the new European Union, a chance to restore the economic, political, and cultural influence of Europe and to embark on the road to a new European society. Mexico wants to become a modern nation-state. China wants to double its per capita GDP by the start of the next century. South Korea wants to reunite with North Korea and become an advanced nation-state ready for membership in the Western club of the OECD by the end of the decade.

But what does Canada want? Our goal should be to transform our economy so that it becomes a knowledge-based, sustainable economy that generates the wealth to make Canada a Sweden of North America, with a strong commitment to social values and public goods, and to be an active member of the new world community that is just as much at home in Japan, Europe, India, Mexico, or Brazil as it is in the United States. With a renewed sense of self-confidence, Canada should be a part of the world, not just part of North America.

Notes

Introduction
1. John Robert Colombo, *Colombo's Canadian Quotations* (Edmonton: Hurtig Publishers, 1984).

CHAPTER 1
The Canadian Challenge
1. *Financial Post*, 27 September 1991.
2. Statistics Canada, *Daily Bulletin*, 17 September 1990.
3. Roger Love and Susan Poulin, "Family Inequality in the 1980s," *Perspectives on Labour and Income*, Autumn 1991, Statistics Canada cat. no. 75-001.
4. Statistics Canada, *Income Distributions by Size in Canada, 1990* (Ottawa: Ministry of Industry, Science and Technology, 1991), cat. no. 13-207.
5. Paul Krugman, *The Age of Diminished Expectations* (Cambridge, Mass.: MIT Press, 1990).
6. Michael E. Porter, *Canada at the Crossroads: The Reality of a New Competitive Environment* (Ottawa: Monitor Co., 1991).
7. Judith Maxwell, "The Impact of Productivity Growth," *Au Courant*, 1991, no. 1.
8. Ibid.
9. Vivien Walsh, "Technology, Competitiveness, and the Special Problems of Small Countries," OECD *STI Review*, 1987, no. 2.
10. Ibid.
11. Edward Carmichael, Katie Macmillan, and Robert York, *Ottawa's Next Agenda* (Toronto: C.D. Howe Institute, 1989).

12. Larkin Kerwin, speech, 1988.
13. Science Council of Canada, *Gearing Up for Global Markets* (Ottawa: SCC, 1988).
14. Canadian Institute for Advanced Research, *Innovation and Canada's Prosperity: The Transforming Power of Science, Engineering and Technology* (Toronto: CIAR, 1988).
15. Canadian Manufacturers' Association, *The Aggressive Economy: Daring to Compete* (Toronto: CMA, 1989).
16. Department of Industry, Science and Technology. Policy Sector, "Innovation: The Key to Competitiveness in the Nineties," confidential draft discussion paper, 10 September 1990.
17. National Advisory Board on Science and Technology, *Science and Technology, Innovation and National Prosperity: The Need for Canada to Change Course* (Ottawa: NABST, 1991).
18. Porter, *Canada at the Crossroads.*
19. "Nice Country, Nice Mess," *Economist*, 29 June 1991.
20. Paul Volcker, speech to Symposium on Policy Implications of Trade and Currency Zones, Kansas City, 1991.
21. U.N. Centre for Transnational Corporations, *World Investment Report 1991: The Triad in Foreign Direct Investment* (New York: United Nations, 1991).
22. *Toronto Star*, 12 September 1991.
23. UNCTC, *World Investment Report 1991.*
24. *Toronto Star*, 28 October 1987.
25. Joel Garreau, *The Nine Nations of North America* (New York: Houghton Mifflin, 1981).
26. M. Delal Baer, "North American Free Trade," *Foreign Affairs*, Fall 1991.
27. World Bank, *Global Economic Prospects and the Developing Countries* (Washington: World Bank, 1992).
28. Buom-Jong Choe, "Global Trends in Raw Materials Consumption," International Economics Department, Working Paper 804 (Washington: World Bank, 1991).
29. Janet Halliwell, "Mapping the Parameters of Canadian Competitiveness," *Science Bulletin*, May 1991.
30. *Financial Times*, 11 October 1990.
31. Porter, *Canada at the Crossroads.*
32. Michael E. Porter, *The Competitive Advantage of Nations* (Toronto: Collier Macmillan, 1990)

33. Hiroshi Kakaza, "Industrial Technology Capabilities in Asian Developing Countries," *Asian Development Review*, 1990, no.2.

34. OECD Forum for the Future, *Long-Term Prospects for the World Economy* (Paris: OECD, 1992).

35. C. E. Ritchie, speech, Bank of Nova Scotia annual shareholders' meeting, Halifax, N.S., 21 January 1992.

36. Canadian Press, 4 April 1989.

37. Charles McMillan, *Services: Japan's 21st Century Challenge* (Ottawa: Canada-Japan Trade Council, 1991).

38. J. Fraser Mustard, "Innovation and Prosperity," paper presented to Canadian Institute for Advanced Research, November 1990.

39. Peter F. Drucker, "Japan: New Strategies for a New Reality," *Wall Street Journal*, 2 October 1991.

40. Science and Technology Task Force, "Pacific Science and Technology Profiles 1991," report for the Pacific Economic Cooperation Conference, Singapore, 1991.

41. Richard G. Lipsey, *Economic Growth: Science and Technology and Institutional Change in a Global Economy* (Toronto: Canadian Institute for Advanced Research, 1991).

42. *Toronto Star*, 2 June 1991.

CHAPTER 2
Aging Canadians and Young Mexicans

1. United Nations Population Fund, *The State of the World Population 1991* (New York: United Nations, 1991).

2. United Nations Population Fund, *The State of the World Population 1990* (New York: United Nations, 1990).

3. Kemper Securities *Economic Review*, 23 March 1992.

4. World Bank, *Global Economic Prospects and the Developing Countries* (Washington: World Bank, 1992).

5. United Nations Population Fund, *The Prospects of World Urbanization* (New York: United Nations, 1987).

6. Organisation for Economic Co-operation and Development, *Development Assistance Committee Annual Report, 1989* (Paris: OECD, 1989).

7. UNPF, *World Population 1991*.

8. Ibid.

9. Organisation for Economic Co-operation and Development, *DAC Aid Review of Canada* (Paris: OECD, 1990).

10. International Labor Organization, *Economically Active Population: Estimates and Projections 1950–2025* (Geneva: ILO, 1986).

11. International Finance Corporation, *Exporting to Industrial Countries: Prospects for Business in Developing Countries* (Washington: IFC, 1990).

12. Richard B. Freeman, "Canada in the World Labor Market to the Year 2000," in *Perspective 2000* (Ottawa: Economic Council of Canada, 1990).

13. James E. Austin, *Managing in Developing Countries* (New York: The Free Press, 1990).

14. Ibid.

15. General Agreement on Tariffs and Trade, *International Trade 1987–88*, vol.1 (Geneva: GATT, 1988).

16. William Johnston, "Global Work Force 2000: The New World Labor Market," *Harvard Business Review*, March–April 1991.

17. *UNESCO Statistical Yearbook, 1990* (Paris: UNESCO, 1990).

18. Statistics Canada, *Population Projections for Canada, Provinces and Territories 1989–2011* (Ottawa: Ministry of Industry, Science and Technology, 1990), cat. no. 91-520.

19. National Health and Welfare Demographic Review Secretariat, *Charting Canada's Future* (Ottawa: Government of Canada, 1989).

20. Office of the Superintendent of Financial Institutions, *Old Age Security Program: First Statutory Actuarial Report* (Ottawa: Government of Canada, 1990).

21. National Health and Welfare, *Charting Canada's Future.*

22. Economic Council of Canada, *Legacies: 26th Annual Review* (Ottawa: ECC, 1989).

23. Economic Council of Canada, *New Faces in the Crowd* (Ottawa: ECC, 1991).

24. Ibid.

25. David Foot, House of Commons Standing Committee on Labour, Employment and Immigration, 24 May 1990.

26. David Foot, *Migration: The Demographic Aspects* (Paris: OECD, 1991).

27. Superintendent of Financial Institutions, *Old Age Security Program.*
28. Michael C. Wolfson, "Perspectives on the Economics of Aging," paper presented to the Canadian Seniors Network Annual Conference, Moncton, N.B., 8 June 1991.
29. David Foot, "Demographics: The Human Landscape for Public Policy," in *Canada at Risk? Canadian Public Policy in the 1990s* (Toronto: C.D. Howe Institute, 1991).
30. Robert B. Fairholm, "Canadian Forecast Summary: Long-Range Market Outlook," *Canadian Review* (Data Resources of Canada), Fall 1900 – Winter 1991.
31. Ibid.
32. *Economic Report of the President, 1990* (Washington: U.S. Government Printing Office, 1990).
33. Christine Keen, speech to the National Conference of the Society for Human Resources Management, Atlanta, Ga., 25 June 1990.
34. Kaori Shoji, "The Changing Face of Japanese Labor," *Business Tokyo*, January 1991.

CHAPTER 3
The New Economy and the Environment
1. Statistics Canada, *Daily Bulletin*, 30 January 1992.
2. World Bank, *World Development Report 1992: Development and the Environment* (Washington: World Bank, 1992).
3. World Commission on Environment and Development, *Our Common Future* (New York: Oxford University Press, 1987).
4. Science Council of Canada, *The Conserver Society*, Report 27 (Ottawa: SCC, 1977).
5. Jean-Philippe Barde, "The Path to Sustainable Development," *OECD Observer*, June–July, 1990.
6. *Business Week*, 30 December 1991.
7. William D. Ruckelhaus, "Toward a Sustainable World," *Scientific American*, September 1989.
8. Environment Canada, *A State of the Environment Report: Understanding Atmospheric Change* (Ottawa: Ministry of Supply and Services, 1991), SOE no. 91-2.
9. International Energy Agency, *Global Energy: The Changing Outlook* (Paris: IEA, 1992).

10. *Financial Times,* 19 October 1990.
11. Environment Canada, SOE no. 91-2.
12. Maurice Strong, speech to Agenda 21 Conference, Vienna, 29 November 1991.
13. Gro Harlem Brundtland, speech to World Economic Forum, Davos, Switzerland, February 1991.
14. *Financial Resources and Mechanisms,* Report of the Secretary General of the Conference, Preparatory Committee for the U.N. Conference on Environment and Development, 4th session, New York, 2 March – 3 April 1992. UN/A Conf. 151/PC/18.
15. Quoted by Janet E. Halliwell in "The Servant and Master of Nature: A Science Perspective on Capturing Canada's Forest Ethic," speech to the annual general meeting of the Canadian Institute of Forestry, 25 September 1991.
16. Environment Canada, SOE no. 91-2.
17. Government of Canada, *Canada's Green Plan* (Ottawa: Ministry of Supply and Services, 1990).
18. Brian Mulroney, speech to the World Conference on the Changing Atmosphere, 27 June 1988.
19. *Globe and Mail,* 5 June 1990.
20. Carl Sonnen, "Environment-Economy Linkages: A Quantitative Analysis of the Federal Green Plan and Policy Implications," paper presented to the CABE/CEA Joint Session on Resources and Sustainable Development, Ottawa, 3 June 1991.
21. G. Bruce Doern, *Shades of Green: Gauging Canada's Green Plan,* C. D. Howe Institute commentary, Toronto, April 1991.
22. J. W. Chuckman, "The Environment and the Economy: Aspects from an Industry Point of View," speech to the Society of Management Accountants, Toronto, 17 May 1990.
23. *Globe and Mail,* 17 November 1990.
24. Science Council of Canada, *Environmental Peacekeepers: Science, Technology and Sustainable Development in Canada* (Ottawa: SCC, 1988).
25. Michael E. Porter, *The Competitive Advantage of Nations* (Toronto: Collier Macmillan, 1990).
26. Doug Macdonald, *The Politics of Pollution* (Toronto: McClelland & Stewart, 1991).

27. *Report of the Auditor General of Canada to the House of Commons, 1991* (Ottawa: Government of Canada, 1991).

28. William F. Sinclair, "Controlling Effluent Discharges from Canadian Pulp and Paper Manufacturers," *Canadian Public Policy*, 1991, 1-86-105.

29. Norman C. Bonsor, "Water Pollution and the Canadian Pulp and Paper Industry," in *In Getting It Green*, ed. G. Bruce Doern (Toronto: C.D. Howe Institute, 1990).

30. Organisation for Economic Co-operation and Development, *OECD Environmental Data: Compendium 1991* (Paris: OECD, 1991).

31. Organisation for Economic Co-operation and Development, *Energy Balance of OECD Countries, 1987–88* (Paris: OECD, 1990).

32. Organisation for Economic Co-operation and Development, *OECD Economic Survey: United States* (Paris: OECD, 1991).

33. Peter Hoeller and Markku Wallin, *Energy Prices, Taxes and Carbon Dioxide Emission Levels*, Working Paper 6, Economics and Statistics Department (Paris: OECD, 1991).

34. The World Wide Fund for Nature, *Caring for the Earth: A Strategy for Sustainable Living*, World Conservation Union, U.N. Environment Program (Gland: World Wide Fund, 1991).

35. Morris Miller, *Debt and the Environment: Converging Crises* (New York: United Nations, 1991).

36. Environment Canada, SOE No. 91-2.

37. Environment Canada, "Climate Change and Canadian Impacts: The Scientific Perspective," *Climate Change Digest*, 1991, cat. no. CCD 91-01.

38. Information supplied by the Office of Energy Research and Development, Ministry of Energy, Mines and Resources, Ottawa, 1991.

39. *Toronto Star*, 2 March 1991.

40. Richard Lipsey, *Economic Growth: Science and Technology and Institutional Change in the Global Economy* (Toronto: Canadian Institute for Advanced Research, 1991).

41. Jim MacNeill, Pieter Winsemius, and Taizo Yakushiji, *Beyond Interdependence* (New York: Oxford University Press, 1991).

42. Lipsey, *Economic Growth*.

278 THE NEXT CANADIAN CENTURY

43. *Issues in Technology,* Fall 1991.
44. Science Council of Canada, *Environmental Peacekeepers.*
45. International Energy Agency, *Annual Report on Energy Policies and Programs: Japan* (Paris: IEA, 1991).
46. Ibid.
47. *Financial Post,* 15 November 1990.
48. *Environmental Industries Sector Initiative* (Ottawa: Ministry of Industry, Science and Technology, April 1990); and *The Environmental Industries Sector Initiative: An Overview and Progress Report,* ibid., June 1990.
49. Canada's Environmental Services Industry: Consultation Document, Commercial Services Industries Directorate. Ministry of Industry, Science and Technology, 1991.
50. Maurice Strong, speech to the United Nations Association of Canada, Toronto, 15 October 1991.

CHAPTER 4
Our Competitors Try Harder

1. Christopher Freeman, Margaret Sharp, and William Walker, eds., *Technology and the Future of Europe* (London: Pinter Publishers, 1991).
2. Ibid.
3. Michael H. Best, *The New Competition: Institutions of Industrial Restructuring* (London: Polity Press, 1990).
4. Kenneth S. Courtis, "Japan in the 1990s," paper, Deutsche Bank Capital Markets Asia, Tokyo, December 1991.
5. Lawrence B. Krause, "Japanese Capitalism: A Model for Others?" *International Economic Insights,* November–December 1991.
6. Daniel J. Okimoto, *Between MITI and the Market: Japanese Industrial Policy for High Technology* (Stanford, Ca.: Stanford University Press, 1989).
7. Richard R. Nelson, *High-Technology Policies: A Five-Nation Comparison* (Washington: American Enterprise Institute, 1984).
8. Okimoto, *Between MITI and the Market.*
9. Jonah Levy and Richard Samuels, "Industries and Innovation: Research Collaboration as a Technology Strategy in Japan," in *Strategic Partnerships: States, Firms and International*

Competition, ed. Lynn Krieger Mytelka (London: Pinter Publishers, 1991).

10. "Japanese Firms Form Advanced Aircraft Industry," *Aviation Week and Space Technology*, 29 July 1991.

11. Levy and Samuels, "Industries and Innovation."

12. *Report on the Research and Development Program on Basic Technologies for Future Industries.* JISEDAI Program (Tokyo: MITI, 1991).

13. Agency of Industrial Science and Technology, *National Research and Development Program: Large-Scale Project, 1991* (Tokyo: MITI, 1991).

14. Industrial Structure Council, *International Trade and Industrial Policy in the 1990s: Towards Human Values in the Global Age* (Tokyo: MITI, 1990).

15. Ibid.

16. *Research and Technological Development Policy*, European Documentation CB-PP-88-01-EN-C Luxembourg.

17. Council decision of 23 April 1990 concerning the framework program of the Community in the field of research and techno-logical development, 1990–94. *Euratom*, EEC 90/221 (official journal of the EC), 8 May 1990, L 117.

18. Freeman et al., *Technology and the Future of Europe.*

19. Commission of the European Communities, *Industrial Policy in an Open and Competitive Environment: Guidelines for a Community Approach*, COM 90 556 Final, Brussels, 16 November 1990.

20. Ibid.

21. Konrad Seitz, "Can Europe's High-Tech Industries Survive?" *World Link*, 1991, no.3.

22. Ibid.

23. Commission of the European Communities, *The European Electronics and Information Technology Industry: State of Play, Issues at Stake and Proposals for Action*, SEC 91 565 Final, Brussels, 3 April 1991.

24. Commission of the European Communities, *From the Single Act to Maastricht and Beyond: The Means to Match Our Ambitions*, COM 92 2000 Final, Brussels, 11 February 1992.

25. Commission of the European Communities, Directorate-General 12, *Research after Maastricht: An Assessment, a Strategy*, Brussels, 13 April 1992.
26. Competitiveness Policy Council, *Building a Competitive America*, 1st annual report to the President and Congress (Washington: CPC, 1991).
27. Kenneth Flamm, *Creating the Computer* (Washington: Brookings Institution, 1988).
28. Kenneth Flamm, *Targeting the Computer: Government Support and International Competitiveness* (Washington: Brookings Institution, 1987).
29. Office of Technology Assessment, U.S. Congress, *The Defense Technology Base* (Washington: OTA, 1988).
30. Lynn E. Browne, "Defense Spending and High Technology Development: National and State Issues," *New England Economic Review*, September–October 1988.
31. Council on Competitiveness, *A Competitiveness Assessment of the President's February 1993 Budget* (Washington: Council on Competitiveness, 1992).
32. National Science Foundation, PR 91-18.
33. Ibid., PR 87-21.
34. Council on Competitiveness, *Gaining New Ground: Technology Priorities for America's Future* (Washington: Council on Competitiveness, 1991).
35. Executive Office of the President, Office of Science and Technology Policy, *U.S. Technology Policy*, Washington, 26 September 1990.
36. President George Bush, speech to the American Academy for the Advancement of Science, 15 February 1991.
37. President Roh Tae Woo, speech to the Korean Institute of Science and Technology, Seoul, 22 February 1991.

CHAPTER 5
Losing the Canadian Team

1. Paul Labbé, House of Commons Committee on Industry, Science and Technology, 21 June 1989.
2. *Financial Post*, 13 March 1989.

3. Premier's Council, *Competing in the Global Economy* (Toronto: Government of Ontario, 1988).

4. Statistics Canada, *Canada's International Investment Position 1988–1900* (Ottawa: Ministry of Industry, Science and Technology, 1991), cat. no. 67-202.

5. Statistics Canada, *Annual Report of the Minister of Industry, Science and Technology under the Corporations and Labour Unions Returns Act: Part 1 — Corporations 1988* (Ottawa: Ministry of Industry, Science and Technology, 1991). cat. no. 67-210.

6. Investment Canada, *The Business Implications of Globalization,* Working Paper 5 (Ottawa: Investment Canada, 1990).

7. CALURA corporations 1987, cat. no. 61-210.

8. *Capital Markets Report,* 27 September 1991.

9. Statistics Canada, *Canada's International Balance of Payments, 4th Quarter 1990* (Ottawa: Ministry of Industry, Science and Technology, 1990), cat. no. 67-001.

10. Statistics Canada, *Canada's International Transactions in Services, 1991* (Ottawa: Ministry of Industry, Science and Technology, 1991), cat. no. 67-203.

11. Michael E. Porter, *The Competitive Advantage of Nations* (Toronto: Collier Macmillan, 1990).

12. Ibid.

13. Michael E. Porter, *Canada at the Crossroads: The Reality of a New Competitive Environment* (Ottawa: Monitor Co., 1991).

14. Department of Regional Industrial Expansion, *Competitiveness Profiles,* reports on various industrial sectors, Ottawa 1986.

15. National Advisory Board on Science and Technology, *Science and Technology, Innovation and National Prosperity: The Need for Canada to Change Course* (Ottawa: Government of Canada, 1991).

16. Michael Porter, *Canada at the Crossroads.*

17. C. Fred Bergsten, "Exxon-Florio after Three Years: An Assessment and Proposals for Future Change," submission to the U.S. Senate Committee on Commerce, Science and Transportation, 19 November 1991.

18. "North American Free Trade Agreement," U.S. Embassy backgrounder 91-21, Ottawa, 26 March 1991.

19. *Toronto Star*, 28 April 1987.
20. Richard Leet and Patrick Early of Amoco Corporation, speech to the San Francisco Society of Financial Analysts, 7 May 1991.
21. Carlo De Bendetti, "Europe's New Role in a Global Market," in *A High Technology Gap? Europe, America and Japan*, ed. Andrew J. Pierre (New York: Council on Foreign Relations, 1987).
22. United Nations Centre on Transnational Corporations, *World Investment Report 1991: The Triad in Foreign Direct Investment* (New York: United Nations, 1991).
23. Ibid.
24. United Nations Centre on Transnational Corporations, *Transnational Corporations in World Development: Trends and Prospects* (New York: United Nations, 1988).
25. *Canada's Technology Industries in the 1990s: How to Win in a World of Change* (Toronto: Ernst & Young, 1990).
26. Ibid.
27. "Innovation: The Key to Competitiveness in the Nineties," confidential draft discussion paper, ISTC Policy Sector, Ottawa, 10 September 1990.
28. Paul Labbé, Investment Canada workshop. University of Toronto, 29 November 1990.
29. Robert B. Reich, "Who Is Us?" *Harvard Business Review*, January–February 1990; "Who Is Them?" *Harvard Business Review*, March–April 1991; and *The Work of Nations* (New York: Knopf, 1991).
30. Ethan B. Kapstein, "We Are US: The Myth of the Multinational," *National Interest*, Winter 1991–92.
31. Ibid.
32. Reich, "Who Is Them?"
33. Ibid.
34. National Advisory Board on Science and Technology, *Science and Technology, Innovation and National Prosperity*.
35. Gilles Paquet, *Globalization and the Nation State* (Ottawa: North-South Institute, 1991).
36. Gunnar Hedlund, letter to the editor, *Harvard Business Review*, May–June 1991.
37. *Economist*, 4 August 1990.

CHAPTER 6
It All Begins in the Classroom

1. Towers Perrin and the Hudson Institute of Canada, *Workforce 2000* (Toronto: Towers Perrin, 1991).
2. *Toronto Star*, 18 July 1989.
3. Economic Council of Canada, *A Lot to Learn: Education and Training in Canada* (Ottawa: ECC, 1992).
4. Janet Halliwell, speech to the B.C. Science and Engineering Awards Dinner, Vancouver, B.C., 22 October 1991.
5. ECC, *A Lot to Learn.*
6. Ontario Ministry of Skills Development, *Literacy: The Basis of Growth* (Toronto: Government of Ontario, 1989).
7. William E. Nothdurft, *SchoolWorks* (Washington: Brookings Institution, 1989).
8. The Corporate–Higher Education Forum, *To Be Our Best: Learning for the Future* (Montreal: CHEF, 1990).
9. ECC, *A Lot to Learn.*
10. *Computing Research News*, January 1991.
11. Malcolm Skilbeck, *Curriculum Reform: An Overview of Trends* (Paris: OECD, 1991).
12. Economic Council of Canada, *Employment in the Service Economy* (Ottawa: ECC, 1991).
13. *Canadian Economic Observer*, February 1992.
14. Statistics Canada, *Education in Canada: A Statistical Review for 1989–90* (Ottawa: Ministry of Industry, Science and Technology, 1991), cat. no. 81-229.
15. Dave Gower, "Unemployment: Occupation Makes a Difference," *Perspectives on Labour and Income*, Winter 1991.
16. *The World Competitiveness Report 1991* (Geneva: World Economic Forum, 1991).
17. Employment and Immigration Canada, *Success in the Works: A Profile of Canada's Emerging Workforce* (Ottawa: Government of Canada, 1989).
18. Employment and Immigration Canada, *Job Futures: Occupational Outlooks*, vol. 1 (Ottawa: Government of Canada, 1990).
19. National Advisory Board on Science and Technology, Human Resource Development Committee, Ottawa, 1991.

20. Economic Council of Canada, *Good Jobs, Bad Jobs: Employment in the Service Economy* (Ottawa: ECC, 1990).
21. Janet E. Halliwell, "Problem or Paradox? Resources for R & D," speech to the Canadian Research Management Association, Ottawa, 23 September 1991.
22. George S. Papadopoulos, "An Educational Agenda for the '90s," *OECD Observer*, February–March 1991.
23. Skilbeck, *Curriculum Reform*.
24. Jo Oppenheimer, "Guidance Now," *Education Today*, May–June 1991.
25. *Business Week*, 10 December 1990.
26. David Istance, "What Changes for Education?" *OECD Observer*, February–March, 1991.
27. Association of Universities and Colleges of Canada, *Averting Faculty Shortages* (Ottawa, 1991).
28. Premier's Council, *People and Skills in the New Global Economy* (Toronto: Government of Ontario, 1990).
29. Statistics Canada, cat. no. 81-229.
30. Association of Universities and Colleges, *Averting Faculty Shortages.*
31. John McDougall, Standing Committee on Industry, Science and Technology, Regional and Northern Development, Ottawa, 27 March 1990.
32. Graham Orpwood, *The Chemical Professions of Canada: Employment and Education for the Future* (Ottawa: Chemical Institute of Canada, 1991).
33. Employment and Immigration Canada, *Software and National Competitiveness: Human Resource Issues and Opportunities* (Ottawa: Government of Canada, 1992).
34. Robert J. Kavanagh, *New Scientists and Engineers from Canadian Universities* (Ottawa: Natural Sciences and Engineering Research Council, 1991).
35. Arthur May, Standing Committee on Industry, Science and Technology, Regional and Northern Development, Ottawa, 15 March 1990.
36. National Advisory Board on Science and Technology, Human Resource Development Committee, Ottawa, 1991.
37. Royal Society of Canada, *Realizing the Potential: A Strategy for University Research in Canada* (Ottawa: RSC, 1991).

38. "Learning Well . . . Living Well," discussion paper for consultation meetings, Ottawa, 1991.

39. Graham W. F. Orpwood and Isme Alam, *Science Education in Canadian Schools*, vol. 2, *Statistical Database for Canadian Science Education*, Science Council of Canada Background Study 52, Ottawa, 1984.

40. Robert K. Crocker, *Science Achievement in Canadian Schools: National and International Comparisons*, Working Paper 7 (Ottawa: Economic Council of Canada, 1990).

41. David F. Robitaille, *Canadian Participation in the Second International Mathematics Study*, Working Paper 6 (Ottawa: Economic Council of Canada, 1990).

42. Association of Universities and Colleges of Canada, "Canada's Universities and the New Global Reality," pre-budget submission to the minister of finance, Ottawa, December 1990.

43. Stuart L. Smith, Commission of Inquiry on Canadian University Education, AUCC, Ottawa, 1991.

44. DPA Group, *Final Report for the Evaluation of the Equipment Grants Program of the Natural Sciences and Engineering Research Council* (Vancouver: DPA Group, 1990).

45. Royal Society of Canada, *Realizing the Potential*.

46. *Toronto Star*, 31 May 1986.

47. David Vice, Senate Committee on National Finance, Ottawa, January 1986.

CHAPTER 7
Our Science and Technology Building Blocks

1. Canadian Manufacturers' Association, *Competing in Industrial Research and Development* (Toronto: CMA, 1987).

2. *Toronto Star*, 28 November 1988.

3. Sunder Magun and Someshwar Rao, "The Competitive Position of Canada in High-Technology Trade," paper presented to the Canadian Economic Association, Quebec City, 2–4 June 1989.

4. Someshwar Rao, Farah Tcharkari, and Tony Lampriere, "Assessing Trends in Canada's Competitive Position" draft paper for Economic Council of Canada, 1990.

5. Ibid.

6. Department of Industry, Science and Technology; Policy Sector, "Innovation: The Key to Competitiveness in the Nineties," confidential draft discussion paper, 10 September 1990.

7. Organisation for Economic Co-operation and Development, *Technology in a Changing World*, The Technology/Economy Program (Paris: OECD, 1991).

8. Economic Council of Canada, *Pulling Together: Productivity, Innovation, and Trade* (Ottawa: ECC, 1992).

9. Science Council of Canada, Sectoral Innovation Strategies Project, presentation to the National Forum of Science and Technology Advisory Councils, Victoria, B.C., September 1991.

10. Science Council of Canada, *The Canadian Non-Ferrous Metals Sector*, Sectoral Technology Strategy Series, no. 11 (Ottawa: SCC, 1992).

11. Ibid.

12. Science Council of Canada, *The Canadian Iron and Steel Sector*, Sectoral Technology Strategy Series, no. 3 (Ottawa: SCC, 1992).

13. Ibid.

14. Science Council of Canada, *The Canadian Forest-Products Sector*, Sectoral Technology Strategy Series, no. 9 (Ottawa: SCC, 1992).

15. Ibid.

16. Ibid.

17. Science Council of Canada, *The Canadian Automotive Parts Sector*, Sectoral Technology Strategy Series, no. 2 (Ottawa: SCC, 1992).

18. Ibid.

19. Science Council of Canada, *The Canadian Non-Electrical Machinery Industry*, Sectoral Technology Strategy Series, no. 10 (Ottawa: SCC, 1992).

20. Science Council of Canada, *The Canadian Petrochemical and Resins Sector*, Sectoral Technology Strategy Series, no. 6 (Ottawa: SCC, 1992).

21. Science Council of Canada, *The Canadian Telecommunications Sector*, Sectoral Technology Strategy Series, no. 1 (Ottawa: SCC, 1992).

22. Ibid.

23. *Research and Money*, 25 September 1991.

24. David C. Mowery and Nathan Rosenberg, *Technology and the Pursuit of Economic Growth* (Cambridge: Cambridge University Press, 1989).

25. Economic Council of Canada, *Pulling Together.*
26. Kenneth Flamm, *Targeting the Computer: Government Support and International Competition* (Washington: Brookings Institution, 1987).
27. National Academy of Sciences, National Academy of Engineering and Institute of Medicine: Panel, *The Government Role in Civilian Technology* (Washington: National Academy Press, 1992).
28. Canadian Manufacturers' Association, *The Aggressive Economy: Daring to Compete* (Toronto: CMA, 1989).
29. Mowery and Rosenberg, *Technology and the Pursuit of Economic Growth.*
30. Economic Council of Canada, *Pulling Together.*
31. Peter Morici, *A New Special Relationship: Free Trade and U.S.–Canadian Economic Relations in the 1990s* (Halifax: Institute for Research on Public Policy, 1991).
32. Janet Halliwell, Charles H. Davis, and Paul Dufour, *Scientific and Technological Collaboration in North America: In Search of New Paradigms?* (Ottawa: Science Council of Canada, 1992).

CHAPTER 8
MoneyIs the Bottom Line

1. Gordon Sharwood, *At the Threshold: Canada's Medium-Sized Businesses Prepare for the Global Marketplace of the 1990s.* A Special Report by Sharwood and Company, Investment Bankers (Toronto: Sharwood and Company, 1989).
2. Ibid.
3. Mary Macdonald, *Creating Threshold Technology Companies in Canada: The Role for Venture Capital* (Ottawa: Science Council of Canada, 1991),
4. Canada Consulting Group, *Under-Funding the Future: Canada's Cost of Capital Problem* (Toronto: Canada Consulting Group, 1992).
5. National Advisory Biotechnology Committee, *National Biotechnology Business Strategy: Capturing Competitive Advantage for Canada* (Ottawa: Ministry of Industry, Science and Technology, 1991).
6. Canadian Chamber of Commerce, *Focus 2000: Report of the Task Force on Making Investment Capital Available* (Ottawa: Canadian Chamber of Commerce, 1988).

7. Canada Consulting Group, *Under-Funding the Future.*

8. Committee on the Financing of Industrial Innovation, National Advisory Board on Science and Technology, Ottawa, 1991.

9. George N. Hatsopoulos, Paul R. Krugman, and Lawrence H. Summers, "U.S. Competitiveness: Beyond the Trade Deficit," *Science,* 15 July 1988.

10. Karen Wensley, "Tax Incentives for Canadian Information Technology Companies Seeking Further Capital" (Toronto: Ernst & Young, 1922).

11. Pierre Lortie, "Ottawa Should Consider a Federal Version of QSSP," *Globe and Mail,* 5 November 1990.

12. *Wall Street Journal,* 4 October 1990.

13. David Slater, *The Contribution of Investment and Savings to Productivity and Economic Growth in Canada,* Working Paper 10 (Ottawa: Investment Canada, 1992).

14. *New York Times,* 17 March 1992.

15. Premier's Council, *Competing in the New Global Economy: Report of the Premier's Council,* vol. 1 (Toronto: Government of Ontario, 1988).

16. Mary Macdonald & Associates, *Financing Canadian Technology Companies: Selected Initiatives to Increase Access to Capital* (Toronto, 1992).

17. Peter F. Drucker, "Reckoning with the Pension Fund Revolution," *Harvard Business Review,* March–April 1991.

18. John Zysman, *Governments, Markets, and Growth: Financial Systems and the Politics of Industrial Change* (Ithaca: Cornell University Press, 1983).

19. Stephen Woolcock and Michael Hodges, "Euro-Capitalism in Focus," *International Economic Insights,* November–December 1991.

20. W. Carl Kester, *Japanese Takeovers: The Global Contest for Corporate Control* (Boston: Harvard Business School Press, 1991).

21. Masaru Yoshitomi, "Keiretsu: An Insider's Guide to Japan's Conglomerates," *International Economic Insights,* September-October 1990.

22. Kenneth S. Courtis, "Perspectives on the Japanese Keiretsu," speech to the National Advisory Board on Science and Technology symposium, Toronto, 1–2 March 1990.

23. Kester, *Japanese Takeovers.*
24. Courtis, "Perspectives on the Japanese Keiretsu."
25. Yoshitomi, "Keiretsu."
26. Organisation for Economic Co-operation and Development, *OECD Economic Surveys: Japan* (Paris: OECD, 1989).
27. Kester, *Japanese Takeovers.*
28. Pierre Fortier, Senate Standing Committee on Banking, Trade and Finance, 24 October 1989.
29. *Toronto Star*, 5 February 1992.
30. Peter Drucker, "Reckoning with the Pension Fund Revolution," *Harvard Business Review*, March–April 1991.
31. Martin Lipton and Steven A. Rosenblum. "Can Pension Funds Lead the Ownership Revolution?" *Harvard Business Review*, May–June 1991.
32. Peter Drucker, "A Crisis of Capitalism," *Wall Street Journal*, 30 September 1986.

CHAPTER 9
A Workplace for the Year 2000

1. Jacquie Mansell, *Workplace Innovation in Canada* (Ottawa: Economic Council of Canada, 1987).
2. Ibid.
3. United Steelworkers of America, *Empowering Workers in the Global Economy: A Labor Agenda for the 1990s* (Toronto: United Steelworkers, 1992).
4. Economic Council of Canada, *Good Jobs, Bad Jobs* (Ottawa: ECC, 1990).
5. Statistics Canada, "General Social Survey on Education and Work, 1989," *Daily Bulletin*, 23 January 1990.
6. Economic Council of Canada, *Making Technology Work: Innovation and Jobs in Canada* (Ottawa: ECC, 1987).
7. Office of Technology Assessment, *Worker Training: Competing in the New International Economy* (Washington: U.S. Congress, 1990).
8. Ibid.
9. Shoshana Zuboff, *In the Age of the Smart Machine* (New York: Basic Books, 1988).
10. Ibid.
11. *New York Times*, 4 March 1992.

12. Zuboff, *In the Age of the Smart Machine.*
13. Paul C. Weiler, *Governing the Workplace: The Future of Labor and Employment Law* (Cambridge, Mass.: Harvard University Press, 1990).
14. Maryellen R. Kelley and Bennett Harrison, "Unions, Technology, and Labour-Management Co-operation," in *Unions and Economic Competitiveness,* ed. Lawrence Mishel and Paula B. Voos (New York: M.E. Sharpe, 1991).
15. Statistics Canada, *Corporations and Labour Unions Returns Act: Labour Unions 1989* (Ottawa: Ministry of Industry, Science and Technology, 1992), cat. no. 71-202.
16. United Steelworkers of America, *Empowering Workers in the Global Economy.*
17. Weiler, *Governing the Workplace.*
18. Koji Matsumoto, *The Rise of the Japanese Corporate System* (London: Kegan Paul International, 1991).
19. Sheridan M. Tatsuno, *Created in Japan: From Imitators to World-Class Innovators* (New York: HarperCollins, 1990).
20. Ikujiro Nonaka, "The Knowledge-Creating Company," *Harvard Business Review,* November–December 1991.
21. Richard B. Freeman and James L. Medoff, *What Do Unions Do?* (New York: Basic Books, 1984).
22. *Toronto Star,* 28 May 1986.
23. Statistics Canada, "Gail Cook Johnson Speaks Out on Human Resource Issues: Interview by Doreen Duchesne," *Perspectives on Labour and Income,* Spring 1991, cat. no. 75-001E.
24. *Adjusting to Win: Report of the Advisory Council on Adjustment* (Ottawa: Government of Canada, 1989).
25. National Advisory Board on Science and Technology, *Human Resource Development Committee Report* (Ottawa: NABST, 1991).
26. Premier's Council, *People and Skills in the New Global Economy* (Toronto: Government of Ontario, 1990).
27. Economic Council of Canada, *Good Jobs, Bad Jobs.*
28. Peter E. Larsen and Matthew W. Blue, *Training and Development 1990: Expenditures and Policies* (Ottawa: Conference Board of Canada, 1991).
29. Andrew Sharpe, "Training in the Work Force: A Challenge Facing Canada in the '90s," *Perspectives on Labour and Income,* Winter 1990. Statistics Canada cat. no. 75-001E.

30. Premier's Council, *People and Skills in the New Global Economy.*
31. Office of Technology Assessment, *Worker Training.*
32. *Economist,* 20 July 1991.
33. Economic Council of Canada, *Making Technology Work.*
34. F. Anthony Comper, "Training for the Economic Olympics," speech, Toronto, 13 June 1990.
35. Peter Larson, speech to Conference Board of Canada, 26 October 1989.
36. *Globe and Mail,* 19 June 1989.
37. *Toronto Star,* 6 March 1991.
38. Jay W. Lorsch, "The Workings of Codetermination," *Harvard Business Review,* July–August 1991.
39. Bernard Avishai, "A European Platform for Global Competition: An Interview with VW's Carl Hahn," *Harvard Business Review,* July–August 1991.

CHAPTER 10
Getting It All Together

1. Andrew Britton, "Economic Growth in the Market Economies 1950–2000," *Economic Commission for Europe: Discussion Papers,* vol. 1, no. 1 (New York, United Nations, 1991).
2. Alan Blinder, *Hard Heads, Soft Hearts: Tough-Minded Economics for a Just Society* (Reading, Mass.: Addison Wesley, 1988).
3. Howard Oxley and John P. Martin, "Controlling Government Spending and Deficits: Trends in the 1980s and Prospects for the 1990s," *OECD Economic Studies no. 17* (Paris: OECD, 1991).
4. Ibid.
5. James R. Gass, "Towards the 'Active Society,'" *OECD Observer,* June–July 1988.
6. Economic Council of Canada, *Employment in the Service Economy* (Ottawa: ECC, 1991).
7. *Toronto Star,* 11 December 1991.
8. Gass, "Towards the 'Active Society.'"
9. Harvey Lazar, "Investing in People: A Policy Agenda for the 1990s," in *Canada at Risk?,* ed. G. Bruce Doern and Bryne B. Purchase (Toronto: C.D. Howe Institute, 1991).
10. *Globe and Mail,* 31 December 1991.
11. Canadian Institute for Advanced Research, *The Learning Society* (Toronto: CIAR, March 1992).

12. Alain Cregheur and Mary Sue Devereaux, "Canada's Children," *Canadian Social Trends*, Summer 1991. Statistics Canada cat. no. 11-008E.
13. Mary Anne Burke, Susan Crampton, Alison Jones, and Katherine Neggner, "Caring for Children," *Canadian Social Trends*, Autumn 1991. Statistics Canada cat. no. 11-008E.
14. Canadian Institute for Advanced Research, *The Learning Society*.
15. Ibid.
16. Ian A. Stewart, "How Much Government Is Good Government?" in *Canada at Risk?*, ed. Doern and Purchase.
17. Roger Love and Susan Poulin, "Family Inequality in the 1980s," *Perspectives on Labour and Income*, Autumn 1991. Statistics Canada cat. no. 75-001E.
18. *Toronto Star*, 30 January 1992.
19. Robert Blair, speech to the Canadian Club, London, Ontario, 8 March 1989.
20. *Toronto Star*, 14 January 1989.
21. Stephen Woolcock and Michael Hodges, "Euro-Capitalism in Focus," *International Economic Insights*, November–December 1991.
22. Ibid.
23. Economic Council of Canada, *Transitions for the 90s. Twenty-Seventh Annual Review* (Ottawa: ECC, 1990).
24. Canadian Institute for Advanced Research, *Economic Growth: Science and Technology and Institutional Change in a Global Economy*, Program in Economic Growth and Policy (Toronto: CIAR, June 1991).
25. Paul Romer, "Economic Growth," *Fortune Encyclopedia of Economics*, 1992.
26. Janet Halliwell, "The Great Canadian Competitiveness Debate," speech, Science Council of Canada, Ottawa, 27 November 1991.

Index